Strategies and Best Practices in Social Innovation

Marta Peris-Ortiz • Jaime Alonso Gómez
Patricia Marquez
Editors

Strategies and Best Practices in Social Innovation

An Institutional Perspective

 Springer

Editors
Marta Peris-Ortiz
Departamento de Organizacón de Empresas
Universitat Politècnica de València
Valencia, Spain

Jaime Alonso Gómez
School of Business Administration
University of San Diego
San Diego, CA, USA

Patricia Marquez
Joan B. Kroc School of Peace Studies
University of San Diego
San Diego, CA, USA

ISBN 978-3-319-89856-8   ISBN 978-3-319-89857-5   (eBook)
https://doi.org/10.1007/978-3-319-89857-5

Library of Congress Control Number: 2018943693

Printed on acid-free paper

This Springer imprint is published by the registered company Springer International Publishing AG part of Springer Nature.
The registered company address is: Gewerbestrasse 11, 6330 Cham, Switzerland

Contents

Chapter 1
Strategies and Best Practices in Social Innovation: An Overview

Marta Peris-Ortiz, Jaime A. Gomez, and Patricia Marquez

Abstract Within society, changes occur that correspond to incremental or radical innovations. These innovations are rooted in technology and the applications of this technology; in the way that organisations are managed; and in the beliefs and behaviour of citizens. These innovations accumulate and interact with one another to explain social innovation, which can be understood as a change in formal institutions (i.e. the political and legal framework) or informal institutions (i.e. beliefs and behaviour). The chapters in this book all present incremental innovations in one or more of these three fields. Many of these innovations have major implications for the sustainability of the natural environment and the well-being of citizens. Furthermore, an ethical commitment to people or the environment is explicitly or implicitly shown in all chapters. Finally, the compatibility or complementarity between profit-seeking and the well-being of citizens emerges in chapters that do not address public or non-profit activities.

Keywords Social innovation · Sustainability · Ethical behaviour · Technical innovation · Organisational innovation

M. Peris-Ortiz (✉)
Departamento de Organización de Empresas, Universitat Politècnica de València, Valencia, Spain
e-mail: mperis@doe.upv.es

J. A. Gomez
University of San Diego, School of Business Administration, San Diego, CA, USA
e-mail: jagomez@sandiego.edu

P. Marquez
University of San Diego, Joan B. Kroc School of Peace Studies, San Diego, CA, USA
e-mail: pmarquez@SanDiego.edu

1

1.1   Introduction

The emergence and consolidation of social innovations allows us to understand each period of history. These social innovations can stem from multiple incremental changes in production and trade technologies or gradual changes in beliefs and forms of social organisation, potentially without any specific cause or technical or political innovation to explain them. Alternatively, major technical innovations (e.g. improvements in maritime transport in the fifteenth century) or political and institutional changes (e.g. social revolutions) may explain social innovation because of their importance and repercussions. In the former case, the accumulation of incremental developments changes the world, leading to social change and innovation. In the latter case, a unique technical, organisational, or political innovation is substantial enough to drive this social change or innovation by transforming informal institutions (i.e. beliefs) and formal institutions (i.e. laws and regulations).

The following 12 chapters correspond to the kind of incremental innovations that have just been discussed. Three common elements link these chapters. First, some form of social innovation justifies the chapter's inclusion in this book. Second, all chapters show, explicitly or implicitly, an ethical commitment to people or the environment. Third, chapters that do not address public or non-profit activities show the compatibility or complementarity between profit-seeking and the well-being of citizens.

Section 1.2 of this chapter establishes the theoretical framework. Section 1.3 provides an overview of the chapters contained in this book. Finally, Sect. 1.4 presents some conclusions, which also help identify the key common elements that emerge throughout this book.

1.2   Theoretical Framework

Social innovations are inherent to the processes of historical development, even though certain historical periods are characterised by political, social and institutional backwardness (Evans 2003, 2016; North 1981). Social innovations may occur in three separate ways. First, social innovations may occur through historical transformations that stem from broad social change. In such cases, no single action or innovation contributing to this complex transformation can be pinpointed as the root of this change (Chandler 1977; North 1981). Second, social innovations may stem from major technological, organisational, political or institutional changes (e.g. 3D printing, joint-stock companies or the French revolution). These changes are deliberate, identifiable innovations but, because of their extraordinary importance, have unanticipated long-term consequences for society (Jensen 2000; Mcphee 2002; Rayna and Striukova 2016; Schumpeter 1942). Third, social innovations may correspond to innovations or changes to institutions themselves. Such innovations can affect either legal or formal institutions or beliefs and social behaviour (North 1990,

2005). These innovations alter the strategies and practices that shape the behaviour and development of society.

Below the formal level of institutions lies the level of beliefs and social sensibilities that require either stability or political and legal innovations and change (see Chap. 8 of this book). The reciprocal influence of beliefs and the formal institutional framework is what establishes the coexistence and development of technical and organisational innovations. According to North (1990, 2005), stability and uncertainty mitigation allows progress and innovation in technology, organisations, education and science (Chaps. 9 and 10 of this book). These innovations and the entrepreneurial ventures that act as vehicles to implement these innovations (e.g. smart cities in Chap. 5, new forms of sustainable energy in Chap. 7 and organic food in Chap. 4) change society. Such innovations drive change in the beliefs and expectations that underpin private initiatives. This change in turn requires the modification, innovation and redesign of formal institutions.

Thus, the interaction between changes in the beliefs and preferences of citizens and the way these changes are reflected in formal institutions create the framework of technical and organisational innovation. By altering information and production processes, transport facilities, productivity and per capita income, these innovations need new organisational and functional forms of society. In the society of any developed country, three types of innovation that we have not yet discussed are currently converging. First, multiple incremental innovations of a technical and organisational nature progressively modify the behaviour and practices of society. Second, as these incremental innovations accumulate, they require changes in formal institutions. Third, radical technical innovations with massive repercussions (e.g. the Internet or 3D printing) revolutionise communication and production and lead to formal institutional changes. The chapters of this book describe some of the current incremental actions and changes. These changes result from established or ongoing innovations (Anderson 2014; Bryniolfsson and McAfee 2014). These innovations provide a glimpse into the strategies and practices of the future.

Society has numerous dimensions and levels. Accordingly, innovation is nurtured in different ways. For example, growing awareness of the need to resolve social issues manifests itself as social entrepreneurship. As Tracey et al. (2011) report for the case of the homeless, strategic and organisational innovations by nonprofit organisations are also social innovation strategies. The importance of this sector is documented in the bibliometric analysis presented in Chap. 2. This bibliometric analysis shows that in Business, Management, Accounting, Social Science, Economics, Econometrics and Finance journals, the proportion of articles that address social entrepreneurship and social innovation has grown since 2006. This growth implies a steady yet constant increase in the importance attached to these processes of social innovation.

Private sector firms also contribute to change and social innovation through for-profit activities in response to the two fundamental changes that have occurred in developed societies. First, the deterioration of the natural environment has captured the attention of citizens and has affected their tastes and preferences as consumers. Second, technical progress has allowed firms to offer different products and services, characterised by a greater awareness of health and the environment. Chapter 4, in which Moreno-Luzón, Gil-Marques, and Chams-Anturi analyse the Spanish organic food market, exemplifies this phenomenon. This market, which includes all exchanges that relate to the production and distribution of such products, has grown by 465% in the last 15 years. From the demand side, this huge growth reflects previously unmet consumer needs and preferences. Likewise, from the supply side, this growth reflects the emergence of entrepreneurs who have identified market opportunities (Seebode et al. 2012) or have created new products. These products are typified by a respect for nature (i.e. sustainability), a concern for health (i.e. the absence of chemicals) and a desire to build an economy and a society committed to the well-being of the customer as a key strategic element. Thus, the subsector studied in Chap. 4 is characterised by the importance of the customer and the potential for combining profit-seeking with the well-being of citizens. This idea is particularly important because it questions the ideological barrier that suggests that only non-profit firms can place the well-being of citizens at the centre of their strategies. Such studies show that when a consideration for the customer's well-being is fundamental to the firm's competitiveness, it breaches the barrier that separates profit-seeking from the well-being of citizens. Arguably, according to the neoclassical orthodoxy profit-seeking, is strictly speaking what removes the barrier between profits and the well-being of citizens in the long run.

Other types of social innovations that combine profit-seeking with the well-being of citizens are based on the beliefs, culture, ideology and ethics of managers or entrepreneurs. Chapter 6, 'The economy of communion', develops this idea. The economy of communion is based on Christian beliefs and ethics. In the three short cases presented in Chap. 6, the authors stress the relationships that emerge in the organisation of the firm. According to this approach, the firm must uphold the principle of equality and must engage in actions based on gratitude and reciprocity, without jeopardising the firm's competiveness or profit-seeking. Changing tack, this view actually resembles Fayol's (1916) affirmations that equality is important for the management of employees and that equality is based on a mixture of benevolence and justice. This view also resembles Nonaka et al. (2000) Ba idea. Based on considerable support from the literature, these approaches actually help rather than hinder the firm's competitiveness and profits through greater commitment and better relations amongst organisational members. It is social innovation, in this case at the heart of the organisation of each firm, that, with variations depending on the culture of each country and firm, advances managerial thinking from Chester Barnard (1938) and the experiments of Hawthorne.

Chapter 3 analyses another type of organisation, this time in the non-profit sector. The chapter addresses social innovation in public organisations. Public organisations are important for numerous reasons, principally because they create economic externalities for the private sector and, in a broader sense, for citizens and society as a whole. Courts of justice, healthcare and education exemplify how the public sector contributes to the institutional framework of a society, thereby improving the way society functions and reducing uncertainty (North 2005). Like the authors of Chap. 3, we are compelled to ask the following question: How do citizens perceive innovation, and what variables does this innovation depend on? The answer, which lends coherence to the chapters in this book, is that social innovation is perceived in terms of two primary variables: the capacity of public organisations to respond to the demands of citizens and citizens' perceptions of the ethical and moral behaviours of these organisations. In the words of the authors, 'the greater the extent to which organisations in this sector (public sector) raise their "response capacity" and their "ethics and morals", the greater the level of social innovation perceived by citizens.'

This book shows how incremental innovations that individually or jointly create social innovation are developed through applications of technical innovations to the natural environment and the well-being of citizens (Chaps. 4, 7 and 12), through universities (Chaps. 9 and 10) and through profit-seeking and sustainability (Chap. 13). The following section provides an overview of each chapter. As previously discussed, these diverse chapters are linked by three common elements. First, some form of social innovation justifies their inclusion in this book. Second, an ethical commitment to people or the environment is shown, explicitly or implicitly, in each chapter. Finally, the compatibility or complementarity between profit-seeking and the well-being of citizens clearly emerges in some chapters.

1.3 Overview of Book Contents

Chapter 2, 'Entrepreneurship and social innovation for sustainability. Bibliometric analysis,' by Durán-Sánchez, Peris-Ortiz, Álvarez-García, and del Río-Rama, examines the importance of social entrepreneurship in the scientific literature. As previously mentioned, greater awareness of the need to address social issues that the markets and public authorities have failed to resolve manifests itself as social entrepreneurship. In this form of entrepreneurship, the strategic and organisational innovations developed by non-profit organisations are social innovation strategies. The importance of this sector is reflected in the bibliometric analysis presented in Chap. 2. The analysis shows that the proportion of articles that address social entrepreneurship and social innovation in Business, Management, Accounting, Social Science, Economics, Econometrics and Finance journals has grown since 2006. This growth reflects an increase in the importance attached to these social innovation processes. The raison d'être of these firms is their moral commitment to people, as reported by Tracey et al. (2011) for the case of the homeless. If these firms belong to the non-profit sector, they are unable to reconcile profit with the well-being of citizens. If this is not the case, however, compatibility and complementarity between these two goals is possible (Auvinet and Lloret 2015).

Chapter 3, 'Social innovation in Public Organisations: The perspectives of managers', by Ferreira, Fernandes, and Oliveira, shows that the public sector has numerous elements in common with the private sector. The goals in both sectors involve improving efficiency and quality and increasing consumer satisfaction. Chapter 3 studies social innovation in public organisations to understand how social innovation can improve the lives of citizens from the perspective of managers. The measurement of social innovation, whose incremental nature can hinder its identification, is conducted using the perceived satisfaction of users of public organisations. The authors report that citizens' evaluations of these organisations depend on perceived ethical commitment as one of the primary variables. Ethical commitment is therefore one of the necessary variables for the management of public organisations.

Chapter 4, 'Quality and innovation in the organic agro-food sector: Threats and opportunities of social and managerial innovation', by Moreno-Luzon, Gil-Marques, and Chams-Anturi, shows that private sector firms contribute to social change and innovation. The deterioration of the natural environment and the technical progress that has allowed firms to offer products and services that are better for consumers' health and that respect the environment are two forces that have led to the success and rapid development of the organic food sector. This chapter meets the three criteria that, as mentioned in the introduction, are present in all the chapters of this book. Together with cultural changes amongst citizens and changes in consumer tastes, technical innovation is a form of social innovation that creates a new area of the sustainable economy. This is a non-profit sector, where profit-seeking and market share could provide an incentive to increase efficiency and show greater concern for people and the environment. This is also a sector where an increase in profits is seemingly linked to a greater commitment to customer health.

Chapter 5, 'Sustainable social innovations in Smart Cities: Exploratory analysis of the current global situation applicable to Colombia', by Alonso-Gonzalez, Palacios Chacon, and Peris-Ortiz, examines Smart Cities, thereby addressing one of today's most important issues in relation to the social well-being of citizens and the preservation of the natural environment. Because of its global nature, this phenomenon encompasses all social, technical and economic issues as well as the behaviour of citizens and businesses through its ethical dimensions. Therefore, considerable private investment is required to ensure that profit-seeking is compatible with the well-being of citizens and sustainability. The smartest entrepreneurs will probably not act in this way simply to comply with the law but rather because they grasp the potential benefit of initiatives and creativity that achieve profitability, social benefit, and environmental conservation.

Chapter 6, 'The Economy of Communion as a social innovation to humanise business', by Esteso Blasco, Gil-Marques, and Sapena Bolufer, shows how Christian beliefs and ethics can shape behaviour and business management. The three short case studies presented in Chap. 6 stress the relations within the firm as a result of applying these ethics and values. Under this approach, the organisation must follow the principle of equality and actions that are based on gratitude and reciprocity whilst ensuring that these practices do not hinder competitiveness or curb profit-seeking. Indeed, Chap. 6 shows that, the for-profit companies that the authors discuss voluntarily pursue the well-being of citizens via a path that is more direct and deliberate than the path offered by competitive markets.

Chapter 7, 'Methodology for analysing electrical scenarios as a means of sustainable development in emerging countries', by Peñalvo-López, Pérez-Navarro, Cárcel-Carrasco, and Devece, consists of a technical proposal for a method to produce sustainable electricity in developing countries, with emphasis on the Democratic Republic of the Congo. This proposal refers to using different sources of energy (coal, oil, natural gas, renewable and nuclear) and combining these sources to provide energy for consumption in a specific geographic area and population. The proposal involves an ethical commitment to the preservation of the natural environment whilst improving living conditions for the population. Chapter 7 is of particular interest because, as the authors affirm, 'electricity is one of the main driving forces for development, especially in remote areas where access to modern energy is linked to poverty, (and) one of the main challenges of the international community is to minimize the inequality of energy services between OECD and developing countries.'

Chapter 8, 'State legitimacy in France as a determinant of competitiveness and social innovation', by Blanco-González, Prado-Román, and Díez-Martín, deals with the necessary correspondence between political institutions of the state and citizens' needs, desires and expectations. The better the fit between what citizens need or expect and the political and social institutions (legal framework, education system and health system), the more citizens' initiatives in all areas are strengthened and the greater the social development and economic growth. According to the authors, 'within the dimension of legality or acceptance of legal authority, the state exercises its political power in concordance with its citizen's views on laws, rules and customs. These are important because they are generally applied and predictable. Rules create predictability in social life, which is in itself a moral good.' Thus, 'there is a set of shared beliefs that intermediate power relationships. The notion of moral congruency between state and society is the basis of the literature on comparative politics and sociology.' However, society evolves and new problems emerge. Therefore, in many situations, the government needs to promote social innovation to achieve greater legitimacy. This idea is consistent with Douglas North's (1990, 2005) vision of institutions.

Chapter 9, 'Developing Sustainability Awareness in Higher Education', by Lopes, Mesquita, del Río-Rama, and Álvarez-García, examines 15 universities to determine whether they have made a great enough commitment to sustainability. Chapter 9 addresses this issue using an innovative method based on the analysis of language through data mining. The authors thus study the degree to which the teaching curricula in different knowledge areas (course contents, learning outcomes and methodologies) and scientific output reflect sustainability awareness and sustainable thinking through the language they use. The authors also study the energy efficiency and waste management of university infrastructures. In a chapter that stands out for the quality of certain reflections, the authors underline the fact that despite the importance of the attention that these institutions devote to sustainability, it is necessary to create and adopt a strategy that combines sustainable development with all functions in all areas. The different areas of study should encourage a more integrated and more realistic view of the world. Methodologies should be created to enable synthesis and evaluation of the full range of areas to develop critical thinking about sustainability in economics, society and the environment.

Chapter 10, 'Corporate Universities as a new paradigm and source of social innovation, sustainability, technology and education in the XXI century corporations', by Alonso-Gonzalez, Peris-Ortiz, and Palacios Chacon, offers a university model that, with certain adjustments, could be applied to any organisation in any sector. The study presents an extensive review of the current literature regarding the concept to analyse the latest trends in relation to corporate universities. The influence of universities is important for the development of organisations' human capital, based on knowledge management as a factor that enables social innovation. The purpose is to meet the strategic goals and objectives with the highest levels of efficiency in the structures and processes of the firm. Based on a new paradigm of universities, Chap. 10 shows how this can be translated into social innovation.

Chapter 11, 'Finland's Centennial Anniversary 2017 – the first 100 years of Finnish social innovations that work for gender equality', by Koponen and Isopoussu-Koponen, highlights different social innovations resulting from initiatives that have arisen within society or from state policies throughout Finnish history. Examples include the actions of the master brewer Gideon Aberg against alcoholism and the decision to grant women the right to vote in 1913, which made Finland a pioneer in gender equality and democracy. Finland was also the first country in Europe to introduce canteens in primary and secondary education and provide state aid for university canteens. The ethical commitment to people, which is a trait of culturally advanced countries, and the social innovations that derive from this commitment play a central role in Chap. 11.

Chapter 12, 'Innovation and Knowledge in the Social Economy: ICT Accessibility', by Juárez Tarraga, Estelles-Miguel, Palmer Gato, and Albarracín Guillem, studies the case of Technosite S.A. Technosite specialises in e-business developments, business intelligence, usability, e-learning, integral management of web portals and, especially, web accessibility. Its goal is to ensure that a website can be navigated by all users, regardless of any possible disabilities. The company has achieved this goal whilst satisfying its responsibilities as a member of the social economy. This study of Technosite also shows the way that companies do business in the social economy, where 'positive economic performance should be balanced with social performance'. Efficiency and economic profit should support social action. Once again in this book, profit-seeking is shown to be compatible with the pursuit of the well-being of citizens.

Finally, Chap. 13, 'Management Systems for Sustainability Practices in the Wine Sector. The Case of Bodegas y Viñedos Fontana, S.L., a Spanish Winery', by Calle, Carrasco, and González, examines a social context characterised by growing concern for environmental problems and an increasingly competitive global wine market. In response to this scenario, companies in the wine sector are adopting different strategies. Some strategies are defensive, and certain companies have stepped up production to increase sales and compensate for lower profit margins, thereby increasing their carbon footprint. Other companies, however, have opted to implement social innovations, seeking to reduce the impact of their production activities on the environment whilst gaining in competitiveness. This case study contributes to the literature on economic profitability and environmental proactivity within the framework of social innovations.

1.4 Conclusions

This book presents contributions related to incremental innovations of a technical nature (Chap. 7), social nature (Chaps. 6, 8 and 11) and a combined technical and social nature (Chaps. 2, 3, 4, 5, 12 and 13), along with Chaps. 9 and 10, which study how universities contribute to sustainability. If any of these innovations has major repercussions for society (e.g. the energy production proposal presented in Chap. 7 or the sustainable environmental awareness investigated in Chap. 9), it can be considered a social innovation. Similarly, the accumulation of different incremental innovations leads to broader changes in the beliefs and behaviour of citizens as well as in the legal and regulatory framework. This process of change represents social innovation and transformation. Different social innovations, such as École 42 in education (Peris-Ortiz 2016) or the initiative by Tracey et al. (2011) to involve the homeless, show that the world, despite the law of large numbers – or perhaps, in fact, because of it – can be transformed. This book offers a modest contribution in this direction.

Acknowledgements The co-editors of this book would like to express their gratitude to the authors and to the anonymous referees.

References

Anderson, C. (2014). *Makers: The new industrial revolution*. New York: Crown Business.

Auvinet, C., & Lloret, A. (2015). Understanding social change through catalytic innovation: Empirical findings in Mexican social entrepreneurship. *Canadian Journal of Administrative Sciences, 32*, 221–223.

Barnard, C. (1938). *The functions of the executive*. Cambridge, MA: Harvard University Press.

Brynjolfsson, E., & McAfee, A. (2014). *The second machine age: Work, progress, and prosperity in a time of brilliant technologies*. New York: Norton & Company.

Chandler, A. C., Jr. (1977). *The visible hand*. Cambridge, MA: Harvard University Press.

Evans, R. J. (2003). *The coming of the Third Reich. How the Nazis destroyed democracy and seized power in Germany*. London: Penguin.

Evans, R. J. (2016). *The pursuit of power. Europe 1815–1914*. London: Penguin.

Fayol, H. (1916). *Administration industrielle et générale*. Paris: Dunot.

Jensen, M. C. (2000). *A theory of the firm. Governance, residual claims, and organizational forms*. Cambridge, MA: Harvard University Press.

McPhee, P. (2002). *The French Revolution 1789–1799*. London: Oxford University Press.

Nonaka, I., Toyama, R., & Konno, N. (2000). SECI, Ba and leadership: A unified model of dynamic knowledge creation. *Long Range Planning, 33*, 5–34.

North, D. C. (1981). *Structure and change in economic history*. New York: Norton and Company.

North, D. C. (1990). *Institutions, institutional change, and economic performance*. Cambridge, MA: Cambridge University Press.

North, D. C. (2005). *Understanding the process of economic change*. Princeton: Princeton University Press.

Peris-Ortiz, M., Alonso Llera, J. J., & Rueda-Armengot, C. (2016). Entrepreneurship and innovation in a revolutionary educational mode: Ecole 42. In M. Peris-Ortiz, F. Teulon, & D. Bonet-Fernandez (Eds.), *Social entrepreneurship in non-profit and profit sectors* (pp. 85–97). New York: Springer.

Rayna, T., & Striukova, L. (2016). From rapid prototyping to home fabrication: How 3D printing is changing business model innovation. *Technological Forecasting and Social Change, 102,* 214–224.

Schumpeter, J. A. (1942). *Capitalism, socialism and democracy.* New York: Harper and Brothers.

Seebode, D., Jeanrenaud, S., & Bessant, J. (2012). Managing innovation for sustainability. *R&D Management, 42*(3), 195–206.

Tracey, P., Phillips, N., & Jarvis, O. (2011). Bringing institutional entrepreneurship and the creation of new organizational forms: A multilevel model. *Organization Science, 22*(1), 60–80.

Chapter 2
Entrepreneurship and Social Innovation for Sustainability. Bibliometric Analysis

Amador Durán-Sánchez, Marta Peris-Ortiz, José Álvarez-García, and María de la Cruz del Río-Rama

Abstract The economic crisis has called the current economic models into question, emerging new ways of understanding the role that companies play in society. As the proliferation of academic articles shows, social innovation and entrepreneurship are currently playing a relevant role as an instrument for satisfying social needs from the business field, adding social utility to the technical and financial viability of companies. Due to the increasing interest in the social economy, the main objective of this chapter was to conduct a study of the scientific production related to innovation and social entrepreneurship, using for this purpose bibliometric techniques and the longitudinal statistical analysis of articles published in journals indexed in the multidisciplinary database Scopus (Elsevier) up to the year 2016. Thus, through an advanced search for terms, more than 1400 documents were obtained, of which 791 articles were selected to make up the ad-hoc database, which the analysis is based on. As a result, it is concluded that since 2006, there has been a considerable increase in the number of studies that address the social economy from different areas of knowledge, standing out from the rest Business, Management and Accounting, Social Sciences and Economics, Econometrics and Finance, studies which are published in a limited number of specialized journals by authors from countries such as the United States, United Kingdom, Spain or Canada.

A. Durán-Sánchez
Area of Public Law, University of Extremadura, Plasencia, Cáceres, Spain

M. Peris-Ortiz
Departamento de Organización de Empresas, Universitat Politècnica de València, Valencia, Spain
e-mail: mperis@doe.upv.es

J. Álvarez-García (✉)
Department of Financial Economics and Accounting, University of Extremadura, Cáceres, Extremadura, Spain
e-mail: pepealvarez@unex.es

M. de la C. del Río-Rama
Department of Business Organisation and Marketing, University of Vigo, Ourense, Spain
e-mail: delrio@uvigo.es

© Springer International Publishing AG, part of Springer Nature 2018   11
M. Peris-Ortiz et al. (eds.), *Strategies and Best Practices in Social Innovation*,
https://doi.org/10.1007/978-3-319-89857-5_2

Keywords Social entrepreneurship · Social innovation · Social economy · Bibliometric study · Scopus

2.1 Introduction

Innovation and *entrepreneurship* are two closely related concepts. Innovation is at the heart of the dynamics of entrepreneurship, whereas *entrepreneurship* is a way of innovating, or otherwise expressed, innovation is the specific instrument of the entrepreneurial spirit (Drucker 1985). In the specific case of social innovation, it has become a new way of thinking and acting that challenges existing paradigms, aiming to provide more effective, efficient or sustainable solutions than the existing ones to current social problems, creating value for the whole society rather than private individuals.

In recent years, significant scientific literature has developed around the concept of enterprise and social entrepreneurship, contributing new ideas to the classic notions of enterprise, whose main objective was to obtain benefits and maximize the value of the owners. In these studies, this motivation is not questioned, but managers of profit-making enterprises are encouraged to take into account not only the interests of owners, but also those of stakeholders and people who may be affected by the entrepreneurial activity (Mitchell et al. 1997). Consequently, the underlying motivation for social entrepreneurship is the creation of both shareholder wealth and social value. Thus, corporations can generate value by using strategies and practices that contribute to a more sustainable world, while maintaining shareholder value (Hart and Milstein 2003).

Although the previous literature uses the terms *social innovation* and *social entrepreneurship* in the same way on a large number of occasions, sharing common overlaps, especially in the process of identifying opportunities for solving unsatisfied social needs, their concepts also reflect particular aspects. While social entrepreneurship focuses on contributing to society based on the initiatives developed in the business field, social innovation achieves this from a broader scope, not only through change in companies, but also in organizations, institutions or in society as a whole. In this way, the field of activity of social entrepreneurship is smaller than that of social innovation (Phills et al. 2008).

In short, in the academic field it is accepted that the style and standards of prevailing Western life are inadmissible, so the transition to a sustainable society requires radical changes in the way we live. From this perspective, Manzini (2015) claims that social innovations are necessary to move from the unsustainable current life models to more sustainable ones, where social entrepreneurship applies these innovative approaches to solving social problems (Tukamushaba et al. 2011).

As a particular field of academic literature develops, it is useful to stop occasionally to record the work that has been done and to identify new directions and challenges for the future (Low and MacMillan 1988). Based on this fact, the objective this paper is to present an in-depth analysis of the current state of research concerning social innovation and social entrepreneurship through its bibliometric study, that is to say, through the use of mathematical and statistical methods to evaluate the existing scientific production to.

A first step for the preparation of the bibliometric analysis is to select the available databases, assessing their suitability and the consequences of using one or another, because this will depend largely on their validity. Thus, in order to reach the proposed objectives, the documents published in journals indexed within the multidisciplinary database Scopus (Elsevier) were reviewed, which provides an overview of international research production, which makes it an ideal instrument for the approach to bibliometric studies. Through an advanced search of terms with a time limit in 2016, a set of 791 documents were selected, that constitute the empirical basis of the study and that were processed later through the bibliographic manager Refworks.

This chapter is organized into four main sections. First, and after this introduction, we proceed to the review of the academic literature in order to establish the theoretical framework of the research. A second point describes both the sources and the methodological process used to obtain the references that form the empirical basis of the study. Subsequently, in the third part, the main results obtained in the calculation of bibliometric indicators are analysed and discussed, in order to conclude, in the fourth and last section, the main conclusions reached, as well as the limitations of the research.

2.2 Theoretical Framework

The development of a bibliometric study on Social Innovation (SI) and Social Entrepreneurship (SE), as in any other field of knowledge, requires a prior definition of the concepts to be analysed. However, the definitions of SI and SE seem to have different versions due to different academic backgrounds, geographic locations and economic context.

2.2.1 Definition of Social Innovation

Authors like Godin (2012) trace the origin of the concept of SI to the nineteenth century, specifically at the beginning of the French Revolution. While for others, its origin as an object of study is in the decade of the seventies of the last century and in the studies of Weber and Schumpeter (Hillier et al. 2004).

The ambiguous character of the SI concept often leads to misunderstandings with other terms such as philanthropy, Corporate Social Responsibility (CSR), entrepreneurship or non-profit making practices (Adams and Hess 2010). But there is no doubt that the greatest confusion is established between SI and technical innovation. Although many authors defend the non-existence of differences between the two concepts (Alquézar-Sabadie 2014), most academic literature agrees to differentiate between the two (Dawson and Daniel 2010). While the former seeks to improve social welfare and breaking with established practices (Dawson and Daniel 2010), the latter focuses on achieving greater profitability and success at corporate level (Mulgan 2007). As Munshi (2010) points out, in technical innovations the income derived from the competitive advantage that innovation generates falls on the innovator, whereas in SI it falls on the end user or society.

Numerous SI definitions are found in the literature, which has provoked intense debate about the true meaning of this concept and what constitutes SI (Elliot 2013). In a review of these definitions, Cunha and Benneworth (2013) classified the main features present in the SI definitions into two distinct categories. The first group addresses the issue of social justice focused on social and human needs as a whole (Moulaert and Nussbaumer 2005) and on value creation and community development (Dawson and Daniel 2010). The second group includes SI practices, characterized by their interdisciplinary, intersectoral and adaptive nature to the different contexts (Brackertz 2011). Based on this duality of characteristics, Cunha and Benneworth (2013) defined social innovation as "A true social innovation is systems-changing by developing novel solutions in border spanning learning communities to create social value and promote community development, challenging existing social institutions through collaborative action developing wider networks".

Due to its great acceptance, we highlight the definition made by Neumeier (2012). This author interprets SI as "the changes in attitudes, behaviours or perceptions of a group of people that are united in an aligned network of interests and that lead to new and better forms of collaboration within a group and beyond it".

The interest aroused by SI is reflected in the exponential increase in studies that analyse social innovation in recent years from different fields of knowledge (Edwards-Schachter et al. 2012; urban and regional development (Moulaert et al. 2005), public policies (Guth 2005), business management (Clements and Sense 2010), open innovation Chesbrough 2003), social psychology (Mumford 2002), public policies (Guth 2005), business management (Clements and Sense, 2010) or social entrepreneurship (Choi and Majumdar 2014).

2.2.2 Definition of Social Entrepreneurship

Demographic changes, technological advances, the liberalization of markets or the failure of governments to meet social needs have promoted the emergence of so-called SE movements (Zahra et al. 2009). As in the case of SI, SE as a field of research was well received and accepted by authors from various disciplines, such as sociology (Kriauciunas et al. 2011), entrepreneurship (Corner and Ho 2010), public administration (Bagnoli and Megali 2009), politics and institutions (Dey and Steyaert 2010) or psychology and education (Chand and Misra 2009). However, as the academic interest increased, a great controversy was generated around its precise meaning. For this reason, much of the scientific work has focused on conceptualizing this phenomenon. Dacin et al. (2011) claim that the current state of conceptual stops further progress in this field of knowledge.

For Gray (2012), the term SE was first used in the literature on social change in the 1960s and 1970s in relation to CSR and in response to the challenges of a new globalized economic environment. However, it was not until the 1990s that this concept was extended with the work of Leadbeater (1997) and Dees (1998). In these studies, Leadbeater emphasizes that social entrepreneurs create social value by finding new solutions to existing social problems, or in the words of Dees, social entrepreneurs seek the most effective methods to fulfil their social missions.

Among the existing definitions we can highlight the one given by Witkamp et al. (2011), for whom SE is a new business model that combines a social objective with a business mentality and promotes a new way of creating social value in a sustainable way. Mair and Marti (2006) consider SE as a process of creating value by allocating current resources to new uses, mainly to explore and exploit opportunities to create social value, stimulate social change or meet new social needs.

One aspect in which all definitions seem to coincide is that the main mission of SE is to contribute to the well-being of society (Austin et al. 2006), address its problems (Light 2006) and satisfy its needs (Seelos and Mair 2005).

The concept of SE has sometimes been confused with that of commercial entrepreneurship. Thus, authors such as Chell (2007) compare both these concepts, since every entrepreneurial process involves both social and economic-commercial behaviour, generating in turn, social value and economic value. Despite this, part of the literature differentiates between both concepts. While the main mission of commercial entrepreneurship is the generation of private benefit, the mission of SE is to create social value for society as a whole (Murphy and Coombes 2009). However, it must be taken into account that the distinction between the SE and the commercial one is not dichotomous, but that enterprises are situated on a continuum that ranges from the purely social to the purely economic, with none of them being on the extremes (Austin et al. 2006).

2.2.3 Differences Between Concepts

In spite of the popularity acquired by the SI and SE concepts, their novelty causes a great deal of confusion when it comes to differentiating their meaning (Mulgan 2007), leading to using on many occasions both concepts interchangeably (Bornstein 2007). However, following the review of the literature, we can see certain differences between both concepts (Phills et al. 2008).

Numerous studies consider SE a form of SI or an opportunity to create SI. For Phills et al. (2008), however, SE is not appropriate for analysing all forms of creation of social change, being the notion of SI more precise, as it includes all types of organizations, both public and private, both profit and non-profit. Thus, SI does not necessarily arise within an entrepreneurial process, and can grow within a collective process organized by multiple actors to create social value and solve social problems (Moulaert et al. 2013).

Some of the main differences between SI and SE that we can find are (Alonso et al. 2015):

1. As we have seen, SI refers to a broader field of action that extends beyond sectors and levels of analysis to a greater extent than SE (Phills et al. 2008), focused on solving problems that affect society but from the business point of view, and its field of action is therefore smaller (Short et al. 2009).

   It should be mentioned, on the other hand, that unlike the authors who understand that the field of action of SI is greater than that of SE, other authors consider that SI is a tool of SE (Peredo and McLean 2006). For these authors SE is seen as a conglomerate of several sub-concepts among which SI would be included (Choi and Majumdar 2014).
2. The processes, strategies, tactics and theories of change generated by SI produce a more lasting impact on society than those carried out by SE (Westley and Antadze 2010).
3. While SE has tended to focus on the individual (or agent) that drives social change, SI studies refer to the motive(s) that generate(s) social change or the processes and results that lead to a change in the system (Chalmers 2012).
4. Although the aim of both is to generate social value, the way in which they achieve it differs. On the one hand, SE generates social value through the enterprise and business (Bacq and Janssen 2011) and on the other hand, SI is achieved through governmental, economic, legal, cultural changes, etc. (Westley and Antadze 2010).
5. While SE refers mainly to tangible improvements (products and services), SI puts greater emphasis on the intangible ones (behavioural, attitude, perception, ideological, etc. changes) (Moulaert and Nussbaumer 2005).
6. Some authors consider that SI is not always necessary for SE, although they all agree that it favours the achievement of greater social results (Pearson 2006).

2.2.4 Bibliometric Studies

The fundamental task of scientific work is the communication of its results with scientific publications being the perfect means for the diffusion and use of knowledge (Vessuri 1995). Through publications, science feeds back and advances. As Martín-Sempere et al. (2000) point out, journals and articles not only serve to communicate and disseminate science, but also to evaluate research and its interests. Bibliometric studies are used to process and analyse these documents.

As in practically all areas of knowledge, there are several bibliometric studies that approach SI and SE, although to date these types of studies are scarce. We emphasize the one done by Phillips et al. (2015), who concluded that both SE and SI share significant common overlaps in the process of identifying opportunities for solving problems and unsatisfied social needs.

However, the number of bibliometric studies that analyse SE and SI separately is higher. Studies such as those by Granados et al. (2011) found that in the UK and USA where the study of SE is more established, without any author standing out above the rest, or the study by Sassmannshausen and Volkmann (2013), who found that almost half of the most cited articles on SE had not been published in journals, but in books. With regard to reviews on SI literature, mention should be made of Bekkers et al. (2013), where, through the review of the most relevant publications in the public administration literature, the factors (in terms of controllers and barriers) that influenced the SI process in the public sector were considered or the one performed by Sharra and Nyssens (2010), who, carrying out a critical and interdisciplinary review of the diverse conceptions of SI as the first and essential step to promote discussion on the subject, found that, although at first glance this concept seems fragmented and refers to different realities, when comparing the different uses and conceptions of SI, there appeared to be more similarities and complementarities than was expected beforehand.

2.3 Methodology

2.3.1 Databases: Scopus

Since access to the entire scientific production is an unreachable goal (Arguimbau Vivo et al. 2013), any bibliometric analysis is limited by the availability, relevance and reliability of information (Rueda et al. 2007). Bibliographic databases are the main source of information used in bibliometric studies and their validity depends to a great extent on the fact that the selected base adequately covers the area under study. The different databases, both multidisciplinary and specialized, differ in thematic coverage, selection criteria of journals and /or documents, geographical and linguistic biases. All these characteristics must be taken into account prior to conducting the bibliometric analysis (Bordons and Zulueta 1999).

SCOPUS, created by the publisher Elsevier in 2004, is the main multidisciplinary bibliographic database, with around 53 million references published in more than 21,000 peer-reviewed scientific journals (Falagas et al. 2008). It is a valuable tool for tracking, viewing and analysing citations since 1996. It includes 390 commercial publications, 370 series of books, 5.5 million papers, 25.5 million patents or 376 million web pages. The journals are classified into 295 thematic categories grouped into 27 areas within the four knowledge blocks: Health Sciences, Life Sciences, Physical Sciences, Social Sciences, Sciences (Table 2.1), becoming an essential instrument for the analysis of any discipline and whose advantages and benefits for this type of studies have been analysed and demonstrated in studies such as those by Goodman and Deis (2005), Bar-Ilan (2010) and Leydesdorff (2012), among others. Its ability to manage bibliographic references and to quantify the citations received enables to evaluate the scientific activity of a journal, the performance of an institution or the international presence of an author, providing a prospect of the world research output.

Table 2.1 Classification of thematic areas in Scopus

Subject area	Subject area classifications
Health sciences (32%)	Medicine; nursing; veterinary; dentistry; health professions; multidisciplinary
Life sciences (15%)	Agricultural and biological sciences; biochemistry, genetics and molecular biology; immunology and microbiology; neuroscience; pharmacology, toxicology and pharmaceutics; multidisciplinary
Physical sciences (30%)	Chemical engineering; chemistry; computer science; earth and planetary sciences; energy; engineering; environmental science; material science; mathematics; physics and astronomy; multidisciplinary
Social sciences (23%)	Arts and humanities; business, management and accounting; decision sciences; economics, econometrics and finance; psychology; social sciences; multidisciplinary

Source: www.elsevier.com

2.3.2 Tracking Methodology

Following the outline of similar studies for developing bibliometric indicators, only articles published in scientific journals are analysed for three main reasons; being high-quality references through a peer review process; being the primary means of transmission of research results (Maltrás-Barba 2003) and forming a representative sample of the academic activity at international level (Benavides-Velasco et al. 2011).

In order to delimit the results of the search to the field of SI and SE, we chose to use the search equation modality. This variety has the advantage of enabling to reach classified journals within all the thematic areas of knowledge resulting in this way, the search more extensive (Corral and Cánoves 2013).

Search Equation: **TITLE ("social entrepreneur*") OR TITLE ("social innovat*") AND PUBYEAR < 2017 AND (LIMIT-TO (DOCTYPE, "ar") OR LIMIT-TO (DOCTYPE, "ip"))**

Once the documents were selected, the necessary ad hoc database was developed to analyse each of the basic variables of the bibliometric indicators. After debugging articles not related to the study area, the final result was 791 articles published in 425 journals and written by 1598 authors, all processed with the bibliographic reference manager Refworks.

2.4 Results and Discussion

2.4.1 Documents

In the search process for SI and SE studies carried out in Scopus, a total of 1438 documents between 1966 and 2016 (Fig. 2.1) were initially found and selected, of which 331 (23%) were books or book chapters, 159 (11%) conference papers, 78

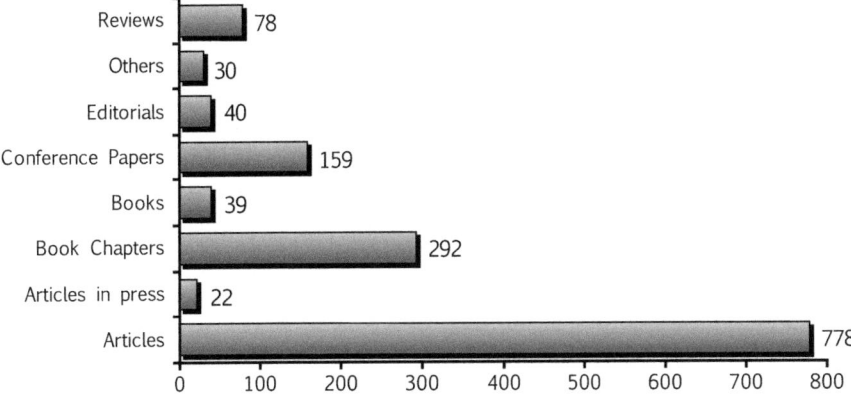

Fig. 2.1 Documents related to SI and SE in Scopus. (*Source:* Authors)

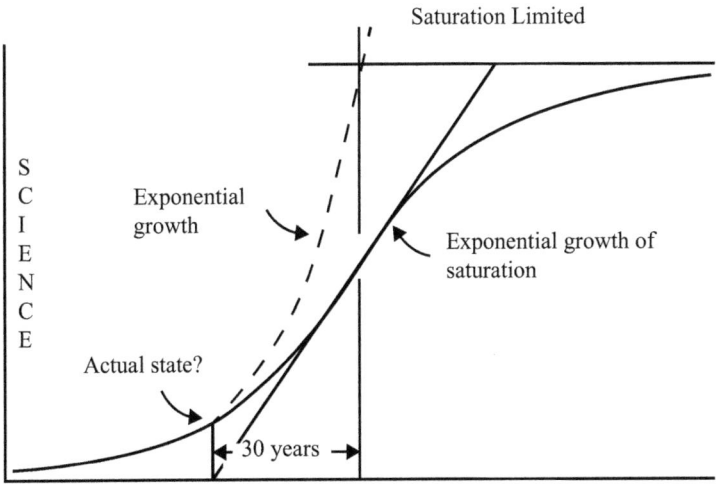

Fig. 2.2 Graphical representation of Price's Growth Law. (*Source:* Valencia et al. 2016)

(5%) reviews, 40 (3%) Editorials and 30 (2%) other formats. The remaining 800 (56%) are articles, which after debugging for the last time were reduced to 791, which make up the ad hoc empirical basis used for the bibliometric analysis.

Price's law assures that the growth of scientific information is exponential, so that every 10–15 years existing global information doubles (Price 1956). However, as shown in Fig. 2.2, each discipline undergoes its own evolution through several stages: Precursors (first publications); Exponential growth (becomes research focus); Linear growth (growth slows down, review and archive of knowledge).

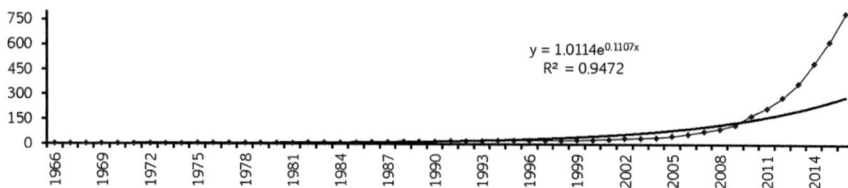

Fig. 2.3 Evolution of articles published and their cumulative. (*Source:* Authors)

Table 2.2 Ranking of the most cited articles

Title	Author	Year	Cited by
Social entrepreneurship research: A source of explanation, prediction, and delight	Mair, J. & Martí, I.	2006	647
A typology of social entrepreneurs: Motives, search processes and ethical challenges	Zahra, S.A. et al.	2009	396
Social entrepreneurship: Why we don't need a new theory and how we move forward from here	Dacin, P. et al.	2010	239
Social entrepreneurship: Creating new business models to serve the poor	Seelos, C. & Mair, J.	2005	239
The world of the social entrepreneur	Thompson, J.L.	2002	192
Social entrepreneurship: A critique and future directions	Dacin, M.T. et al.	2010	176
The legitimacy of social entrepreneurship: Reflexive isomorphism in a pre-paradigmatic field	Nicholls, A.	2010	171
Conceptions of social enterprise and social entrepreneurship in Europe and the United States: Convergences and divergences	Defourny, J. & Nyssens, M.	2010	164

Source: Authors

Based on what is observed in Fig. 2.3, the studies on SI and SE are in the exponential growth phase, adjusting the accumulated production function to an exponential equation with R2 = 0.9472.

With respect to the number of citations received by the articles in Scopus (Table 2.2), one stands out over the rest; Social Entrepreneurship Research: A source of explanation, prediction, and delight (Mair and Marti 2006) with 647 citations, followed by A typology of social entrepreneurs: Motives, search processes and ethical challenges (Zahra et al. 2009) with 396 and Social Entrepreneurship: Why we do not need a new theory and how we move forward from here (Dacin et al. 2010) and Social entrepreneurship: Creating new business models to serve the poor (Seelos and Mair 2005) with 239. It must be highlighted that at the date of accomplishing this study, 14 articles received more than 100 citations.

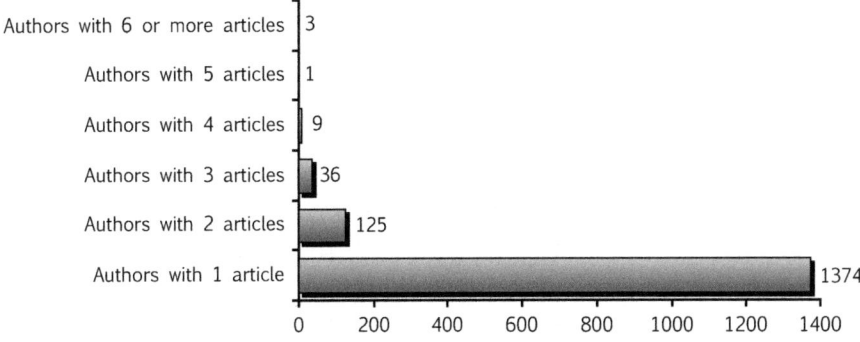

Fig. 2.4 Productivity of authors of SI and SE articles in Scopus. (*Source:* Authors)

Table 2.3 Ranking of the most productive authors

Author	Articles	h-index	Lotka
Westley, F.	12	18	1.079181246
Bacq, S,	8	6	0.903089987
Kickul, J.R.	6	20	0.77815125
Dey, P.	5	4	0.698970004
Antadze, N.	4	3	0.602059991
Handy, F.	4	16	0.602059991
Mair, J.	4	15	0.602059991
Miller, T.L.	4	12	0.602059991
Nadin, S.	4	13	0.602059991
Prieto, L.C.	4	3	0.602059991
Renko, M.	4	10	0.602059991
Shier, M.L.	4	11	0.602059991
Williams, C.C.	4	28	0.602059991

Source: Authors

2.4.2 Authors

Productivity of authors (both primary and secondary) is calculated based on the number of articles published by each of them (Fig. 2.4). According to the criteria proposed by Lotka (1926), they are classified as:

- Small producers: Authors with only one published article
- Medium producers: Authors with between two and nine published articles
- Large producers: Authors with 10 or more published articles.

Within the field of SI and SE, Westley, F. is the only author considered a large producer, having published a total of 12 articles (Table 2.3). Following Lotka,

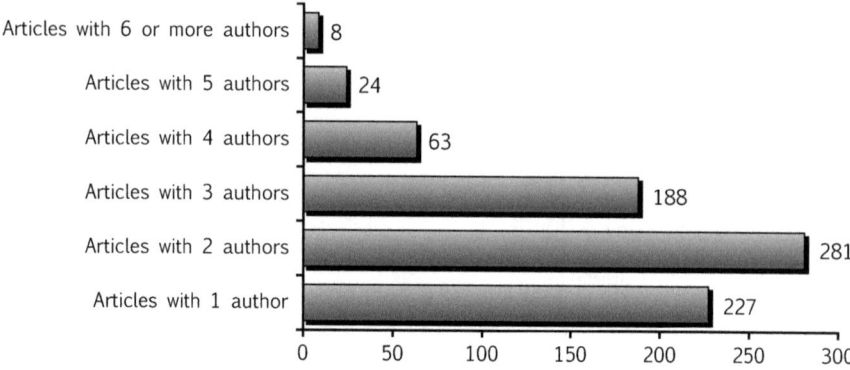

Fig. 2.5 Authors per article. (*Source:* Authors)

Table 2.4 Affiliation of authors by country

Country	Authors	%	Centers	%	Authorships	%
United States	334	21.58	156	21.88	409	22.73
United Kingdom	148	9.56	62	8.70	193	10.73
Spain	108	6.98	38	5.33	124	6.89
Canada	91	5.88	36	5.05	126	7.00
Italy	69	4.46	29	4.07	72	4.00
Australia	65	4.20	22	3.09	71	3.95
Germany	63	4.07	35	4.91	78	4.34
Netherlands	52	3.36	22	3.09	60	3.34

Source: Authors

11.2% (173) of the authors are medium producers, while the remaining 88.8% (1374) are considered small producers having a single published work. The average productivity per author was 1.16 articles.

The collaboration index, number of signatures on average, for the whole period was 2.27. As shown in Fig. 2.5, 5564 articles (71.3%) are written by more than one author, with 2 or 3 authors per article being the most common, 469 (59.3%).

By country (Table 2.4), the United States stands out with more than 21% of the authors affiliated to some center of this country (334 authors – 156 centers – 409 authors). It is followed by the United Kingdom (148 – 62 – 193) and Spain (108 – 38 – 124) as the most relevant countries in the academic literature indexed in the Scopus database on SI and SE of a total number of 71 countries.

Table 2.5 Journals indexed in Scopus that form the Bradford's core on SI and SE

Title	Articles
Journal of social entrepreneurship	45
Journal of business ethics	19
Voluntas	15
International journal of entrepreneurship and small business	11
Entrepreneurship and regional development	10
Journal of entrepreneurship	10
Technological forecasting and social change	10
Journal of business research	9
Academy of management learning and education	8
Innovation	8
Ecology and society	7
Information systems management	7

Source: Authors

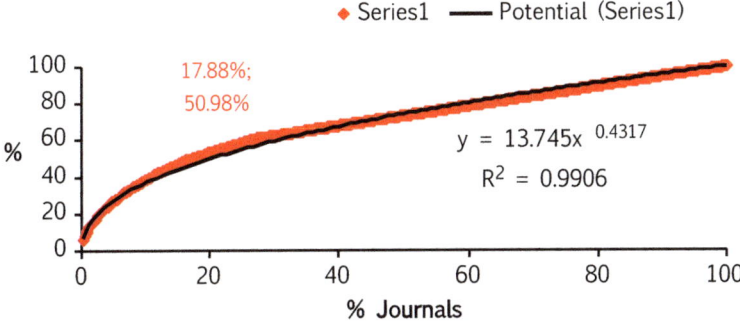

Fig. 2.6 Lorenz Curve and Bradford's core. (*Source:* Authors)

2.4.3 Journals

The total number of 791 selected articles on SI and SE were published in 424 different journals, 309 of them (72.88%) published a single study (39.06% of the total), and only 115 (27.12%) included two or more papers (Table 2.5).

According to Bradford's Law (1934), a small number of journals group most of the articles published related to an area, a fact that helps us to identify the journals most used by researchers for the dissemination of their work (Fig. 2.6). Minimum Bradford Zone (MBZ) is defined as the number of articles equal to half the quantity that appears in the last range of the list of journals arranged by production (those that produce a single article) (Spinak 1996).

$$MBZ = \frac{NR1a}{2}; \quad MBZ = \frac{309}{2}; \quad MBZ = 154.5$$

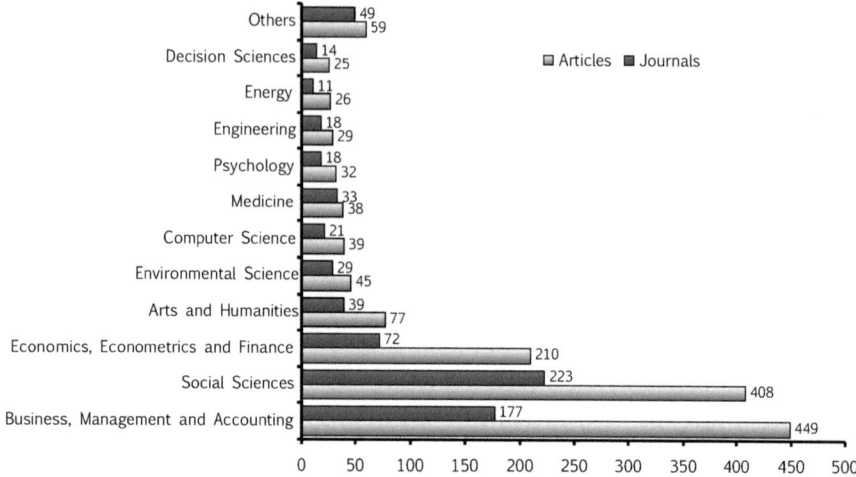

Fig. 2.7 Classification of articles by subject areas. (*Source:* Authors)

Where:

MBZ: Minimum Bradford Zone
NR1a: Total number of journals with a single published article

Once the MBZ value has been calculated, and from the ranking of journals arranged in descending order of productivity, the MBZ is made up of those journals whose sum of articles was equal to the value of MBZ (155). In our bibliometric analysis on SI and SE, the MBZ is made up of 12 journals, with the Journal of Social Entrepreneurship standing out from the rest with 45 published articles (5.7%).

The thematic classification of documents carried out by the Scopus database, according to the areas to which the journals in which they are published belong to (Fig. 2.7), shows a great variety of areas (24), which include articles on SI and SE, highlighting 3 over the rest: Business, Management and Accounting with 449 articles (56.76%); Social Sciences with 408 (51.58%) and Economics, Econometrics and Finance with 210 (26.55%).

2.4.4 *Keywords*

The correct selection of search terms is an essential issue when locating documents related to a specific field of research. The analysis of the keywords used by the authors of articles indexed in Scopus on SI and SE (Fig. 2.8), points out that it is precisely the words Social Innovation and Social Entrepreneur that are most frequently repeated, followed by far by Human, Social Capital or Sustainability.

Fig. 2.8 Most used keywords in articles on Sport Management in Scopus. (*Source:* Authors)

2.5   Conclusions

The main objective of this work was to perform a review of the academic literature related to SI and SE, contained within the Scopus databases, in order to know and summarize the state in which research is found within this particular area of knowledge. Based on the analysis of the results, and the extensive literature consulted, to summarize, useful ideas for future researchers can be drawn.

(a) As in other fields, the article published in scientific journals is the authors' favourite transmission means on SI and SE to make their research known. After a few years with a small number of published papers, it is from 2006 when a second stage of exponential growth begins that continues until today, demonstrating the interest that currently awakens everything concerning SI and SE.

(b) Westley, F. is the only author considered a large producer, having published a total of 12 articles. The high percentage of articles signed by a single author causes the average productivity per author to be very low, close to 1. With a collaboration index of 2.27, the analysis of co-authors shows a high percentage of articles with two or more authors, which favours receiving a larger number of citations (Granda-Orive et al. 2009).

(c) By country, the United States stands out with more than 21% of the authors affiliated to some center of this country. It is followed by the United Kingdom, Spain and Canada as the most relevant countries within the academic literature indexed in the Scopus database on SI and SE.

(d) Through Bradford's Law with a larger number of papers published and which make up the so-called Bradford's core were identified. In our bibliometric analysis on SI and SE, the MBZ is made up of 12 journals, where the *Journal of Social Entrepreneurship* stands out with 45 published articles.
(e) Thematic classification of documents, according to the areas which the journals in which they are published belong to, reveals a great variety of fields in which the articles are included and proves the great multi-direction of the concepts SI and SE. *Business, Management and Accounting; Social Sciences;* and *Economics, Econometrics and Finance* are the areas that include a greater number of articles.
(f) The terms belonging to the category of *Social Innovation* and *Social Entrepreneurship* are those that most frequently appear as keywords of the articles. It is advisable to use them by means of an advanced search of documents within Scopus. Other words that appear on a greater number of occasions are: *Human, Social Capital* or *Sustainability.*

In summary, this literature review shows that research on SI and SE has increased during the last decade, accelerating in the last 5 years and attracting attention from a wide range of disciplines.

When interpreting the results of any bibliometric study, these should be contextualized within the area under study, in this case SI and SE, and taking into account the limitation of choosing a single source of information (Scopus) and defining a specific search profile. On the other hand, the aim was not to carry out an analysis of the quality of the content of the selected articles, which can be studied in a later research, but a descriptive-quantitative analysis of the studies related to the field of SI and SE. In order to expand this chapter, it would be interesting to examine the documents indexed in other databases, in addition to considering the possibility of including comparative analyzes among them or to deepen the analysis of citations.

References

Adams, D., & Hess, M. (2010). Social innovation and why it has policy significance. *The Economic and Labour Relations Review, 21*(2), 139–155.
Alonso, D., González, N., & Nieto, M. (2015). Emprendimiento social vs innovación social. *Cuadernos Aragoneses de Economía, 24*(1–2), 119–140.
Alquézar-Sabadie, J. (2014). Technological innovation, human capital and social change for sustainability. Lessons learnt from the industrial technologies theme of the EU's research framework programme. *Science of the Total Environment, 481*, 668–673.
Arguimbau Vivo, L., Fuentes Pujol, E., & Gallifa Calatayud, M. (2013). Una década de investigación documental sobre cienciometría en España: Análisis de los artículos de la base de datos ISOC (2000–2009). *Revista Española de Documentación Científica, 36*(2), 1–9.
Austin, J., Stevenson, H., & Wei-Skillern, J. (2006). Social and commercial entrepreneurship: Same, different, or both? *Entrepreneurship Theory and Practice, 30*(1), 1–22.
Bacq, S., & Janssen, F. (2011). The multiple faces of social entrepreneurship: A review of definitional issues based on geographical and thematic criteria. *Entrepreneurship and Regional Development, 23*(5–6), 373–403.

Bagnoli, L., & Megali, C. (2009). Measuring performance in social enterprises. *Nonprofit and Voluntary Sector Quarterly, 20*(10), 1–17.

Bar-Ilan, J. (2010). Citations to the 'Introduction to infometrics' indexed by WOS, Scopus and Google Scholar. *Scientometrics, 82*(3), 495–506.

Bekkers, V. J. J. M., Tummers, L. G., & Voorberg, W. H. (2013). *From public innovation to social innovation in the public sector: A literature review of relevant drivers and barriers.* Rotterdam: Erasmus University Rotterdam.

Benavides-Velasco, C. A., Guzmán-Parra, V., & Quintana-García, C. (2011). Evolución de la literatura sobre empresa familiar como disciplina científica. *Cuadernos de Economía y Dirección de la Empresa, 14*(2), 78–90.

Bordons, M., & Zulueta, M. A. (1999). Evaluación de la actividad científica a través de indicadores bibliométricos. *Revista Española de Cardiología, 52*(10), 790–800.

Bornstein, D. (2007). *How to change the world: Social entrepreneurs and the power of new ideas.* New York: Oxford University Press.

Brackertz, N. (2011). Social innovation, Australian policy online, topic guide, 5 December.

Bradford, S. C. (1934). Sources of information on specific subjects. *Engineering, 137,* 85–86.

Chalmers, D. (2012). Social innovation: An exploration of the barriers faced by innovating organizations in the social economy. *Local Economy, 28*(1), 17–34.

Chand, V. S., & Misra, S. (2009). Teachers as educational-social entrepreneurs: The innovation-social entrepreneurship spiral. *Journal of Entrepreneurship, 18*(2), 219–228.

Chell, E. (2007). Social enterprise and entrepreneurship towards a convergent theory of the entrepreneurial process. *International Small Business Journal, 25*(1), 5–26.

Chesbrough, H. W. (2003). *Open innovation: The new imperative for creating and profiting from technology.* Cambridge, MA: Harvard Business School Press.

Choi, N., & Majumdar, S. (2014). Social entrepreneurship as an essentially contested concept: Opening a new avenue for systematic future research. *Journal of Business Venturing, 29*(3), 363–376.

Clements, M. D., & Sense, A. J. (2010). Socially shaping supply chain integration through learning. *International Journal of Technology Management, 51*(1), 92–105.

Corner, P. D., & Ho, M. (2010). How opportunities develop in social entrepreneurship. *Entrepreneurship Theory and Practice, 34*(4), 635–659.

Corral, J. A., & Cánoves, G. (2013). La investigación turística publicada en revistas turísticas y no turísticas: análisis bibliométrico de la producción de las universidades catalanas. *Cuadernos de Turismo, 31*(1), 55–81.

Cunha, J., & Benneworth, P.S. (2013). *Universities' contributions to social innovation: Towards a theoretical framework.* Paper presented at the annual European urban research association conference, Enschede.

Dacin, P. A., Dacin, M. T., & Matear, M. (2010). Social entrepreneurship: Why we don't need a new theory and how we move forward from here. *The Academy of Management Perspectives, 24*(3), 37–57.

Dacin, M. T., Dacin, P. A., & Tracey, P. (2011). Social entrepreneurship: A critique and future directions. *Organization Science, 22*(5), 1203–1213.

Dawson, P., & Daniel, L. (2010). Understanding social innovation: A provisional framework. *International Journal of Technology Management, 51*(1), 9–21.

Dees, G. (1998). *The meaning of 'social entrepreneurship'.* Center for Social Innovation, Stanford University, Graduate School of Business. Working paper.

Dey, P., & Steyaert, C. (2010). The politics of narrating social entrepreneurship. *Journal of Enterprising Communities. People and Places in the Global Economy, 4*(1), 85–108.

Drucker, P. (1985). *Entrepreneurship and Innovation: Practice and Principles.* New York: Harper Business.

Edwards-Schachter, M. E., Matti, C. E., & Alcántara, E. (2012). Fostering quality of life through social innovation: A living lab methodology study case. *Review of Policy Research, 29*(6), 672–692.

Elliot, G. (2013). Character and impact of social innovation in higher education. *International Journal of Continuing Education and Lifelong Learning, 5*(2), 71–82.

Falagas, M. E., Pitsouni, E. I., Malietzis, G. A., & Pappas, G. (2008). Comparison of PubMed, Scopus, Web of Science, and Google Scholar: Strengths and weaknesses. *FASEB Journal, 22*(2), 338–342.

Godin, B. (2012). Social innovation: Utopias of innovation from 1830 to the present. *Project on the intellectual History of innovation*, INRS, Montreal, Working paper N. 11.

Goodman, D., & Deis, L. (2005). Web of Science (2004 version) and Scopus. *The Charleston Advisor, 6*(3), 5–21.

Granados, M. L., Hlupic, V., Coakes, E., & Mohamed, S. (2011). Social enterprise and social entrepreneurship research and theory: A bibliometric analysis from 1991 to 2010. *Social Enterprise Journal, 7*(3), 198–218.

Granda-Orive, J. I., Villanueva-Serrano, S., Aleixandre-Benavent, R., Valderrama-Zurían, J. C., Alonso-Arroyo, A., García-Río, F., et al. (2009). Redes de colaboración científica internacional en tabaquismo. Análisis de co-autorías a través del Science Citation Index durante el periodo 1999–2003. *Gaceta Sanitaria, 23*(3), 34–43.

Gray, E. (2012). For-profit social entrepreneurship. In T. S. Lyons (Ed.), *Social entrepreneurship: How businesses can transform society* (pp. 47–70). Santa Barbara: ABC-CLIO.

Guth, M. (2005). Innovation, social inclusion and coherent regional development: A new diamond for a socially inclusive innovation policy in regions. *European Planning Studies, 13*(2), 333–349.

Hart, S. L., & Milstein, M. B. (2003). Creating sustainable value. *Academy of Management Executive, 17*(2), 56–67.

Hillier, J., Moulaert, F., & Nussbaumer, J. (2004). Trois essais sur le rôle de l'innovation sociale dans le développement territorial. *Géographie, Économie, Société, 6*(2), 129–152.

Kriauciunas, A., Parmigiani, A., & Rivera-Santos, M. (2011). Leaving our comfort zone: Integrating established practices with unique adaptations to conduct survey-based strategy research in nontraditional contexts. *Strategic Management Journal, 32*(9), 994–1010.

Leadbeater, C. (1997). *The rise of the social entrepreneur*. London: Demos.

Leydesdorff, L. (2012). World shares of publications of the USA, EU-27, and China compared and predicted using the new Web of Science interface versus Scopus. *El Profesional de la Información, 21*(1), 43–49.

Light, P. C. (2006). Reshaping social entrepreneurship. *Stanford Social Innovation Review, 4*, 47–51.

Lotka, A. J. (1926). The frequency distribution of scientific productivity. *Journal of the Washington Academy of Sciences, 16*(12), 317–323.

Low, M. B., & MacMillan, I. C. (1988). Entrepreneurship: Past research and future challenges. *Journal of Management, 14*, 139–161.

Mair, J., & Marti, I. (2006). Social entrepreneurship research: A source of explanation, prediction, and delight. *Journal of World Business, 41*(1), 36–44.

Maltrás-Barba, B. (2003). *Los indicadores bibliométricos: Fundamentos y aplicación al análisis de la ciencia*. Gijón: Trea.

Manzini, E. (2015). *Design, when everybody designs* (1st ed.). Cambridge, MA: The MIT Press.

Martín-Sempere, M. J., Rey-Rocha, J., & Plaza-Gómez, L. (2000). Assessment of Spanish scientific journals on Geology. *Interciencia, 25*(8), 372–378.

Mitchell, R. K., Agle, B. R., & Wood, D. (1997). Towards a theory of stakeholder identification and salience: Defining the principle of who and what really counts. *Academy of Management Review, 22*, 853–886.

Moulaert, F., & Nussbaumer, J. (2005). The social region: Beyond the territorial dynamics of the learning economy. *European Urban and Regional Studies, 12*(1), 45–64.

Moulaert, F., Martinelli, F., Swyngedouw, E., & Gonzáles, S. (2005). Towards alternative model(s) of local innovation. *Urban Studies, 42*(11), 1969–1990.

Moulaert, F., McCallum, D., Mehmood, D., & Hamdouch, A. (dir) (2013). *International handbook of social innovation: Collective action, social learning and transdisciplinary research*. Cheltenham: Edward Elgar Publishing.

Mulgan, G. (2007). *In and out of sync: The challenge of growing social innovations*. London: Nesta.

Mumford, M. D. (2002). Social innovation: Ten cases from Benjamin Franklin. *Creativity Research Journal, 14*(2), 253–266.

Munshi, N. V. (2010). Value creation, social innovation, and entrepreneurship in global economies. *Journal of Asia-Pacific Business, 11*(3), 160–165.

Murphy, P. J., & Coombes, S. M. (2009). A model of social entrepreneurial discovery. *Journal of Business Ethics, 87*(3), 325–336.

Neumeier, S. (2012). Why do social innovations in rural development matter and should they be considered more seriously in rural development research?–proposal for a stronger focus on social innovations in rural development research. *Sociologia Ruralis, 52*(1), 48–69.

Pearson, K. A. (2006). *Accelerating our impact: Philanthropy, innovation and social change.* Montreal: The J.W. McConnell Family Foundation.

Peredo, A. M., & McLean, M. (2006). Social entrepreneurship: A critical review of the concept. *Journal of World Business, 41*(1), 56–65.

Phillips, W., Lee, H., Ghobadian, A., O'Regan, N., & James, P. (2015). Social innovation and social entrepreneurship: A systematic review. *Group & Organization Management, 40*(3), 428–461.

Phills, J. A., Deiglmeier, K., & Miller, D. T. (2008). Rediscovering social innovation. *Stanford Social Innovation Review, 6*, 34–43.

Price, D. J. S. (1956). The exponential curve of science. *Discovery, 17*(6), 240–243.

Rueda, G., Gerdsri, P., & Kocaoglu, D. F. (2007). Bibliometrics and social network analysis of the nanotechnology field. In *PICMET'07-2007 Portland international conference on management of engineering & technology* (pp. 2905–2911). IEEE.

Sassmannshausen, S. P., & Volkmann, C. (2013). *A bibliometric based review on social entrepreneurship and its establishment as a field of research* (No. 2013-003). Schumpeter Discussion Papers.

Seelos, C., & Mair, J. (2005). Social entrepreneurship: Creating new business models to serve the poor. *Business Horizons, 48*(3), 241–246.

Sharra, R., & Nyssens, M. (2010). *Social innovation: An interdisciplinary and critical review of the concept* (pp. 1–15). Louvain-la-Neuve: Université Catholique de Louvain Belgium.

Short, J. C., Moss, T. W., & Lumpkin, G. T. (2009). Research in social entrepreneurship: Past contributions and future opportunities. *Strategic Entrepreneurship Journal, 3*(2), 161–194.

Spinak, E. (1996). *Diccionario Enciclopédico de Bibliometría, Cienciometría e Informetría.* Caracas: UNESCO.

Tukamushaba, E., Orobia, L., & George, B. (2011). Development of a conceptual model to understand international social entrepreneurship and its application in the Ugandan context. *Journal of International Entrepreneurship, 9*(4), 282–298.

Valencia, A., Montoya, I. A., & Montoya, A. (2016). Intención emprendedora en estudiantes universitarios: un estudio bibliométrico. *Intangible Capital, 12*(4), 884–922.

Vessuri, H. (1995). Estrategia de valoración de las revistas científicas latinoamericanas. In A. M. Cetto, & K.-I. Hillerud (Comp.), *Publicaciones científicas en América Latina* (pp. 200–2010). México: Fondo de Cultura Económica.

Westley, F., & Antadze, N. (2010). Making a difference: Strategies for scaling social innovation for greater impact. *The Innovation Journal: The Public Sector Innovation Journal, 15*(2), 1–19.

Witkamp, M. J., Royakkers, L. M., & Raven, R. M. (2011). Strategic niche management of social innovations: The case of social entrepreneurship. *Technology Analysis & Strategic Management, 23*(6), 667–681.

Zahra, S., Gedajlovic, E., Neubaum, D., & Shulman, J. (2009). A typology of social entrepreneurs: Motives, search processes and ethical challenges. *Journal of Business Venturing, 24*(5), 519–532.

Chapter 3
Social Innovation in Public Organisations: The Perspectives of Managers

João J. Ferreira, Cristina I. Fernandes, and Valter R. M. Oliveira

Abstract The world today is not only becoming increasingly competitive but this competition is also increasingly intense and, for organisations, innovation emerges as one solution to the problems they face. Thus, innovation has attracted increased interest as the means to acquire and develop skills to address and/or inspire organisations in a globally competitive and economically uncertain environment. Furthermore, in such a competitive world, not even the public sector escapes the need to evolve towards providing better services and satisfying its citizens. However, just what is the need to evaluate social innovation in public organisations? Is there the drive to compete and/or market share to conquer? Profits to achieve? The public sector has many points in common with the private sector with the goals in both sectors involving the raising of efficiency and quality levels and better satisfaction for customers. Thus, this research aims at studying social innovation in public organisations and understanding how social innovation can better the lives of citizens from the perspective of managers. As the data collection method, we applied a questionnaire based on the constructs and scales already validated by Vigoda-Gadot (Public Administration 86(2):307–329, 2008) before then analysing the results through recourse to PLS. The results identify how responsiveness and ethics and morals are important factors in the perceptions of innovation as perceived by citizens. In turn, the findings also demonstrate the importance of this capacity for innovation to the image of the public sector as well as the confidence and satisfaction of its citizens.

Keywords Social innovation · Public organizations · Manager perspectives · Citizens · Institutional theory

J. J. Ferreira (✉) · C. I. Fernandes
Management and Economics Department, University of Beira Interior and NECE – Research Unit in Business Sciences, Covilhã, Portugal
e-mail: jjmf@ubi.pt

V. R. M. Oliveira
Management and Economics Department, University of Beira Interior, Covilhã, Portugal

© Springer International Publishing AG, part of Springer Nature 2018
M. Peris-Ortiz et al. (eds.), *Strategies and Best Practices in Social Innovation*,
https://doi.org/10.1007/978-3-319-89857-5_3

3.1   Introduction

Innovation has attracted the greatest level of interest as the most appropriate means of acquiring and developing competences able to resolve and/or inspire organisations against a backdrop of global competition and economic uncertainties. There is no single, concrete definition of the term innovation, in part because the meaning has been undergoing constant change, despite all of the efforts applied to achieving a consensual definition (Halvorsen et al. 2005).

Generally, the understanding of innovation involves behavioural changes (Halvorsen et al. 2005) even while changes are normal in every organisation (Green et al. 2001). For the change to rank as an innovation, it must meet three criteria: newness (Koch and Hauknes 2005), impact and reapplication (Borins 2001). While there are these different definitions, in accordance with the role held in society, whether academic, political decision maker or business manager (Massa and Testa 2008), innovation contains new ideas that function in operational practice (Green et al. 2001; Mulgan and Albury 2003). Hence, innovation holds importance to organisations and has gathered increasing proportions of their attentions (Dundon 2002; Green et al. 2001; Mulgan and Albury 2003; Windrum and García-Goñi 2008). However, where does the need to evaluate social innovation in the public sector stem from? Is there the competition to compete against? Market share to win over? Profits and gains to achieve? While there is the presumption that the economy adjusts to the markets of its own accord, reality demonstrates how they constantly depend on the decisions of governments (Maroto and Rubalcaba 2005) and institutions (North 1990, 1991).

Despite recent progress, and in keeping with its status as a research field under development, there remains deep and ongoing discussions about the role of institutions in economic development. Nevertheless, the institutionalist theory has gained a rising profile and attributed importance whether for explaining the workings of the economy or for observing how institutional change impacts on the ways of life of peoples and productive organisations across different countries (North 2005).

When taking reality into account, we soon grasp the extent of the influence and weighting of the public sector in the daily realities of both people and the economy. The public sector employs persons, the public sector is a client, the public sector "facilitates" through security and social action programs, children attend schools, everybody is out and about in public parks, benefitting from highways and other public services and goods (Maroto and Rubalcaba 2005). We may correspondingly begin to understand how the private sector is not the main factor of competitive advantage to a nation as the public sector reaches far further and everything that the state involves reflects in major consequences for the economy in general and its institutions in particular.

According to North (2005), we live in a non-ergodic world, in an environment in which changes are continuous, atypical and human beings need to engage in enormous cognitive efforts to begin to grasp economic and social phenomena. Hence, the traditional principle of rationality, as incorporated into economic models, turns out to be insufficient either for understanding the choices or how to process the ongoing changes and the innovations and correspondingly grow the performances of institutions and organisations.

There thus arises the need to analyse social innovation in the public sector (Maroto and Rubalcaba 2005; Snow 2007). The public sector shares many points in common with the private sector. Various authors (Bloch and Bugge 2013; Omachonu and Einspruch 2010) detail aspects such as the objectives that both sectors strive to obtain through not only raising their levels of efficiency and quality but also better satisfying their clients. These aspects end up by reflecting the same concept and processes of innovation. Taking into consideration these shared aspects, the public sector might be able to obtain valuable lessons about administrative techniques and practices were it capable of incorporating private sector practices and values (DeLeon and Denhardt 2000; Kay and Goldspink 2013). According to Mulgan and Albury (2003), effective government and efficient public services depend on the success of their innovations. Innovations directly improve the quality of services and rarely return any associated negative effects (Election Commission 2000; Salge and Vera 2012). In this context, the objectives of the present research are the following: (a) undertaking a survey of the literature existing on social innovation in the public sector and comparing this with innovation in the private sector; (b) proposing and testing a conceptual research model for a specific concrete reality.

3.2 Literature Review

We may characterise innovation as efficient (which incorporates alterations designed to improve on that already existing), evolutionary (innovations that do something already done but in a new and better way) and revolutionary (radical innovation as regards that which was previously happening) (Dundon 2002).

Organisational innovation has received increasing levels of attention in the literature on marketing and long term management (Frambach and Schillewaert 2002). The isolated vision of the process of generating and applying innovations does not result in consistent and reliable approaches according to the theories of generating or implementing innovation (Damanpour and Daniel Wischnevsky 2006). The industrial sector is no longer perceived as the main factor in establishing the competitive advantage of a nation (Matthews et al. 2009; Snow 2007).

In turn, there is growing recognition as to the importance of the public sector and social innovation in this sector for the growth in long term national productivity (Matthews et al. 2009; Snow 2007). The influence of the public sector reflects in the taxes paid. Almost everybody has at some stage received a transfer from the state, for example some form of social security payment or the payment of wages in the case of state sector workers. Most children attend public schools and there is cross-society enjoyment of public parks, highways and other services and infrastructures (Maroto and Rubalcaba 2005). The public sector is wide reaching and what happens in the sector holds major consequences for the economy in general (Halvorsen et al. 2005). Thus, there emerges the corresponding need to analyse social innovation in the public sector (Matthews et al. 2009; Snow 2007).

Public service is an activity of interest to the population in general, the responsibility of governments and their respective institutions. However, this also recognises the nature of public services with private companies undertaking activities in the general interest even if doing so with economic and learning objectives (Bon and Louppe1980). This learning drives constant modifications in the mental models, which get reviewed, redefined or rejected depending on their abilities to interpret the prevailing environment (North et al. 2004; North 2005). The learning process results in individual cognitive models responsible for modelling and framing reality.

Chapman and Cowdell (1998) define the public sector as the term normally applied to collectively reference the institutions that societies deem necessary for the basic wellbeing of their members. North (1990) strives to demonstrate how the long term development and the historical evolution of any society remains conditioned by the formation and evolution of its institutions (institutional dynamic). The market adds costs to the economy and reducing those costs stems from the existence of institutions independent of the sector of activity.

The public sector falls into the classification of four categories of products and producers: the primary or agricultural sector, the secondary or industrial sector, the tertiary sector that refers to commercial services and the quaternary sector that spans non-commercial services (Kuhry and Torre 2002). There is a broad perception of the public sector as rendering non-commercial services and with this description susceptible to organisation into two fields: (1) an institutional definition strictly based upon the juridical status of the producers, thus spanning public services and non-profit private services; (2) a functional definition – a list of service categories that cover the range of interventions by governments and/or by similar non-profit private organisations (Kuhry and Torre 2002). Effective governance and public services depend on the success of innovations as these constitute the means of developing the best ways of meeting needs, resolving problems, making the best utilisation of resources and technologies with innovation not so much representing an option but rather a fundamental activity for any organisation (Mulgan and Albury 2003).

Koch and Hauknes (2005) identify how public sector innovation may include the production of "things", materials or products while public social sector innovation implies the application of already existing "things" or the delivery of services in keeping with either organisational changes or policy developments. Potts (2010) complements this with the concept of negative innovation; hence, as an attempt to create value (as any innovation does) by eliminating a negative value (that logically emerges as equivalent to a positive value). According to this author, innovation may therefore work in the inverse sense with the creation of value deriving from a controlled elimination approach.

There are then difficulties in applying methods and theories from the private sector to the public sector as, while there may be public organisations that operate in similar fashions to the private sector, the majority of such institutions continue to work in different contexts (Halvorsen et al. 2005). Institutional change correspondingly assumes an incremental nature, which emphasises the role played by the path dependence of the institutional matrix and holds core implications for any understanding of the differences in levels of economic development among states (North 1990).

The particular case of the public sector is also highly sensitive to time and the quality of ideas in a way that does hold true for the private sector. Furthermore, political initiatives may get introduced with relatively little prior warning and with their range limited to the modification or adaptation at the departmental level. Consequently, public managers become far more adept at reacting to new and highly uncertain ideas than their peers in the private sector (Kay and Goldspink 2013).

The public sector also closely interconnects and indeed depends upon its interactions with the private sector and the consumers of public services as regards innovation (Bloch and Bugge 2013). Amara et al. (2008) maintain these contacts with the exterior interrelate with the presence of greater levels of innovation even while not with the level of its newness.

According to the Election Commission (2000), innovations improve the work of the public administrative and rarely incur the aforementioned negative effect. The positive effects of innovation include: improvements to accessing information through innovating services; higher consumer satisfaction; better focused services; swifter service delivery; simplified administrative procedures; improvements to working conditions and/or employee satisfaction levels; and innovation achieved cost reductions. Salge and Vera (2012) report on a direct effect of innovation activities on the quality of public services and more than any client or learning focused orientations that both return only moderately positive effects.

Social innovation projects, in the service sector, incorporate a deep understanding of a particular problem or a clear understanding of the service able to resolve it, furthermore identifying the key consumers and defining viable tactics, drawing upon resources such as time and money and not making any recourse to external investments. Planning for organisational success assumes that project managers have attained the competences for building alliances with the key interested parties in order to guarantee the service gets successfully adopted. The core parties holding such interests include the consumers as well as the line managers and other governmental agencies (Bygstad et al. 2007).

There is an implicit understanding that men are more innovative than women and capacities such as self-confidence and knowledge represent important factors for understanding why some ideas do not transform into innovations (Nählinder 2010). The absence of public sector innovations oriented towards personality constitutes the most notable difference when compared with the private sector where such innovations take a leading role in the profile of success (Kay and Goldspink 2013), perhaps stemming from how public sector values discourage personal aggrandisement over the work produced.

Becheikh et al. (2006) identify how one of the most important decisions for policy formulators seeking to foster innovation would be to introduce competition among the diverse economic sectors, removing barriers to the entrance of new players and avoiding strategies undertaken by companies striving to attain monopoly or almost monopoly positions in their sector. Denham and Kaberon (2012) highlight the continuous need to foster innovation as its absence might jeopardise the stability and performance of institutions.

This recognition extends to the importance and utility of innovations able to impact not only on the technical systems but also on their social systems with Naranjo-Gil (2009) thus suggesting that executives formulate the structural and human resource strategies in conjunction with the technical strategies.

Ongkittikul and Geerlings (2006) report that radical reforms are susceptible to sustaining long term innovations more than merely moderate reforms. Therefore, managers wishing to nurture the introduction of social innovations to leverage improvements to organisational efficiency need to recognise the situational factors for the implementation of both administrative and technical innovations.

Concerns about society are important to motivation and should correspondingly receive the scope for seeking out ideas able to contribute towards the public interest. Hence, civil servants and state sector employees should have access to the means for exercising influence and creativity in addition to other incentives, for example financial bonuses, among other efforts focusing on establishing a dynamic and entrepreneurial climate that nurtures learning, intellectual challenges and personal growth underpinning the feeling that they are engaging in public service of social significance (Özcan and Reichstein 2009).

The public sector needs furthermore to dedicate more attention in relation to the acquisition of knowledge, supporting and contributing to the sharing of skills (Micheli et al. 2012). Holm (2009) agrees on this importance attributed to knowledge and also identifies how intellectual property needs protecting in order to serve as a competitive advantage.

Public sector organisations are increasingly aware of the need to leverage the innovation capacities of their members of staff (Savory 2009). Social innovation and entrepreneurship inherently interlink in the public service (Bartlett and Dibben 2002; Parry and Proctor-Thomson 2002). Additionally, studies of the career dynamics implicitly reveal that government and state sector employees are not entrepreneurial (Özcan and Reichstein 2009).

The public sector manager therefore plays a fundamental role in ensuring success in implementing some of the recent policy initiatives taken within the international context of the public sector, which contrasts with the public organisation stereotype depicting large bureaucracies that hinder innovation and in which there is little scope for any entrepreneurial spirit (Bartlett and Dibben 2002).

3.3 Methodology

Taking into consideration the rising importance of the state and its public organisations for the growth of a nation (Maroto and Rubalcaba 2005; Matthews et al. 2009; Snow 2007), the analytical perspective of this study focuses on public organisations under the auspices of the state. As already referenced, while there is recognition of the public organisational character of all public organisations and even their private peers whenever the latter undertake activities in the general interest (Bon and Louppe 1980), even when displaying this public service characteristic, private organisations contain differences to their public counterparts (Halvorsen et al. 2005).

Of the public organisations eligible for study, we selected only those from the public sectors accounting for the greatest proportion of the Portuguese State Budget [S.B.] ("Citizen Budget – State Budget 2015" 2014). The difficulties imposed by the crisis and recession that Europe and consequently Portugal have experienced, the lack of budgetary means represents one of the greatest problems (Stockhammer and Sotiropoulos 2014). We therefore seek to expose this problem to the power of social innovations for resolving problems or improving situations.

In the case of the 2015 S.B., 44% of public expenditure goes on social security and related actions, 12% on health and 10% on education. Together, these three sectors account for 66% of total public expenditure and well ahead of the next sector, the relatively small transport and communications section back on 5%.

Within the same framework, IDH, an index that measures national development, focuses upon three core points: average life expectancy, number of years of education and individual income. The sectors bearing greatest direct influence on each of these three factors are education, healthcare and social action (United Nations Development Program 2014).

This also demonstrates the importance of the sectors chosen for analysis. It is fundamental to gaining a vision of innovation in these sectors, whether deployed to resolve problems related to the crisis, as these are the core state costs, or to help the country develop in keeping with the key points of the IDH.

As the data collection method, we drafted questionnaires based upon those already constructed and applied in the research by Vigoda-Gadot et al. (2008). According to the method of these same authors, the respondents, mid-ranking managers at the respective organisations, answered the questionnaires online. While seeking to obtain results based on citizen perspectives, these authors defend that this target audience enables the reduction in response biases given its minimisation of problems over the lack of knowledge about the results of public services and word-of-mouth based evaluations. We correspondingly request respondents to serve as citizen representatives while also with thorough knowledge about public entities and agencies.

The study sent out 385 emails with a request to respond to the questionnaire, which received a total of 57 answers and resulting in a response rate of approximately 15%.

The profile of respondents was the following: an average age of 44, 58% female, 90% had higher education qualifications, 75% earned a wage above the national average and with representation by sector seeing 39% of respondents from the health sector, 40% from education and 21% from social security and action.

Due to the sample size ($N = 57$), the Amos software does not run a structural equation model (SEM). According to Kline (2011), the sample size is too small for such a technique to hold validity and requires $N > 200$ that is not the case here ($N = 57 < 200$). Therefore, as an alternative, the study applies PLS-SEM with the SmartPLS software. According to Hair et al. (2011), this is a promising method with great research potential especially in the field of marketing and management and working effectively even with very small samples, as in the case of the study by Tenenhaus et al. (2005) with its sample of $N = 6$.

3.4   Analysis of Results

In order to verify the reliability of the constructs incorporated into this research study, we carried out Cronbach's Alfa test. Table 3.1 displays the results of the analysis alongside the descriptive statistics for the variables.

According to Streiner (2013), there are two points for consideration in these results. Firstly, the study should exclude any constructs returning values of below 0.6. Therefore, in accordance with the recommendations handed down by this author, "Internal policy" and "Innovation", which returned values below those stated as recommended, were then excluded from consideration by the model of analysis.

Secondly, the author identifies values of over 0.8 as ideal for reliable constructs.

In other words, of the eleven constructs for evaluation, we exclude two, as recommended by the literature, and, of the remaining nine, we may report that six turn in values equal to or greater than 0.8. Figure 3.1 displays the model of analysis.

When tested, the model returned the following results (see Fig. 3.2). The model obtained a squared R of 0.69, thus, "Public sector leadership / vision" "Professionalism of staff", "Response capacity", "Ethics and morals" and "Connectivity" account for almost 70% of the capacity for innovation of these organisations.

Table 3.1 Descriptive statistics

Reliability statistics			
Constructs	Cronbach's Alfa	Average	Standard deviation
Capacity for innovation	0.797	3.23	0.830
Internal policy	0.501	3.56	0.754
Image of the public sector	0.728	3.35	0.949
Professionalism of staff	0.772	3.40	1.07
Public sector leadership / vision	0.826	3.02	1.11
Response capacity	0.922	2.35	1.07
Innovation	0.471	3.18	0.869
Ethics and morals	0.696	3.40	0.953
Connectivity	0.730	3.11	1.07
Satisfaction	0.878	2.77	1.07
Trust	0.851	2.58	0.762
N	57		

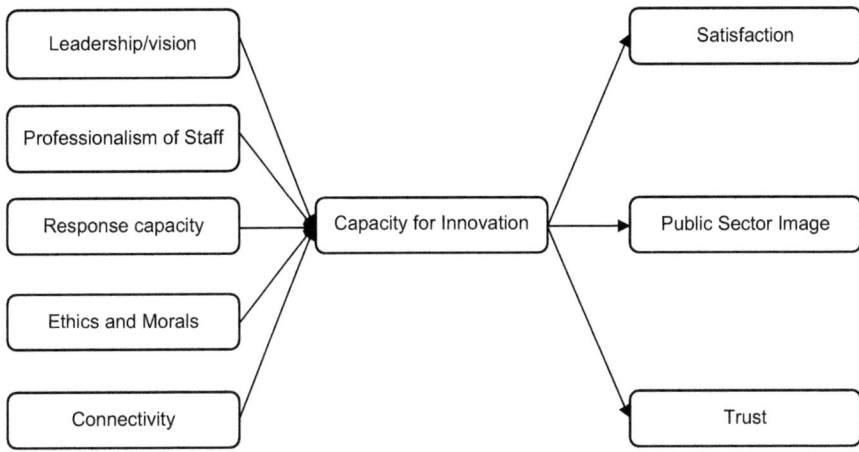

Fig. 3.1 Model of analysis

When analysing the factors impacting on the capacity for innovation, "professionalism of staff" and "leadership/vision" return a negative relationship with the capacity for innovation of −0.16 and −0.20 respectively. The remaining factors, "connectivity", "ethics and morals" and "response capacity" report positive relationships of 0.19, 0.60 and 0.45 respectively.

These relationships demonstrate a low value due to their proximity to 0 (Aparasu and Bentley 2014) and, when analysing the significance of the five factors, two attain a significant relationship with the capacity for innovation factor, which are "response capacity" P value 0.001 < 0.05 and "ethics and morals" P value 0.017 < 0.05.

Observing the effects of "capacity for innovation", especially as regards the relationship with "image" "satisfaction" and "trust", we find that this relationship is significant with a P value of 0.000 < 0.05 for each of the three cases. This relationship also proves strong on 0.77 for the "image of the public sector", 0.66 for "trust" and 0.68 for "satisfaction". Following R^2, each of these constructs obtains 0.59, 0.66 and 0.47 respectively.

Another observed dimension encapsulates how the variables that Vigoda-Gadot et al. (2008) define as influencing the capacity for innovation, when posing the question to the contrary and analysing the relationship that capacity for innovation holds over them, we find that this is far greater. This may reflect the explanation given in the literature as regards how social innovation brings major improvements and solutions that rarely incur negative effects (Borins 2000; Election Commission 2000; Green et al. 2001; Mulgan and Albury 2003).

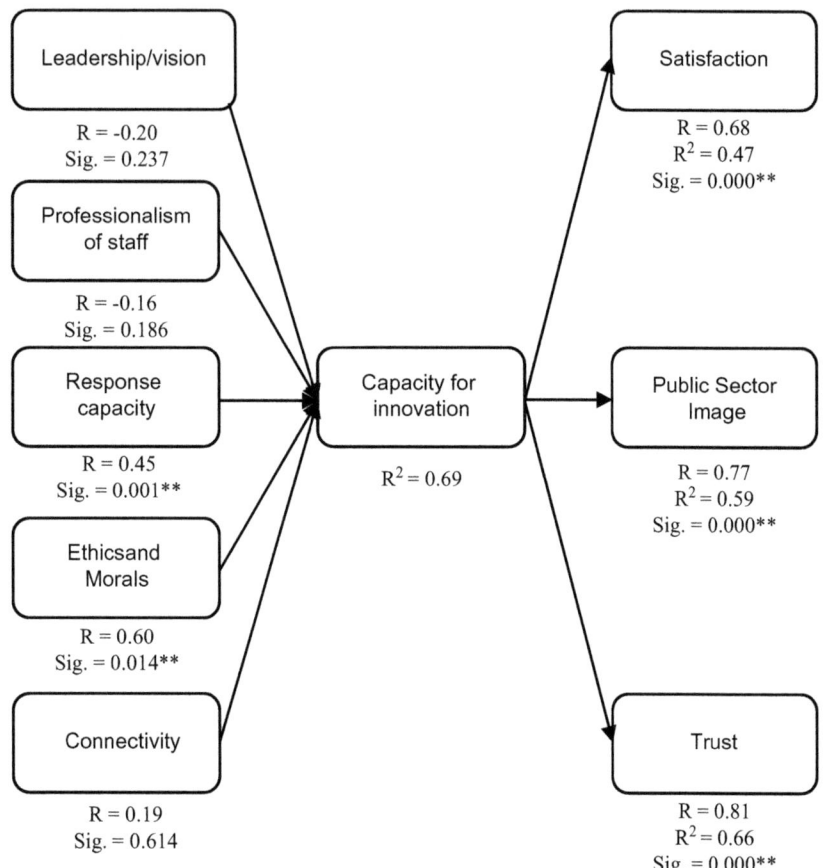

Note: ** p value <0.005

Fig. 3.2 Model analysis results. (Note: ** p value <0.005)

3.5   Conclusion and Discussion

In keeping with the existing literature, the present research approached a fundamental theme to contemporary societies worldwide. Social innovation in the public sector is critical to the development of societies and economies and efforts have focused on better understanding how such processes take place (Bloch and Bugge 2013; Dundon 2002; Green et al. 2001; Maroto and Rubalcaba 2005; Mulgan and Albury 2003; Snow 2007; Windrum and García-Goñi 2008).

The public sector is fairly broad, displays differences to the private sector and what happens in the former sector holds a major impact for ongoing daily life (Ettlie and Rosenthal 2011; Kay and Goldspink 2013; Koch and Hauknes 2005; Maroto and Rubalcaba 2005; Mulgan and Albury 2003; Snow 2007).

Despite the efforts applied to returning a better understanding of such processes, there are still shortcomings to our understanding (Bloch and Bugge 2013; Halvorsen et al. 2005). Hence, this research correspondingly seeks to add more knowledge to that existing on innovation processes in the public sector. More specifically, we took into account the recommendations suggested by Vigoda-Gadot et al. (2008) and tested a model. The model proposed by these authors and tested in this present research consists of a set of important variables explaining innovation in the public sector based upon the literature review we carried out.

We tested the importance of "internal policy", "professionalism of staff", "public sector leadership / vision", "response capacity", "innovation", "ethics and morals" and "connectivity" as regards explaining and understanding the "capacity for innovation" in the public sector. The model furthermore evaluates the results of this respective "capacity for innovation". Hence, this approaches the ways in which the "capacity for innovation" impacts on "satisfaction", "trust" and the "image" of this sector.

While seeking citizen perspective based analysis, our questionnaire surveyed mid-ranking managers. This stems from the objective of avoiding bias in the answers received. With a response rate of approximately 15%, we made recourse to PLS for analysis in keeping with the method Hair et al. (2011) recommend as best for such cases.

The conclusions point to how the "response capacity" and "ethics and morals", based upon the perspectives of citizens, provide the factors that best explain the "capacity for innovation" in the public sector. Hence, the greater the extent to which organisations in this sector (in this case, those most closely related with activities in the field of social security, health and education) raise their "response capacity" and their "ethics and morals", the greater the level of social innovation perceived by citizens.

Thus, in keeping with the findings of the study by Vigoda-Gadot et al. (2008), the "response capacity" emerges as an explanatory variable of significant importance. As regards the independent variables, we may also report similar results for both research projects. However, contrary to the Vigoda-Gadot et al. (2008) study, which describes "Ethics and morals" as lacking in importance in relation to the "capacity for innovation", the present research findings identify this as the factor with the greatest weighting. The variable "Leadership / Vision" represents a similar case with the results obtained demonstrating its lack of significance and even reporting negative relationships, although at very low levels.

The current study finds that the "response capacity" holds importance to the innovation perceived by citizens and in alignment with the study by Vigoda-Gadot et al. (2008). Another conclusion stems from how Portuguese citizens consider "ethics and morals" as the most important factor to their perceptions of the capacity for innovation in this sector. This gains due recognition in the literature. This interest reflects in articles and studies ranging from those attempting to understand how to explain this (Mujtaba et al. 2011) and others that strive to grasp the impact on the public sector (Hawkins et al. 2011; Small 1995; Stensöta 2010). The second conclusion confirms the position of Stensöta (2010) that stipulates how this factor is a need for attaining implementation and performance standards in public sector activities.

Another conclusion worth highlighting stems from how, when considering the independent variables as dependent, therefore when testing the influence that the "capacity for innovation" holds over "leadership and vision", "staff professionalism", "response capacity", "ethics and morals" and "connectivity", the results report a very positive relationship among the variables. The literature also accounts for this facet (Borins 2000; Election Commission 2000; Green et al. 2001; Mulgan and Albury 2003) in keeping with both how rarely there are negative effects and how innovation may bring major improvements.

When incorporating the influence that "capacity for innovation" holds over "image", "satisfaction" and "trust", these results underpin the conclusion that the capacity for innovation in this sector closely interrelates with aforementioned variable, thus, the greater the capacity for innovation, the higher the image of this sector as well as reflecting greater levels of satisfaction and trust. This conclusion also receives support from the similarities of these results to those returned by Vigoda-Gadot et al. (2008).

We would highlight how the "image" of the sector closely relates to and explains "satisfaction" and "trust" in keeping with that also observed earlier by the aforementioned authors. The observed influence of "image" over the aforementioned variables actually reports higher values than those returned specifically by "capacity for innovation".

This encapsulates the sheer importance of tending to the image of organisations with the pertinence of this research conveyed by the contribution made towards gaining greater citizen satisfaction and trust. Indeed, other studies have already identified this relationship in other fields (Ar and Kara 2014; Chen 2010; Orth and Green 2009; Wu 2011). Furthermore, this approaches relations not forecast by the initial model, "Trust" returned a more significant relationship with "Image" than did "Capacity for innovation".

These represent the main theoretical contributions towards innovation in the public sector.

In practical terms, this study contributes with some advice for policy makers in making clear the importance and the level of need over paying more attention to the response capacity of organisations, and the ethics and morals of their members of staff in order to raise both the trust and the satisfaction prevailing among citizens while also simultaneously improving on the image of the organisations that they represent.

This also highlights the need to foster greater levels of social innovation given how this provides an important tool for generating improvements in organisations, whether to their intrinsic variables (not only those demonstrated as holding the greatest importance, such as response capacities and ethics and morals but also the remaining variables) or to the variables stemming from the activities undertaken (image, satisfaction and trust).

Rather than any specific recommendation (as the relationship values were rather low and, as such, this observation requires interpreting with caution), this study draws attention to the need for staff professionalism and for the leadership and vision able to reduce perceptions of innovation as resulting in poor organisational results.

3.5.1 Limitations and Future Lines of Research

Despite the contributions made by this research, there are some limitations. The low response rate and the correspondingly low number of eligible questionnaires meant the study contained only a small sample. Were the sample larger, the results would hold greater reliability even while (following Vigoda-Gadot et al. 2008) considering that N > 50 represents a satisfactory benchmark and nationally representative.

Another limitation arises from recourse to PLS. While the literature does support and defend the idea that this provides the most accurate method for analysing results, in fact, there remains a great deal of controversy surrounding this type of analysis (Hair et al. 2011). These methodological issues also limit the extent and rigorousness of any comparison with the study by Vigoda-Gadot et al. (2008). The absence of any specific constructs for each variable and the small number of cases may also signal difficulties in obtaining more reliable results.

Taking into account these current limitations, future research projects might deploy different constructs as well as benefitting from applying better evaluation procedures to them. Another dimension that might well be worth developing involves adding other sectors of activity to the model applied. The focus of this study remained on the three branches of activity with the greatest weighting in the S.B. and are fundamental to human development.

However, the other branches of government that fell beyond the scope of this research still represent major sources of expenditure, great public utility and are also fundamental to economic development, for example the case of the public transportation sector. Furthermore, valuable lessons may arise from the study of such organisations. Correspondingly, should future research projects benefit from larger samples, the comparison between sectors might serve as the foundation for comparisons at the respective national level.

Acknowledgements The authors would like to thank to NECE – Research Unit in Business Sciences funded by the Multiannual Funding Programme of R&D Centres of FCT – Fundação para a Ciência e a Tecnologia, under the project «UID/GES/04630/2013».

References

Amara, N., Landry, R., Becheikh, N., & Ouimet, M. (2008). Learning and novelty of innovation in established manufacturing SMEs. *Technovation, 28*(7), 450–463. https://doi.org/10.1016/j.technovation.2008.02.001.

Aparasu, R. R., & Bentley, J. P. (2014). *Principles of research design and drug literature evaluation.* Burlington: Jones & Bartlett Publishers.

Ar, A. A., & Kara, A. (2014). Emerging market consumers' country of production image, trust and quality perceptions of global brands made-in China. *Journal of Product and Brand Management, 23*(7), 491–503.

Bartlett, D., & Dibben, P. (2002). Public sector innovation and entrepreneurship: Case studies from local government. *Local Government Studies, 28*(4), 107–121. https://doi.org/10.1080/714004159.

Becheikh, N., Landry, R., & Amara, N. (2006). Lessons from innovation empirical studies in the manufacturing sector: A systematic review of the literature from 1993–2003. *Technovation, 26*(5–6), 644–664. https://doi.org/10.1016/j.technovation.2005.06.016.

Bloch, C., & Bugge, M. M. (2013). Public sector innovation—From theory to measurement. *Structural Change and Economic Dynamics, 27*, 133–145. https://doi.org/10.1016/j.strueco.2013.06.008.

Bon, J., & Louppe, A. (1980). *Marketing des services publics: l'étude des besoins de la population (French Edi.)*. Paris: Editions d'organisation.

Borins, S. (2000). Loose cannons and rule breakers, or enterprising leaders? Some evidence about innovative public managers. *Public Administration Review, 60*(6), 498–507.

Borins, S. (2001). Innovation, success and failure in public management research: Some methodological reflections. *Public Management Review, 3*(1), 3–17.

Bygstad, B., Lanestedt, G., & Choudrie, J. (2007). Successful broadband projects in the public sector – A service innovation perspective. In *40th Hawaii international conference on system sciences* (pp. 1–7).

Chapman, D., & Cowdell, T. (1998). *New public sector marketing* (4th ed.). Great Britian: Financial Times Professional Lmt.

Chen, Y. (2010). The drivers of green brand equity: Green brand image, green satisfaction, and green trust. *Journal of Business Ethics, 93*(2), 307–319. https://doi.org/10.1007/s10551-009-0223-9.

Commission, E. (2000). *Innovation policy in a knowledge-based economy*. Luxembourg: Enterprise Directorate-General.

Damanpour, F., & Daniel Wischnevsky, J. (2006). Research on innovation in organizations: Distinguishing innovation-generating from innovation-adopting organizations. *Journal of Engineering and Technology Management, 23*(4), 269–291. https://doi.org/10.1016/j.jengtecman.2006.08.002.

DeLeon, L., & Denhardt, R. B. (2000). The political theory of reinvention. *Public Administration Review, 60*(2), 89–97.

Denham, J., & Kaberon, R. (2012). Culture is king: How culture contributes to innovation. *Journal of Product Innovation Management, 29*(3), 358–360. https://doi.org/10.1111/j.1540-5885.2012.00908.x.

Dundon, E. (2002). *The seeds of innovation: Cultivating the synergy that fosters new ideas*. New York: AMACOM.

Ettlie, J. E., & Rosenthal, S. R. (2011). Service versus manufacturing innovation. *Journal of Product Innovation Management, 28*(2), 285–299.

Frambach, R. T., & Schillewaert, N. (2002). Organizational innovation adoption a multi-level framework of determinants and opportunities for future research. *Journal of Business Research, 55*, 163–176.

Green, L., Howells, J., & Miles, I. (2001). *Services and innovation: Dynamics of service innovation in the European Union*. PREST and CRIC, Manchester, UK: University of Manchester.

Hair, J. F., Ringle, C. M., & Sarstedt, M. (2011). PLS-SEM: Indeed a silver bullet. *Journal of Marketing Theory and Practice, 19*(2), 139–152. https://doi.org/10.2753/MTP1069-6679190202.

Halvorsen, T., Hauknes, J., Miles, I., & Røste, R. (2005). *Inovation in the public sector, on the diferences between public and private sector innovation* (D9 ed.). Publin Report. Oslo: NIFU STEP.

Hawkins, T. G., Gravier, M. J., & Powley, E. H. (2011). Public versus private sector procurement ethics and strategy: What each sector can learn from the other. *Journal of Business Ethics, 103*(4), 567–586. https://doi.org/10.1007/s10551-011-0881-2.

Holm, A. S. (2009). *Incentives for innovation does today's patent system work as intended?* University of Aarhus, Denmark: Aarhus School of Business.

Kay, R., & Goldspink, C. (2013). Public versus private sector innovation — A case of apples and oranges. *Keeping Good Companies, 65*(1), 17–23.

Kline, R. B. (2011). *Principles and practice of structural equation modeling* (3rd ed.). New York: Guilford Press.

Koch, P., & Hauknes, J. (2005). *Innovation in the public sector: On innovation in the public sector* (D20 ed.). Publin Report. Oslo: NIFU STEP.

Kuhry, B., & van der Torre, A. (2002). *De vierde sector*. Den Haag: Sociaal en Cultureel Planbureau.

Maroto, A., & Rubalcaba, L. (2005). *Inovation in the public sector, the structure and size of the public sector in an enlarged Europe*. (D14, Ed.). Publin Report. Oslo: NIFU STEP.

Massa, S., & Testa, S. (2008). Innovation and SMEs: Misaligned perspectives and goals among entrepreneurs, academics, and policy makers. *Technovation, 28*(7), 393–407. https://doi.org/10.1016/j.technovation.2008.01.002.

Matthews, M., Lewis, C., & Cook, G. (2009). *Public sector innovation: A review of the literature, Report on a project carried out to support the preparation of an ANAO better practice guide on public sector innovation*. (Final Report). Australia: Australian National Audit Office.

Micheli, P., Schoeman, M., Baxter, D., & Goffin, K. (2012). New business models for public-sector innovation: Successful technological innovation for government. *Research-Technology Management, 55*(5), 51–57. https://doi.org/10.5437/08956308X5505067.

Mujtaba, B. G., Tajaddini, R., & Chen, L. Y. (2011). Business ethics perceptions of public and private sector Iranians. *Journal of Business Ethics, 104*(3), 433–447. https://doi.org/10.1007/s10551-011-0920-z.

Mulgan, G., & Albury, D. (2003). *Innovation in the public sector*. Strategy Unit, London, UK: Cabinet Office.

Nählinder, J. (2010). Where are all the female innovators? Nurses as innovators in a public sector innovation project. *Journal of Technology Management & Innovation, 5*(1), 13–29.

Naranjo-Gil, D. (2009). The influence of environmental and organizational factors on innovation adoptions: Consequences for performance in public sector organizations. *Technovation, 29*(12), 810–818. https://doi.org/10.1016/j.technovation.2009.07.003.

North, D. C. (1990). *Institutions, institutional change and economic performance*. Cambridge, MA: Cambridge University Press.

North, D. C. (1991). Institutions. *Journal of Economic Perspectives, 5*(1), 97–112.

North, D. C. (2005). *Understanding the process of economic change*. Princeton/Oxford: Princeton University Press.

North, D. C., Mantzavinos, C., & Shariq, S. (2004). Learning, institutions, and economic performance. *Perspectives on Politics, 2*(1), 1–19.

Omachonu, V. K., & Einspruch, N. G. (2010). Innovation in healthcare delivery systems: A conceptual framework. *The Innovation Journal: The Public Sector Innovation Journal, 15*(1), 1–20.

Ongkittikul, S., & Geerlings, H. (2006). Opportunities for innovation in public transport: Effects of regulatory reforms on innovative capabilities. *Transport Policy, 13*(4), 283–293. https://doi.org/10.1016/j.tranpol.2005.12.003.

Orçamento do Cidadão – Orçamento do Estado 2015 (2014): Lisboa, Portugal, Ministério das Finanças.

Orth, U. R., & Green, M. T. (2009). Consumer loyalty to family versus non-family business : The roles of store image , trust and satisfaction. *Journal of Retailing and Consumer Services, 16*(4), 248–259. https://doi.org/10.1016/j.jretconser.2008.12.002.

Özcan, S., & Reichstein, T. (2009). Transition to entrepreneurship from the public sector: Predispositional and contextual effects. *Management Science, 55*(4), 604–618. https://doi.org/10.1287/mnsc.1080.0954.

Parry, K., & Proctor-Thomson, S. (2002). Leadership, culture and performance: The case of the New Zealand public sector. *Journal of Change Management, 3*(4), 376–399. https://doi.org/10.1080/714023843.

Potts, J. (2010). Innovation by elimination : A proposal for negative policy experiments in the public sector. *Innovation: Management, Policy and Practice, 12*(2), 238–248.

Salge, T. O., & Vera, A. (2012). Benefi ting from public sector innovation: The moderating role of customer and learning orientation. *Public Administration Review, 72*(4), 550–560. https://doi. org/10.1111/j.1540-6210.2012.02529.x.550.

Savory, C. (2009). Building knowledge translation capability into public-sector innovation processes. *Technology Analysis & Strategic Management, 21*(2), 149–171. https://doi.org/ 10.1080/09537320802625223.

Small, M. W. (1995). Business ethics and commercial morality : Report of the Royal Commission into commercial activities. *Journal of Business Ethics, 14*(8), 613–628.

Snow, C. C. (2007). Moderator comments innovation. *Strategic Entrepreneurship Journal, 1*, 101–102. https://doi.org/10.1002/sej.

Stensöta, H. O. (2010). The conditions of care: Reframing the debate about public sector ethics. *Public Administration Review, 70*(2), 295–304.

Stipak, B. (1979). Citizen satisfaction with urban services: Potential misuse as a performance indicator. *Public Administration Review, 39*(1), 46–52.

Stockhammer, E., & Sotiropoulos, D. P. (2014). Europe in crisis: Introduction. *Review of Political Economy, 26*(2), 167–170. https://doi.org/10.1080/09538259.2014.881012.

Streiner, D. L. (2013). *A guide for the statistically perplexed: Selected readings for clinical researchers.* Toronto: University of Toronto Press.

Tenenhaus, M., Pages, J., Ambroisine, L., & Guinot, C. (2005). PLS methodology to study relationships between hedonic judgements and product characteristics. *Food Quality and Preference, 16*, 315–325. https://doi.org/10.1016/j.foodqual.2004.05.013.

United Nations Development Program (2014). Sustaining human progress: Reducing vulnerabilities and building resilience, human development report, Published for the United Nations Development Programme (UNDP), New York, USA, avaiable at http://hdr.undp.org/sites/ default/files/hdr14-report-en-1.pdf.

Vigoda-Gadot, E., Shoham, A., Schwabsky, N., & Ruvio, A. (2008). Public sector innovation for Europe: A multinational eight-country exploration of citizens' perspectives. *Public Administration, 86*(2), 307–329. https://doi.org/10.1111/j.1467-9299.2008.00731.x.

Windrum, P., & García-Goñi, M. (2008). A neo-Schumpeterian model of health services innovation. *Research Policy, 37*(4), 649–672. https://doi.org/10.1016/j.respol.2007.12.011.

Wu, G. (2011). Country image, informational influence, collectivism/individualism, and brand loyalty: Exploring the automobile purchase patterns of Chinese Americans. *Journal of Consumer Marketing, 28*(3), 169–177.

Chapter 4
Quality and Innovation in the Organic Agro-Food Sector: Threats and Opportunities of Social and Managerial Innovation

Maria D. Moreno-Luzon, Maria Gil-Marques, and Odette Chams-Anturi

Abstract This study seeks to understand how innovation in the organic agro-food sector has evolved, studying the main challenges facing the sector as a consequence of its growth. Through the study and analysis of literature we reflect on the threats and opportunities facing the sector. We also used two expert panels to help us cross-reference and complete the information available from previous studies. The organic agro-food sector was born as a social and radical innovation based on specific values and principles, which include respect for nature and sustainability, ecology, no pollution, equity and a close relationship with consumers. In this chapter, we explain how regulations and the interplay of different actors have sustained the sharp growth and development of the sector, mainly in the USA and Europe. However, the sector is currently facing major challenges, due precisely to this sharp growth. We identify the main challenges as the need to develop an ambidextrous capability, balancing exploration and exploitation, together with a second group of challenges, related to integrating formal and informal rules as well as new actors in the sector. There is a need to maintain the core values of the organic agro-food sector and its genuine social differentiation as well as to develop the standards and regulations required to maintain the high levels of food safety and quality of organic agro-food, given that nowadays it is distributed in supermarkets and major chains, and is consumed by a new type of customer. New actors in the organic agro-food sector (conventional distribution, mass consumers, and international traders) have been attracted by the sector's growth. This means rules and requirements are needed to create certainty in economic activity and international trade. Institutional change constitutes a crucial component to secure the future development of the sector. We have seen that

M. D. Moreno-Luzon (✉) · O. Chams-Anturi
Department of Management, Faculty of Economics, University of Valencia, Valencia, Spain
e-mail: maria.moreno@uv.es; ochamsan@alumni.uv.es

M. Gil-Marques
Department of Management, Faculty of Economics, Catholic University of Valencia, Valencia, Spain
e-mail: maria.gil@ucv.es

© Springer International Publishing AG, part of Springer Nature 2018   47
M. Peris-Ortiz et al. (eds.), *Strategies and Best Practices in Social Innovation*,
https://doi.org/10.1007/978-3-319-89857-5_4

although these challenges arise from the social and economic trends that the sector is facing, there are also opportunities linked to all of them. Looking at the sector as a whole, the innovation trend has changed from paradigmatic, value-based, social and radical innovation to one of incremental managerial innovation aimed at overcoming the challenges associated with growth.

Keywords Quality management · Innovation · Social change · Social innovation · Ambidexterity · Exploration · Exploitation

4.1 Introduction

Based on traditional origins and solid values and principles, including health, respect for nature, sustainability, ecology, no pollution, equity and a close relationship with consumers, the organic agro-food sector has constituted a radical social and managerial innovation for the conventional agro-food sector. It can be classified as a paradigmatic innovation - in terms of Tidd and Bessant (2015) - because it has implied substantial changes in the framework of values and principles, not only in products, but also in processes, technologies and markets.

The sector is progressively facing major challenges that put some of the core values at the heart of its original revolution at risk. These challenges have mainly arisen as a result of the sharp and sustained growth in the demand for organic products, and of the strict requirements imposed in the specific regulations applicable to firms in this industry. These formal regulations are necessary to create a secure environment for international trade and economic development but they should not replace core values, which are already embedded in the traditional actors in this sector, though they will need to be assumed by new entrants. Improvements in efficiency bring cost and price adjustments that are essential to ensure competitiveness. Although organic products are still considerably more expensive than non-organic goods, the fact that the sector is maturing is bringing with it greater competition in terms of prices, making the need for improved, more efficient processes absolutely essential. Therefore, companies in this sector need to reduce operating costs and be competitive pricewise.

Looking at the sector as a whole, the innovation trend has changed from paradigmatic, value-based, social and radical innovations to incremental managerial innovations aimed at overcoming the challenges associated with growth.

The purpose of this paper is then to understand how social and managerial innovations are evolving in the organic agro-food sector, and to assess the main challenges and opportunities facing the sector as a result of the dramatic growth it has undergone. To approach the phenomenon, the study starts by analyzing relevant theoretical and empirical studies to reflect on the threats and opportunities facing the sector. It also uses the results of two expert panels to help cross-reference and complete the information available from previous studies. The analysis of existing studies and the use of expert panels have yielded proposals which could be used in future research.

This study opens up new lines of research related to the challenges identified. In terms of its relation with innovation management and ambidexterity, it can be stated that although ambidexterity has been extensively analyzed in conceptual and empirical terms, up until now its implications in terms of social and managerial innovation in this specific sector have not been explored. This study has several theoretical and practical implications. On one hand, an in-depth analysis of this sector enables us to discuss core issues in management literature, such as the flexibility/efficiency dilemma and the exploration/exploitation dilemma, which can be avoided by developing ambidextrous capabilities. On the other hand, when firms improve quality and innovation, and simultaneously reduce costs by improving the efficiency of their processes, they are able to lower prices, thus facilitating greater consumer access to these products and enabling sustainable production to spread.

From the perspective of an institutional analysis (North 2005), we can see how formal and informal rules have evolved and changed in the last decade. Formal rules (regulations, standards) have grown very fast during this period, while informal rules need longer to be learned. While social motivation was the driving force for traditional actors, new actors with economic rather than social objectives have now entered the sector. This fact can put original values in danger. We can explain this generalized problem in the sector by differentiating between three related challenges, which center on changes generated by new entrants: conventional channels, mass consumers and new business with economic motivations, rather than social innovations.

The second challenge, the use of conventional and specialized distribution channels, is also related to managerial decisions about efficiency and consumer access to these products, but it is not without difficulties which are mainly associated with the fact that retailers within the organic food sector attempt to ensure the integrity of their organic supplies via the imposition of standards that exceed mandatory government requirements, thus potentially exerting pressure on suppliers.

The third challenge, formalization, standards and high levels of food safety and quality, focuses on the great burden of regulation already present in the agro-food industry, which is even greater for this sector with specific organic certifications. However, this could be an advantage for the organic agro-food industry since it can guarantee consumers greater food safety and quality than the conventional agro-food sector.

Finally, the fourth challenge is the danger that the success of organic products could distance the organic sector from its original values. This challenge can be seen as an opportunity because the irruption of conventional agro-food companies in the organic sector can serve to massively disseminate its original values.

The present study contains five sections: (1) The organic agro-food sector: Principles and objectives, (2) The organic agro-food sector and social innovation, (3) The sector's growth, (4) Challenges and opportunities, and (5) Final discussion and conclusions.

4.2　The Organic Agro-food Sector: Principles and Objectives

The organic agro-food sector encompasses the set of agents that produce, transform and distribute products grown using organic agriculture. Organic agriculture is a production management system that uses cultural practices that maintain ecological harmony aiming at profitability with no or minimal impact on the environment (Dorais 2007).

There are different agents involved in the value chain of organic food products, including those dealing with production, processing, distribution and consumption. The IFOAM (International Federation of Organic Agriculture Movements) was created in 1972, and it is the international umbrella organization for the organic world, uniting a diversity of stakeholders that contribute to the organic vision.

In 2005, IFOAM established the principles of organic agriculture at its general assembly in Adelaide and grouped them into four areas: health, ecology, fairness and care (IFOAM 2005).

1. **Health:** This principle states that organic agriculture should sustain and enhance the health of soil, plant, animal, human and planet as one and indivisible. It is broadly understood as the maintenance of physical, mental, social and ecological well-being. Soils must be healthy to produce foods that promote the health of animals and people, and to maintain the health of the ecosystem. For this reason, organic agriculture should avoid the use of fertilizers, pesticides, veterinary products and additives in foods that could cause negative effects on health (IFOAM 2005).

   Ecological consumers were initially a minority, but have grown rapidly given that many people recognize the value of organic products from a health viewpoint (DuPuis 2000). Consumer distrust of conventional food supplies remains high and though organic certification is not based on explicit health claims, the majority of consumers identify organic labels as symbols of food safety and quality (Raynolds 2004).

2. **Ecology:** This implies that organic agriculture should be based on living ecological systems and cycles, should work with them, emulate them and help sustain them. These cycles are universal but their operation is specific to the place, reducing inputs through the reuse, recycling and efficient management of materials and energy in order to maintain and improve the environmental quality and conservation of the resources, and the upkeep of genetic diversity and agriculture (IFOAM 2005). This principle includes respect for nature, sustainability, and no pollution. It avoids the hidden social costs of industrial agriculture that generates increasing environmental problems.

3. **Fairness:** This principle emphasizes that those involved in organic agriculture should conduct human relationships in a manner that ensures fairness at all levels and for all parties - farmers, workers, processors, distributors, traders and consumers. People around the world buy organic food because they see it as being safer, not only for themselves, but also for farmers, and for the environment (FAO 2000).

The aim is to achieve good quality of life, contribute to food sovereignty and reduce poverty. Animals must have living conditions that they are commensurate with their physiology, natural behavior and well-being. Resources must be managed fairly, socially and ecologically, and should be kept as a legacy for future generations (IFOAM 2005).

4. **Care:** It implies that technologies need to be evaluated and existing methods reviewed so that increases in efficiencyand productivity do not compromise health and well-being. Organic agriculture must prevent significant risks by adopting appropriate technologies and rejecting unpredictable ones, such as genetic engineering. Decisions should reflect the values and needs of all those potentially affected through transparent and participatory processes (IFOAM 2005).

In order to regulate the application of these principles and define the obligations that this type of agriculture and industrial activity implies, several standards have been developed to regulate the sector. Organic standards are sets of requirements which define the organic practices that are applicable to organic operators. The IFOAM estimates that there are hundreds of organic standards throughout the world. Some are government regulations, others are private standards. Some have a very localized scope of application (e.g. one country or even one region in a given country), whereas others are applied internationally. To facilitate the acceptance of different standards, the IFOAM has developed the IFOAM Family of Standards, which is a list of all standards officially endorsed as being organic after a detailed technical assessment of each standard by the IFOAM's Organic Guarantee System.

From an institutional perspective (North 2005), we can differentiate formal institutions (laws, formal regulations and governmental procedures) from informal institutions (ideas, beliefs, attitudes and values) from the culture of a specific society. Correct coherence of the state system and the motivation behind the behavior of certain actors in the social economic environment will allow long-term rooting of the informal norms.

We can observe that since the early 1970s, when the sector was born, economic performance has largely been determined by the quality of the institutions that support this sector. The creation of standards and governmental regulations by different political, economic and social institutions and organizations has been fundamental in influencing behavior and has provided stability for the organic agro-food sector. They have provided a transparent and efficient framework, which is certainly one of the cornerstones of the sector's economic development.

4.3   The Organic Agro-food Sector and Social Innovation

Social innovation has mainly grown out of practice, focusing on implementation, with lack of consideration to theory development. The main aim of social innovation is to improve the well-being of people, communities and society. Recently, there has been much promising research on the issue but there are no clearly defined schools of thought and no continuing theoretical arguments (Mulgan 2012).

Everyone appears to agree that social innovation is essential but the exact meaning of this term is often unclear (Bock 2012). Unlike innovations that are driven by profit or competitive business pressures, social innovations are prompted by an interest in improving the well-being of people in society, with social matters being the main driver behind the development and application of new ideas to solve problems (Dawson and Daniel 2010).

As Bock (2012) argued, to acquire more knowledge about how to support social innovation, it is important to explore and monitor its operations and contribution to processes of social change and renewal. In their search of key journals, Edwards et al. (2012) found that research is highly fragmented and includes studies from different disciplines such as sociology, social entrepreneurship, management, creativity and human development economics.

The Guide to Social Innovation (European Commission 2013) states that social innovations are innovations that are social in both their ends and their means, and defines them as new ideas that simultaneously meet social needs and create new social relationships or collaborations.

Following Franz et al. (2012), our proposal aims to conceptualize social innovation as a new paradigm for innovation management, research and assessment rather than considering it as a distinct form of innovation in itself. Innovation generates outputs that potentially have social outcomes and impacts, and sometimes they meet social needs quite straight. However, in general, economic matters are highly relevant in innovation, partly excluding other logics, such as ecological sustainability or social inclusion, and not taking side-effects into account. The social innovation paradigm integrates social rationality, and combines it with conventional economic and technological criteria.

As Bock (2012) stated, social innovation is often appointed as an essential part of agricultural and rural innovation. Social innovation may refer to identifying society's need for more sustainable production methods, the necessity for collaboration and social learning, or the scope of change needed to revitalize rural society. Organic farming seeks to create social and environmental value, in addition to economic returns. The principles and values that support agriculture and the organic industry, and the objectives it pursues are the point of reference to consider this as a social innovation given the benefits that it seeks (IFOAM 2005; Doherty et al. 2014). In addition to providing healthier food, organic products are produced through agricultural systems that favor sustainable land use and biodiversity. Organic farming contributes to the carbon cycle in a variety of ways, such as closing nutrient cycles, self-supplying resources and inputs, and using local resources; maintaining the physical-chemical characteristics of soils; and using a higher percentage of renewable energy sources thus lowering fuel consumption.

The organic agro-food industry has grown rapidly since its origins as a social movement which presented an alternative to conventional food which was related to health problems (Scrinis 2007). It has brought about various changes and new sensitivities around food, such as fair-trade schemes, farmers' markets, box delivery schemes, seed-saving networks, local and community food production movements, food retail co-operatives, the Slow Food Movement, and vegetarianism.

The innovation of organic farming implemented by the different agents involved in the value chain of agro-organic food is a radical disruptive innovation that has meant leaving behind the conventional ways of operating in this sector to develop new routines and to radically modify generalized ones. It has required a process of learning and 'unlearning'. Innovation in the origins of the sector posed a complex challenge for pioneering organizations, requiring a series of complex interactions between independent elements. As Seebode et al. (2012) suggested, innovative activity centering on sustainable development means moving outside the traditional business framework. The sector has been considered as one of paradigmatic radical innovation (Tidd and Bessant 2015), given its radical rethinking of the framework of the principles of agro-food activities and its capacity for research and constant innovation. The innovation generated fits with what Seebode et al. (2012) call co-evolution.

Such system-level innovation has the capacity to generate positive social and environmental impacts rather than simply minimizing negative ones, with the involvement of multiple players who have traditionally not worked together, in co-creating system-level change. Innovations in the organic farming sector have been characterized by collaboration between researchers and people interested in the development and / or application of innovations. Supplier cooperation via advice, research and the encouragement of partnership schemes has been common in this sector (Patel and Woodward 2007). According to Porter and Kramer (2011), the focus on creating 'shared value', which builds connections between social, environmental and economic progress, has the power to unleash the next wave of global growth. From an institutional analysis perspective (North 2005), we can point out that the collaboration between actors in this sector has been based on strong informal rules, social values and shared beliefs, which can be divided into four main areas: health, ecology, fairness and care.

4.4   The Sector's Growth

The organic agro-food sector is experiencing exponential growth globally, and the latest estimates suggest a market value of over €60 billion. In the next few years, a greater presence of organic products is expected in consolidated and emerging markets. Figure 4.1 illustrates the behavior of the world market for organic products up to 2015, where average annual growth was in excess of €3.5 billion. This means the barrier of €100 billion would be reached in 2025. This would support the consolidation and expansion of the sector in the coming years, in addition to highlighting the importance of organic food production in the world (Prodescon 2016).

It should be noted that about 70% of the world's ecological surface area is concentrated in 10 countries: Australia, Argentina, USA, China, Spain, Italy, Uruguay, France, Germany and Canada. Table 4.1 shows the proportion of ecological surface area worldwide (Prodescon 2016).

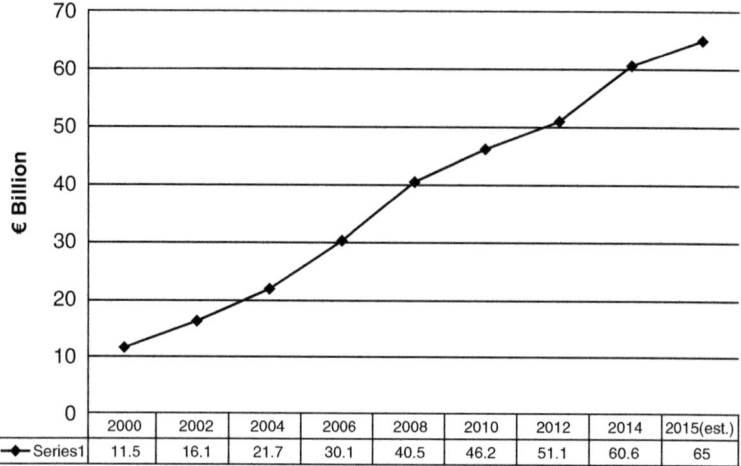

Fig. 4.1 Evolution of the global market for beverages and organic food. (*Source:* Adapted from Prodescon 2016)

Table 4.1 Ecological surface area by countries

Position	Countries	Ecological surface area (Millions of hectares) 2014	% Sup./World total (%)
1	Australia	17.15	39.24
2	Argentina	3.06	7.00
3	USA	2.18	4.99
4	China	1.93	4.42
5	Spain	1.66	3.80
6	Italy	1.39	3.18
7	Uruguay	1.31	3.00
8	France	1.12	2.56
9	Germany	1.05	2.40
10	Canada	0.9	2.06
Others	Rest of the world	11.95	27.35
	World total	**43.70**	**100.00**

Source: Adapted from Prodescon (2016)

As shown in Table 4.1, Australia (39.24%), Argentina (7.00%) and the United States (4.99%) occupied the first three positions in terms of availability of ecologically registered world-wide surface areas.

According to Dorais (2007), in her studies based on statistical data published by IFOAM & FiBL (Willer and Yussefi 2007), demand for products is highest in Europe and North America. They argue that organic agriculture is present in more than 120 countries and approximately 31 million Ha are managed organically on over 600,000 farms worldwide. This constitutes approximately 0.7% of agricultural land.

Specifically, the world's organic land is organized as follows: Oceania has 39%, followed by Europe with 23%, Latin America with 19%, Asia with 9%, North America with 7%, and Africa with 3%. The countries with the greatest organic areas are Australia with 11.8 million Ha, followed by Argentina with 3.1 million Ha, China with 2.3 million Ha, and the United States of America with 1.6 million Ha. (Dorais 2007).

According to Raynolds (2004), global organic market growth is consumer led and its increasing demand is attributed to consumers concerned about health and environmental issues. Organic products, especially in the United States and Europe, have made this the fastest growing segment in the global food sector. Europeans consume more or less half of all the organic products sold worldwide, and sales are still rising by 10% per year. Germany has the largest market, followed by the United Kingdom, Italy, and France.

Organic production represents an important economic and social dimension that contributes to job creation, agricultural production and agro-food trade. At global level, there has been continuous growth in the consumption of organic products in developed markets. In 2014, there were 172 countries cultivating organic produce in the world, a registered ecological surface area of 43.7 million hectares (1.0% of the world's cultivated area), 2.3 million organic producers and 62.000 processors. The number of organic producers in 2013 stood at 50.936. In 2014 a group of 10 countries controlled 73% of the world's ecological surface area; between 2011 and 2014 that area increased by 17% (MAPAMA 2015). Figures 4.2 and 4.3 show the ecological surface and market growth worldwide with optimistic estimates up to 2020 (Prodescon 2016).

The global market for organic products has grown exponentially, supported by strong growth in imports by large consumer markets in developed countries. All indications point to the fact that this trend will continue over the next few years (MAPAMA 2015).

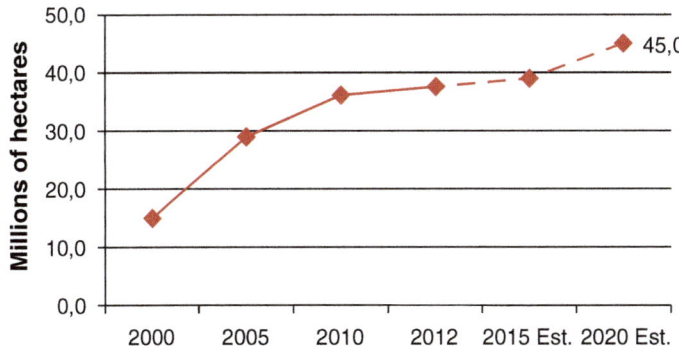

Fig. 4.2 Growth of the global ecological surface area in millions of hectares. (*Source:* MAPAMA 2015)

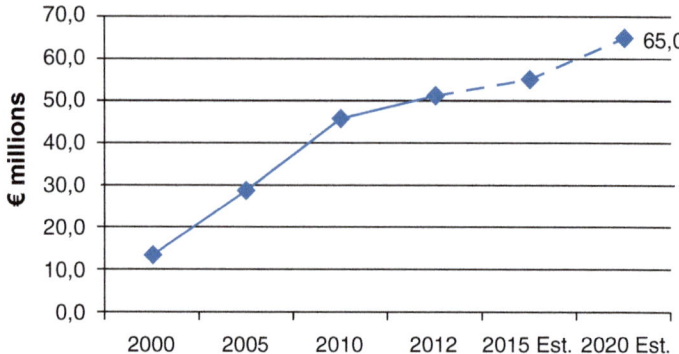

Fig. 4.3 Growth of the world market in € millions. (*Source:* MAPAMA 2015)

Table 4.2 Expert panel participants

Public Sector Participants	Private Sector Participants
General Manager of Rural Development and Common Agricultural Policy (CAP) Valencian Regional Government	CEO of The Muesli Up Company
Chairman of the Spanish Society of Organic Agriculture (SSOA)	Director of Quality, R&D and the Environment, Dulcesol Group
Chairman of the Valencian Region's Organic Agriculture Committee (VOAC)	Technical Director, Herbes del Molí S.L.
Head of Sub-division of Differentiated Quality and Organic Agriculture. Ministry of Agriculture, Fisheries, Food and the Environment.	General Manager of José María Bou S.L.
Representative of IFOAM (International Federation of Organic Agriculture Movements), Organics International.	

4.5   Challenges and Opportunities

The analysis of relevant theoretical and empirical studies enables us to reflect on the threats and opportunities facing the sector. We also used two expert panels to help us cross-reference and complete the information available from previous studies. This section has been compiled from the analysis of previous works as well as from the arguments discussed by the cited experts (Moreno-Luzon et al. 2017).

Table 4.2 specifies the participants taking part in the two panels held. The first took place on January 26, 2017, and included representatives from the public sector and academia. The second was held on May 2, 2017, and featured representatives from private-sector firms. All the experts are very actively involved in the sector studied.

The challenges analyzed have mainly arisen as a result of the sharp and sustained growth in the demand for organic products (Willer and Yussefi 2007) and of the strict requirements imposed in the specific regulations. Looking at the sector as a whole, the innovation trend has shifted from value-based, social and radical innovations to a new need to succeed in managing incremental innovations to overcome the challenges associated with growth and to improve efficiency. Therefore, the main challenge facing the sector is how to maintain the essence of the original values and principles, and to combine radical and incremental innovation. The sector must invest in research to develop the innovations needed to tackle unsolved challenges and, at the same time, incremental innovation is essential to achieve higher levels of efficiency in order to reduce the price differential with the conventional sector and to meet growing demand that the conventional agro-food sector is finding increasingly attractive, and consequently is opening up organic lines of production.

4.5.1 Management Innovation and Ambidexterity

Although organic products are still considerably more expensive than non-organic goods, the fact that the sector is maturing is bringing with it greater competition in terms of prices, making the need for improved, more efficient processes through exploitation activities absolutely essential. Therefore, companies in this sector need to be ambidextrous (Moreno-Luzón and Valls Pasola 2011), combining exploitation in order to reduce operating costs and compete on price, and exploration to be receptive to new markets, technological change and product innovation. This ambidextrous capability is crucial to maintaining balanced innovation for the future of these companies.

   Ambidexterity is described as the ability to use both hands with the same dexterity and has been used as a metaphor to characterize an organizational capacity where exploitation and exploration activities are both sustained, that is, to improve and take advantage of existing resources, and to seek new knowledge and opportunities, respectively. March (1991), who is a pioneer in this subject, argued for the importance of achieving a balance between exploration and exploitation to maintain the competitiveness of companies in the long term. Specifically, exploitation is related to efficiency, certainty, control, reduction of variance, refinement, and the improvement of existing knowledge, skills and technologies (March 1991; Tushman and O'Reilly 1996). It also involves the use of explicit knowledge, from which incremental innovations in existing products or processes originate (Nonaka 1994). In contrast, exploration is related to experimentation, flexibility, risk-taking, increasing variance, and acquiring new knowledge, skills and technologies (Lubatkin et al. 2006; March 1991; Tushman and O'Reilly 1996). It also involves the use of tacit knowledge, and is intended to respond to changes in the environment by creating radical innovations (Tushman and O'Reilly 1996). According to March, carrying out both types of activities in a correct and balanced manner is a source of prosperity and a fundamental survival factor for firms.

   The agro-organic food sector in particular has a strong need and a great opportunity to be ambidextrous. Given clear competition with conventional products and a high export profile, they must pursue exploitation to make continuous improvements in efficiency, improve processes, reduce costs, and be competitive in terms of price. They also require exploration to establish themselves in new markets, improve the quality and efficiency of processes, and be more alert to technological changes and product innovation.

4.5.2   Conventional and Specialized Distribution Channels

The success of a product depends on the place of sale. The challenge lies in the choice of conventional sales channels or specialized channels. In the year 2000, a significant threshold was crossed in the USA, with more organic products being bought in conventional supermarkets than in specialized stores. In the USA, 73% of American supermarkets stock organic products (Dimitri and Greene 2002).

In Europe, supermarket chains are increasing the sale of organic products. This diversity of distribution channels represents an opportunity for producers and processors to channel products more extensively, but it is not without difficulties. Conventional distribution is a new actor which has introduced new formal regulations to ensure the integrity of its organic supplies via the imposition of standards that exceed mandatory governmental requirements, thus potentially exerting pressure on suppliers (Patel and Woodward 2007).

On the other hand, the pricing policies applied by supermarkets constitute a barrier for small local producers, and supermarkets tend to import produce to achieve better prices instead of using domestic sources as the specialized distribution channel has traditionally done. Moreover, supermarket consumers are not the same as those who shop in specialized distribution establishments, who are environmentally aware and very much concerned with health and quality-of-life issues (Patel and Woodward 2007).

4.5.3   Formalization, Standards and High Levels of Safety and Food Quality

In the global organic business, certification systems establish a particular definition of certified organic quality, and impose strict production and documentation requirements on producers. If producers do not adapt to these requirements they will not be able to access global export networks. Certification is actually a new, very powerful form of governance applied by the social, legal, and bureaucratic institutions creating certification regulations. Organic certification is not cheap for small producers; therefore it creates entry barriers and encourages the concentration of organic production and price premiums in the hands of large corporate producers.

Certification is a guaranty for consumers, as they can rely on qualifications and auditing systems controls, to ensure that labeling is correct and that safety and quality norms have been well implemented. Corporate retailers and branders also benefit from organic certification, since the chain of custody and documentation requirements facilitate their control over suppliers, and organic labels facilitate their participation in mainstream markets (Raynolds 2004).

However, excessive regulation and the duplicity of standards and governmental requirements can reduce flexibility and increase complexity, therefore making it more difficult for small innovative entrepreneurs to break into the sector.

However, it is a great challenge to deal with the regulation already present in the agro-food sector and the specific ecological certifications as well. At the same time, it can be a great advantage for the agro-organic food sector since it can guarantee consumers greater food safety and quality than the conventional agro-food sector.

4.5.4   Maintaining Original Values

Along with the recognition of the success of the organic sector and the many hopes for its future, there is still the fear of its accelerated growth and of the approach of the conventional sector, due to the irruption in the conventional sector of large firms that move the organic sector away from its original values (Willer and Yussefi 2007).

There is a debate in the literature on trends and patterns in the development of modern organic agriculture that centers on modernization, institutionalization, globalization, functional differentiation, dis-embedding from local systems, enrollment in mainstream agro-food corporations, conventionalization, industrialization, professionalization, intensification and specialization.

In particular, there has been a lively debate among practitioners and academics on whether and to what extent there is a trend towards 'conventionalization', in which the organic sector becomes more like the conventional agro-food industry (e.g., Guthman 2004; Lockie and Halpin 2005). The implications of this for the transformation potential of the sector are under debate, as it may imply losing core values and principles, and the question to be asked is whether conventionalization is necessary for growth.

In line with Alroe and Noe (2008), we understand there must be a way to achieve growth using industrial production and values. This challenge can be seen as an opportunity because the irruption of conventional agro-food firms in the ecological sector can serve to massively spread its original values.

As one of the participants of the panel of experts mentioned, "Given the high demands of food quality and safety that require continuous improvement of processes and many methodologies and tools of quality management, the conventional industry is a step away from the organic industry, so it can easily apply many of the values that characterize it" (Moreno-Luzon et al. 2017).

The three challenges we have just presented can be analyzed as a whole based on the institutional perspective (North 2005). According to North (1990), institutions are the rules of the game in a society or the constraints that shape human interactions. Growth requires evolution in these rules to face change while maintaining the essence of social focus. If the sector loses its capacity to realize the four founding principles and fails to differentiate itself from similar proposals that can lead to confusion, it may be at risk.

As we have seen, standards and governmental regulations have been fundamental to influence behaviors and have provided a transparent and efficient framework, which is certainly a good basis for the sector's economic development. Yet these rules still need to continue to evolve and change to adapt to new circumstances, which means efforts must be made to continue to adapt them.

New entrants, big food corporations, with greater economic rather than social objectives, are breaking into the organic agro-food sector as it continues to grow, and this economic interest may jeopardize the traditional belief system adopted by the actors in this sector. These global corporations develop standards to regulate international trade and do not share the strong social values of traditional organic businesses working with specialized distribution outlets. We believe that the imbalance towards formal rules in the sector may put the development of the sector at risk.

4.6 Final Discussion and Conclusions

The organic agro-food sector is facing major challenges that are putting some of the core values at the heart of its original revolution at risk. These challenges have mainly arisen as a result of the sharp and sustained growth in the demand for organic products, and of the strict requirements imposed on firms in specific regulations. Improvements in efficiency bring cost and price adjustments that are essential to ensure competitiveness. Although organic products are still considerably more expensive than non-organic goods, the fact that the sector is maturing is bringing with it greater competition in terms of prices, making the need for improved, more efficient processes absolutely essential. Therefore, companies in this sector need to reduce operating costs and compete on price.

After a study of the sector, we can say that the commercial link of organic products is still relatively young, since most of the points of sale began trading between the years 1996 and 2001. Although the demand for organic products is increasingly exponentially, it is still low in the most common sales outlets such as hypermarkets and supermarkets; and medium-high in specialty channels such as herbalists and specialty shops.

Although organic products are more expensive than conventional products, the industry is maturing and is becoming more competitive on price, making the need for improved processes and more efficient processes essential through exploitation activities. When firms in the sector improve quality and innovation as well as reducing costs by improving the efficiency of their processes, they can reduce prices by facilitating greater consumer access to these products and by extension, encourage the spread of sustainable production. Therefore, these firms must combine exploitation to reduce operating costs and compete on price, together with exploration to be receptive to new markets, technological change and product innovation. Thus, they become ambidextrous firms and assure their future.

Together with this need to be ambidextrous, firms in this sector face other important challenges such as the right selection of distribution channels, either conventional or/and specialized; and the election of the correct level of formalization, which has to be high enough to fulfill the demanding standards of premium food safety and quality but not so high as to cause excess rigidity in the processes that stop innovation and impede adaptability to market changes. These three challenges are connected to the need of innovation management to improve managerial and operational processes.

On one hand, when examining the sector as a whole, and taking on board the range of needs that these firms face, we can say that the innovation trend in the sector has changed from paradigmatic, value-based, social and radical innovations when these products began to break into the market to incremental managerial innovations to overcome the challenges associated with growth in a period of maturity.

On the other hand, as we have seen, there are challenges facing the sector that could put its main values and principles at risk, such as the irruption of conventional distribution channels onto the scene in the shape of large manufacturing companies whose objectives are profit-based rather than socially focused. These global corporations develop standards to regulate international trade and do not share the strong social values of the traditional organic industry which operates in the specialized distribution channel. We believe that the imbalance towards formal rules in the sector may jeopardize the development of the sector. According to North (1990), institutions are the rules of the game in a society or the constraints that shape human interactions. Growth requires evolution in these rules to face change while maintaining the essence of social focus. If the sector loses its capacity to realize the four founding principles and fails to differentiate itself from similar proposals, by extension leading to confusion, it may be at risk. As we have seen, standards and governmental regulations have been fundamental to influence behaviors and have provided a transparent and efficient framework, which is certainly a good basis for the sector's economic development. Yet these rules still need to continue to evolve and change to adapt to new circumstances, which means efforts must be made to continue to adapt them.

This study opens up new avenues of research about this sector, especially related to the challenges identified.

Acknowledgements This research is part of the Project ECO2015-71380-R funded by the Spanish Ministry of Economy, Industry and Competitiveness and the State Research Agency. Co-financed by the European Regional Development Fund (ERDF).

References

Alroe, H. F., & Noe, E. (2008). What makes organic agriculture move: Protest, meaning or market? A polyocular approach to the dynamics and governance of organic agriculture. *International Journal of Agricultural Resources, Governance and Ecology, 7*(1–2), 5–22.

Bock, B. B. (2012). Social innovation and sustainability; how to disentangle the buzzword and its application in the field of agriculture and rural development. *Studies in Agricultural Economics, 114*(2), 57–63.

Dawson, P., & Daniel, L. (2010). Understanding social innovation: A provisional framework. *International Journal of Technology Management, 51*(1), 9–21.

Dimitri, C., & Greene, C. (2002). Recent growth patterns in the US organic food sector. *Agriculture Information Bulletin, 777*, 1–21.

Doherty, B., Haugh, H., & Lyon, F. (2014). Social enterprises as hybrid organizations: A review and research agenda. *International Journal of Management Reviews, 16*(4), 417–436.

Dorais, M. (2007). Organic production of vegetables: State of the art and challenges. *Canadian Journal of Plant Science, 87*(5), 1055–1066.

DuPuis, E. M. (2000). Not in my body: BGH and the rise of organic milk. *Agriculture and Human Values, 17*(3), 285–295.

Edwards-Schachter, M. E., Matti, C. E., & Alcantara, E. (2012). Fostering quality of life through social innovation: A living lab methodology study case. *Review of Policy Research, 29*(6), 672–692.

European-Commission. (2013). *Guide to social innovation.* Brussels: European Commission Regional and Urban Policy.

FAO. (2000). *Food safety and quality as affected by organic farming.* Rome: Food and Agriculture Organization.

Franz, H. W., Hochgerner, J., & Howaldt, J. (2012). *Challenge social innovation: Potentials for business, social entrepreneurship, welfare and civil society* (pp. 1–16). Berlin: Springer Science & Business Media.

Guthman, J. (2004). The Trouble with "Organic Lite" in California: A Rejoinder to the "Conventionalisation" Debate. *Sociologia Ruralis, 44*(3), 301–316.

IFOAM. (2005). *Principles of organic agriculture.* Adopted by the IFOAM General Assembly in Adelaide in 2005. https://www.ifoam.bio/

Lockie, S., & Halpin, D. (2005). The "Conventionalisation" thesis reconsidered: Structural and ideological transformation of Australian organic agriculture. *Sociologia Ruralis, 45*(4), 284–307.

Lubatkin, M. H., Simsek, Z., Ling, Y., & Veiga, J. F. (2006). Ambidexterity and performance in small-to medium-sized firms: The pivotal role of top management team behavioral integration. *Journal of Management, 32*(5), 646–672.

MAPAMA. (2015). *Caracterización de la comercialización y distribución de productos ecológicos a través de los canales de venta especializados.* Ministerio de Agricultura, Alimentación Y Medio Ambiente, Madrid, Spain, 1–57.

March, J. G. (1991). Exploration and exploitation in organizational learning. *Organization Science, 2*(1), 71–87.

Moreno-Luzón, M. D., & Valls Pasola, J. (2011). Ambidexterity and total quality management: Towards a research agenda. *Management Decision, 49*(6), 927–947.

Moreno-Luzon, M. D., Gil-Marques, M., LLoria-Aramburo, M. B., Escriba-Moreno, M. A., & Martinez-Perez, J. F. (2017). *Report on threats and opportunities of the organic agro-food sector.* Working Paper. University of Valencia.

Mulgan, G. (2012). The theoretical foundations of social innovation. In *Social innovation* (pp. 33–65). Basingstoke: Palgrave Macmillan.

Nonaka, I. (1994). A dynamic theory of organizational knowledge creation. *Organization Science, 5*(1), 14–37.

North, D. (1990). A transaction cost theory of politics. *Journal of Theoretical Politics. Cambridge University Press, 2*(4), 355–367.

North, D. C. (2005). *Understanding the process of economic change.* Princeton: Princeton University Press.

Patel, A., & Woodward, D. G. (2007). Supermarkets and the organic food supply chain: The potential for waste generation and its mitigation. *International Journal of Global Environmental Issues, 70*(1), 53–87.

Porter, M. E., & Kramer, M. R. (2011). Creating Shared Value. *Harvard Business Review, 89*(1/2), 62–77.

Prodescon, S. A. (2016). Caracterización del sector de la Producción ecológica española En términos de valor y mercado, Referida al año 2015. España.

Raynolds, L. T. (2004). The globalization of organic agro-food networks. *World Development, 32*(5), 725–743.

Scrinis, G. (2007). From techno-corporate food to alternative agri-food movements. *Local-Global: Identity, Security, Community, 4*, 112.

Seebode, D., Jeanrenaud, S., & Bessant, J. (2012). Managing innovation for sustainability. *R&D Management, 42*(3), 195–206.

Tidd, J., & Bessant, J. (2015). *Managing Innovation. Integrating Technological, Market and Organizational Change* (5th ed.). Hoboken: Wiley.

Tushman, M. L., & O'Reilly, C. A. (1996). Ambidextrous organizations: Managing evolutionary and revolutionary change. *California Management Review, 38*(4), 8–30.

Willer, H., & Yussefi, M. (2007). *The world of organic agriculture: Statistics and emerging trends 2007* (9th ed., p. 251). International Federation of Organic Agriculture Movements, Bonn and Research Institute of Organic Agriculture, Frick.

Chapter 5
Sustainable Social Innovations in Smart Cities: Exploratory Analysis of the Current Global Situation Applicable to Colombia

Antonio Alonso-Gonzalez, Lorena A. Palacios Chacon, and Marta Peris-Ortiz

Abstract In the current world most of the population is concentrated in urban areas, where people receive their education, work and leisure activities. Therefore, many challenges have appeared in cities all over the world related to growth, over-population, urban planning, quality of services, competitiveness, environmental factors and citizenship values, which have become main priorities of the managers and mayors of these cities. The Smart City concept emerges as a paradigm that aims to solve these problems and challenges, by developing policies, infrastructure, services and public awareness programs that will transform today cities, for example a future self-sustaining innovation, growth, technological development, civic and ethical citizenship and social progress. This study presents an exploratory analysis in respect of the current global situation related to the concept of Smart City, comparing the different essential definitions and dimensions described in recent literature by cited authors and related to the nomenclature of the term. The effects, challenges and opportunities that Smart Cities can offer to their citizens, has been presented, for example in different programs, projects and initiatives, that cities all over the world have implemented, focusing on sustainable social innovations, economic growth, environmental protection, quality of life, participatory governance, social and community development, citizenship education, efficient urban mobility, tourism services, health and safety. The situation in Bogota and Medellin, the two main cities of Colombia have been reviewed and studied in this work, the aspects

A. Alonso-Gonzalez (✉)
EIAM—PRIME Business School, Universidad Sergio Arboleda, Bogotá, Colombia
e-mail: antonio.alonso@usa.edu.co

L. A. Palacios Chacon
Escuela de Negocios, Universidad del Norte, Barranquilla, Colombia
e-mail: lorenapalacios@uninorte.edu.co

M. Peris-Ortiz
Departamento de Organización de Empresas, Universitat Politècnica de Valencia, Valencia, Spain
e-mail: mperis@doe.upv.es

© Springer International Publishing AG, part of Springer Nature 2018   65
M. Peris-Ortiz et al. (eds.), *Strategies and Best Practices in Social Innovation*,
https://doi.org/10.1007/978-3-319-89857-5_5

previously mentioned have been taken into account to establish a new definition of the Smart City concept. To perform this task, a set of six dimensions and 27 subcategories are essential to define and measure this concept in the Colombian paradigm, which can be used to monitor the current status, in order to approximate evaluations of Colombian cities to the qualification concept described as the Smart City. Due to the lack of studies observed in this work, further research must be focused, not only on getting more data from Bogota and Medellin, but also having the opportunity to observe the situation in other important cities such as Barranquilla, Cali, Bucaramanga or Cartagena, currently no data is available.

Keywords Corporate culture · Dynamic capabilities · Sustainability · SMEs · Non-profit organizations · Innovation · Entrepreneurship

5.1 Introduction

North (1981, 2005) a well-known author, states that related economic development in any society has four different interconnected structures: institutions, technology, population and ideology. This idea is complemented by other works such as the one written by Nasar (2011) and Auvinet and Lloret (2015), in which they analyzed the role of the different inventors, inventions and innovations in the economic development of society and organizations. It is important to take into account that in any observed country, economic growth is associated directly with urban growth. Theoretically, the larger a city, the better the welfare and employability are, as well as investment, quality education, communication systems, and media entertainment and recreation supply that appeal to all tastes. It also implies that information is available to the majority of the population (Hernandez-Escobar and Perez-Hernandez 2015).The concept of what a city is must be explained, so Fernandez-Güell (2015) defines a city as a "complex ecosystem of connected items or parts, where human activities are linked by communications that interact and the system evolves dynamically as a whole, where any spatial or structural alterations of its parts modify other parts of the system".

Perhaps the biggest difference between ancient and modern cities is not about the core concept but their size (Montiel-Casas 2015). Therefore, the city must be analyzed in relation to the current trends in urban development and the impact that cities have in our world today. It is important to highlight that in 2007, for the first time in history, the urban population exceeded the rural population (Sierra 2013). By 2015 more than 6 billion people will live in large cities (Boob 2015). United Nations forecasts that 70% of human beings will live in urban centers by 2050. In real terms, the number of urban residents is growing by nearly 60 million people every year (Casas-Perez 2014).

According to this astonishing growth, our planet is becoming more and more urban, and cities need to become smarter and improve their urbanization plans, requiring new ways of managing the growing complexity of urban living (Rizzo 2015). Cities must become places suitable to provide the best conditions for their inhabitants in a comprehensive and sustainable manner (Cohen and Obediente 2014), and this scenario requires the development of sustainable and intelligent approaches to these urban environments to ensure that cities are optimized for sustainable economic activity, efficient energy consumption, minimal environmental impact and ideal wellness (Boob 2015). Because of this, today the attractiveness of metropolitan areas is no longer based solely on their ability to offer jobs and housing, but also the provision of services is increasingly important, both in quantity and quality, focused on customer satisfaction (Vasquez-Ortega 2012).

Currently, a large number of metropolitan areas around the world are moving towards the model known as Smart City, a term that covers a variety of solutions and approaches, whose prevalent points are the efficient management of resources and the improvements in quality of life. Each concept of Smart City aims to contribute from different perspectives to new benefits for existing cities, to reach greater ecological sustainability, significant reduction in emissions of greenhouse gases, the efficient management of resources in the city, promoting new information economies, and a total connectivity between elements of the city, (Alfaro-Martinez and Soria-Rodriguez 2012).This concept of the Smart City appeared around 20 years ago, and has evolved based on the number of areas and fields that have been included in the urban environment. Originally, the key component of Smart Cities was energy, however it has expanded to include, in some cases, the use of Information and Communication Technology (hereafter ICT), city government and management, or provision of public services such as health (Sierra 2013).

As a matter of fact, the concept of smart cities has been an area of research and development in recent years around the world. There are some very significant projects, for example: the Smart Cities project of the MIT Media Lab, the Smart Cities project of the European Union, and the IBM Smart Cities project. Essentially a smart city seeks to use ICT as an engine for a city's development, promoting sustainable growth and welfare of its inhabitants (Sierra 2013). Since its emergence in the 90s of the last century, the Smart City concept has been strongly influenced by technology, as a key element to address major challenges of concern in contemporary cities (Fernandez-Güell 2015).

The transition from conventional cities to Smart Cities is a priority because of the shortage of essential resources (water, energy, food, etc.) which is becoming a fundamental problem for humanity, according to the Millennium Development Goals, especially relating to sustainability and quality of life. However, it is clear that humanity is transforming urban spaces in different latitudes at different paces. For example, it is a fact that cities like Barcelona and Seoul are taking advantage over other cities, due to their capacity to finance infrastructure improvements, their designation as urban laboratories by major technology companies in the world, but also the existence of a defined digital policy that has been established by their governments to move towards more efficient and sustainable urban environments (Casas-Perez 2014).

5.2 Theoretical Background

5.2.1 Definitions Referred to the Smart City Concept

To better understand the term Smart City, some definitions will be quoted in reference to the concept and recent study results published by the authors. Cohen and Obediente (2014) define Smart Cities as "cities that through the application of technology in different areas become more efficient in the use of resources, energy saving, services provided and sustainable development, solving major problems that citizens have". Hernandez-Escobar and Perez-Hernandez (2015) use a similar definition: "multilevel systems of innovation where technological mechanisms are deployed in physical, institutional and digital spaces. The mainstays of these Smart Cities are innovation systems complemented by digital spaces providing strategic intelligence, digital media, networking and collaboration".

It may be observed, that there is a strong implication of the technological dimension to achieve the objectives defined by the concept. In this line of research, Sierra (2013) defines Smart Cities as "the cities that improve their services through the generation of different applications related to ICT, enhancing the citizens' quality of life, increasing competitiveness in the productive sector, and facilitating interaction with governments. For this purpose, it should be considered that the development of some aspects, for example security, competitive intelligence, data analysis, data mining, and software development on mobile platforms. In this definition, the authors specifically highlight ICT as the most important technology today. Boob (2015) continues defending ICT as a cornerstone of the Smart City concept as "a transformation of the existing urban development and its infrastructure by using and harnessing ICT to improve economic and political efficiency and enable social, cultural and sustainable urban development to reach a high quality of life, with a sustainable management of natural resources, through people, public and participatory governance". Montiel-Casas (2015) follows the same line defining "Smart Cities as a concept that integrates the use of new ICT, energy efficiency, e-government (local participatory democracy), transparency in management (open data), effective recycling and urban waste management, forming a technologically advanced structure that should benefit all populations."

The question is if ICT or technologies in general terms are the only important issues to consider in the definition of the term. Patiño (2014) starts questioning this reasoning explaining that "during the last decade the term Smart City has been used as a concept associated with the ability to maximize the use of ICT to meet the modern challenges of urban issues, although there is still no universal consensus on its meaning". Following this skeptical view relating to the latest definitions that are focused only on the importance of ICT, Casas-Perez (2014) specifies that "a Smart City is not only a digital concept, but also a sustainable entity, in a way that not all digital cities are smart. The fundamental difference lies in the ability of the smart city to solve problems. This implies that smart systems are embedded within the city infrastructure, by automating the delivery of information and delivery of basic services". Villanueva et al. (2014) also defends this point of view of a Smart City as a universe to help citizens to improve their quality of life, explaining that "the concept of Smart City intends to evolve processes and daily activities that citizens carry out from their current situation to a more efficient state from an energy point of view, time and cost. To do so requires the collaboration of different actors in their areas of activity, as well as the introduction of new technologies". Therefore the authors add the importance of the problem solving and introduce the sustainability dimension to the definition of the term.

At this point, it has been mentioned that the authors support the importance of ICT as the core issue of the concept, and others highlight the relevance of problem solving for citizens, and the sustainability of the entire project. However, there is another key trend which includes the importance of the human factor and its combination with the infrastructure, environment and services. Rizzo (2015) introduces a variation of the concept Smart City, using the term "Human Smart Cities (hereafter HSC) as ecosystems where physical and digital infrastructures are introduced and implemented in a systemic relation with the cities human capital. The HSC are both systematic and anthropocentric, and are designed so they can operate at scale, being able to achieve things that cities need, and creating large areas in which social relation and empathy are possible". Ishkineeva et al. (2015) expand the idea that the combination of human, tangible and intangible capital defining a Smart City as "a city where investments in human and social capital and in traditional and modern infrastructure, provide sustainable city development and a high quality of life, with an intelligent use of natural resources and a smart use of the cities potential based on a participative management. A Smart City is a city with an effective networkable business climate, smart professions, clever and free people who are able to make decisions and participate in urban life and development. New ICT will switch to a totally new way of smart management and a method to build conceptually, a new city format. Another interesting definition of the concept related to human capital but focused on the dimension of education, reference Vasquez-Ortega (2012) who introduces another vision related to the term Smart City: "a smart city has smart people in terms of education, referring to the relationship between city government, the administration and its citizens, where the population is taken into account and especially where it is possible to ensure their rights in a legally effective and transparent model. Also, it often refers to the use of new communication channels for citizens, for example, e-governance or electronic democracy".

5.2.2 Different Dimensions to be Considered into to the Smart City Concept Approach

It is necessary to act in multiple and different dimensions in order to advance towards the concept of Smart City, but common elements allow us to develop each of these axis, as defined in the previous section: the use and application of new technologies and specifically ICT, focused on problem solving for citizens', in a sustainable way, and combining human capital, infrastructure and city systems and services. What is necessary now is to recognize how the different authors have defined these dimensions according to a cites infrastructure, services and systems.

Paskaleva (2011) sets three dimensions to measure the level of development of a Smart City: the level of exploitation of network infrastructure (to improve economic and political efficiency and enable social, cultural and urban development), the level of vision and strategy to create a competitive city within the smart city (opportunities of ICT to increase local prosperity and competitiveness at a multi-actor, multi-sector, and multi-level urban perspective towards sustainability), and the level of sustainable and inclusive approach of the cities (placing the main responsibility on the human and social capital of urban development). Casas-Perez (2014) also defines three basic dimensions necessary in order to be considered and developed by a Smart City, but based on other approaches, for example: innovative economy (innovation in industries, clusters and urban districts; workforce education, employment and knowledge; knowledge generators), urban infrastructure (transport; energy, water and other services; environmental protection; safety), and governance (public services management; direct and participatory democracy; services to citizens; and quality of life).

There are other views that increase the number of dimensions to six. A research project performed by the European Smart Cities Association includes six dimensions as essential to define the concept of Smart City: smart governance (political strategies and perspectives, transparency, community participation in decision making), smart people (diversity, creativity, participation in public life), smart living (cultural facilities, housing quality, health and safety issues), smart environment (sustainable resource management, pollution prevention, environmental protection), smart mobility (strong ICT infrastructure, sustainable transport systems), and smart economy (high productivity, entrepreneurship, ability to transform) (Kanter and Litow 2009). Cohen and Obediente (2014) also develop their study six areas or components, grouping 28 indicators that are used to measure and rank smart cities: environment (smart buildings, resources management, sustainable urban development), mobility (efficient transport, multimodal access, technological infrastructure), government (online services, infrastructure, open government), economy (opportunity, local and global productivity, connections and networks), society (integration, education, creativity) and quality of life (culture and personal welfare, security, health). Number six is also used by Hernandez-Escobar and Perez-Hernandez (2015) to define the dimensions of a Smart City, defining the concept as an urban entity that has a sustained outstanding performance in six disciplines: smart economy, smart mobility, smart environment, smart people, smart life and smart government. Each of these disciplines have specific lines of action that are aligned with the central objective of the Smart City model and are subject to measurement, to determine whether the score is within the established parameters. These six dimensions described by the previous authors are also used by Sierra (2013), identifying government, infrastructure, mobility, energy, environment and services as the main dimensions to measure a Smart City.

Vasquez-Ortega (2012) includes two more elements to be considered in the identification and measurement of the Smart City concept, which summarize eight different dimensions that should be taken into account: efficient energy management, business environments and knowledge economy, transport and urban mobility, e-government and citizen participation, environmental issues, urban planning, tourism and cultural activities, and health and personal care. Each of these categories drive the city towards the category of Smart City, committed to the environment, with artistic architectural elements and buildings equipped with the latest technological solutions in order to facilitate and combine a rural citizen interaction with an organized urban environment, and helping ordinary citizens to make their life easier.

5.2.3   Effects Derived from the Smart City Concept Related to Sustainable and Social Innovations

Nowadays, for any city with a population ranging from 0.2 to 1.0 million, it should be mandatory to focus its growth and development towards the Smart City concept, taking the implementation of this model as a whole instead of as a sum of different systems (Boob 2015). But the Smart city concept is also crucial for modern cities that are planning their future existence, sustainability and proper development. An irrational urban development becomes ineffective and hence non-competitive, while the attractiveness of the city for its citizens, prospective investors and partners are strongly connected to its level of competitiveness (Ishkineeva et al. 2015).

In this section a review will be made of some of the advantages that Smart Cities could offer to citizens, due to the different services offered by its urban model. As explained in the previous sections, data is at the heart of many visions of the future city: information about traffic, the movements of people, and air quality. In the smart city, this data can be integrated, monitored, analyzed and visualized to improve city management, highlighting three important objectives: data integration, data analysis and visualization and predictive analytics (Saunders and Baeck 2015). The safety of citizens is another aspect that can be improved as part of Smart Cities projects, using technological surveillance services to increase security or to identify and characterize trends in the application of ICT in city projects that provide support for decision-making, relating to public policies in each of its components, providing citizens a better quality of life within the concept of a sustainable city (Sierra 2013). The importance of public sector information has increased dramatically, and therefore the data that is associated with this area, known as open government data (including availability and access, use and redistribution, and universal participation), is becoming an important source to generate new services and applications (Patiño 2014).

Efficient energy management in Smart Cities is also an added value that should be taken into consideration, due to an observed trend of an increase in the urban population in the next few years, which in these cases must be supported by proper management of green energy (Balaji 2013; Benitez and Ortega 2015; Klingert et al. 2015). Benchmarking this efficiency on the management of energy, is also important, selecting specific indicators to measure the performance in particular key fields related to energy (Fertner and Gorth 2015). So that, Smart ICT can be described as greener sustainable technologies, that not only use less energy but help to improve performance and reduce environmental impact of the whole of society (Cohen and Obediente 2014).

Urban mobility, city logistics and transport management, as well as the regulation of vehicular traffic, can achieve significant improvements through the implementation of smart technologies applied to control and optimization of the traffic flow in a Smart City (Ben Ahmed et al. 2015; De Domenico et al. 2015; Djahel et al. 2015; Klimek and Kotulski 2015). It is important to highlight that there are ecological models and initiatives that have been developed and successfully implemented in Smart Cities, such as public bike rentals (Graham and Zhang 2015).

Another major improvement that Smart Cities can implement in the environment is the combination of technologies and public services in data collection relating to pollution, for example using sensors installed in public transport vehicles, is a way to register this data and save time and energy reducing installation and operational cost of every sensor nodes (Jamil et al. 2015).

Health services is another area that could be improved in Smart City projects, through the concept of electronic health, used to encompass the many possible applications of ICT in this field, whether intended for health authorities, health services providers, health professionals, as well as custom systems for patients and citizens (Sierra 2013).

Another technological use that can be applied in Smart Cities of the future will allow an increase in the efficiency of services and monitoring systems applied to the tourism sector, thanks to the advantages of new technologies such as Near Field Communication technology (hereafter NFC), which offers a high level of security in the recording of information and a low probability of error in data collection, and it can be applied to monitor the data path of a tourist in real time (Agredo et al. 2015).

However, it must be highlighted that the Smart City concept should not only be focused on infrastructure, systems and services offered to citizens to improve their quality of life, but also in the increase of competitiveness for the whole city in terms of the economy, production and logistics for business. As Dattagupta (2014) explains "a Smart city is an attractive card which will attract a large number of foreign investors. It will pave the way for jobs, investment, better lifestyle, and opportunities for global and human capital. As many experts point out, Smart Cities are a great business opportunity, attracting an affluent middle class as well as other social stratum. This effort is encouraged by the planners and decision makers to meet the needs of all origins, sectors and social classes rather than just emulating the western model of cities".

Reviewing successful cases of Smart City models around the world, it is evident how technology solutions have been implemented for almost any kind of activity related to the city: administrative management and e-government, vehicle control and public transport services, sustainable development, efficient energy control, environmental issues, and education of human capital are some of the areas that have been improved (Hernandez-Escobar and Perez-Hernandez 2015). In addition to this, and as Paskaleva (2011) says, "in the era of the digital economy, the performance of cities is influenced not only by their physical infrastructure, but more and more by their knowledge and social capacity (intellectual and human capital)," so technology is important, but it is not the only element that must be taken into account. It should be combined with the development of infrastructure and the education of citizens. Kamel-Boulos et al. (2015) explain this idea: "by focusing on people, smart cities and regions stand better chances of becoming healthier and happier cities, but it should always be remembered that technology is not a panacea but rather an enabler, and that other factors are equally important in creating happier and healthier cities and regions".

Most people perceive work as an important issue in their life. Without work, or with a unstable job, there is no access to small or large ranges of tangible and intangible assets that a city could offer. So a comprehensive dialogue must be undertaken concerning the construction of a Smart City, with the proposal of an understandable productive city concept, implying the real basis for the realization of many human aspirations in the urban context (Mancheno and Teran 2013). Quality of Service must also be considered, in order to impact on the development of Smart City services (Martinez-Ballesteros et al. 2015). But above all, the Smart City concept should be considered as a broader and capable term to reach another important concept: the Happy City, the place where citizens can have the necessary elements to develop the vital, physical, emotional, psychological, playful, and creative fulfilment. Possibly there can be no greater ambition for people than to be happy and develop a transcendent life (Montiel-Casas 2015).

5.2.4 Challenges and Opportunities for Smart Cities

The advance and progress towards the establishment of a true Smart City starting from a conventional city requires financial and human resources in abundance. In many places, the Smart City initiatives are legislated and driven for this purpose by specialized offices and local governments (Hernandez-Escobar and Perez-Hernandez 2015). What is clear is that conventional cities must overcome some challenges to advance towards the Smart City concept:

- Organizational barriers: due to their singular territorial organization, some cities, municipalities, provinces and regions should be consolidated to create a single, integrated, horizontal and global vision that deviates from their vertical and conventional disconnected development, in order to create a real convergent progress for all their citizens (Cohen and Obediente 2014). In fact, in many cases a divergence can be identified between the proponents of the current Smart City term and the group of urban planners and architects, which could question the sustainability of the Smart City concept in the medium and long term (Fernandez-Güell 2015).

- Legal barriers: in relation to the issue of sharing information between different governmental agencies, some public institutions and administrative offices could have relevant and valuable information but it is not correlated and shared with other public entities or government agencies, because of legal obstacles that prevent such compatibility of information sharing, disabling the operation of how a Smart City should work (Cohen and Obediente 2014).
- Citizen participation barriers: if citizens are not aware of what a Smart City means and the benefits it brings or the behaviour of citizens cannot be measured, it is difficult to create a Smart City. Citizen participation is key and it is one of the barriers that must be overcome in the short term (Cohen and Obediente 2014). Complexity, diversity and uncertainty are also challenges inherent to citizenship that must be tackled (Fernandez-Güell 2015). Many Smart City strategies offer citizens little chance to engage in the design and deployment of new technologies. While citizens trend to be the implied beneficiaries of Smart City projects, they are rarely consulted and often ignored about what they want and their ability to contribute to make their city a better place to live (Saunders and Baeck 2015).
- Lack of awareness of how others are trying to improve their cities: Smart City projects are often too insular and too isolated, with developers talking to each other, but not linking their work to others groups that are trying to address urban challenges and improvements, such as people working within the city government in areas from transport and planning to economic development and public participation (Saunders and Baeck 2015).

To tackle and overcome these barriers, some aspects must be taken into account. For example the organizational barriers can be passed through technological developments related to ICT, as for example Web 2.0 technology to allow a direct and immediate access to information by town planners and urban managers to make sustainable decisions based on opinion from all levels of the urban community (Raut and Raut 2015). The CIVITAS project is an example of a software platform for development and support services to deploy in a smart city. This ambitious project aims to develop a logical nervous system that allows the collection and distribution of information generated in daily activities of a Smart City (Villanueva et al. 2014). Improvements in the levels of efficiency and interconnectivity between the different devices and city services must be developed, towards the so-called Internet of Things (hereafter IoT) (Misra et al. 2015). However, it must be taken into account that the use of computers, software and communication technologies are an integral part of smart cities and must be associated with energy efficient controls, the so-called green computing trend (Anusha et al. 2015).

It is quite understandable that Smart Cities will have smart infrastructure (roads, water, solid waste management, and drainage networks), but it is also obvious that the private sector will play a major role through investment in Smart Cities.

To overcome any legal barriers that could be against a Smart City project, the central and regional government need to design specific formats to generate or improve the urban data base in major urban growth variables (such as income, infrastructure, business, finance, and education). Furthermore, the collection of information on basic socio-economic status is essential to enable the various government departments to formulate appropriate urban development strategies at sub national levels. This would help to raise the standard of urban management practices and monitor the implementation of the various urban policies (Tripathi 2015). Smart cities conceived as ecosystems should provide policy makers with some practical guidelines to integrate soft and hard domains. Three areas for smart government should be implemented: economic development, a vibrant political life and strong support to encourage innovation (Rochet and Pinot de Villechenon 2015).

As it has been defined so far, the Smart City concept is generated when technology pervades all human activities, modifying to the extent that can also change their environment (Hernandez-Escobar and Perez-Hernandez 2015). Following this argument, some authors like Biancalana et al. (2015) propose models to overcome the citizen participation challenge, which they call Personalized Extended Government model (PEG), to encourage and facilitate the exchange of public domain and community information in a personalized perspective, respecting the public administration and citizenship information needs. Other authors like Muñoz de Dios et al. (2014) highlight the necessity to emphasize the intelligent character of the environment, and not only focus on the energy efficiency or the incorporation of wireless communications, but also on the specific actions that are able to guarantee and allow multiple benefits towards improving the quality of services that are provided. Papa and Lauwers (2015) mention "one key element is the interactive and participatory process to commit citizens and not just users towards the smarter paradigm. The open and active involvement of people and stakeholders would be far more effective. Thus, broad coalitions should be formed to include specialists, researchers, academics, practitioners, policy makers and activists in the related areas of technology, transport, land use, urban affairs, environment, public health, ecology, engineering, green modes and public transport. It is only when such coalitions form a real debate, that Smart City concept can take place. There must be a willingness to change and accept a collective responsibility. It is crucial to create conditions for a continuous process of learning and innovation".

In general, all these challenges and barriers (organizational, legal, lack of citizen participation, and isolation) can be overcome by involving higher education institutions such as universities in this process, and becoming active members in these ecosystems. A Smart City should be the orchestrator of collaboration with educational institutions, being the most effective way to manage these new networks and ecosystems (Erkkilä 2014). Nowadays, universities can assist in helping public policy makers and activists thanks to their deep understanding of public learning and innovation in the modern city (Hambleton 2015). Cities with greater percentages of their populations possessing a college education are more likely to become active groups pursuing smart growth policies on their urban environment (O'Connell 2008). New postgraduate degrees and urban ITC systems are increasingly being offered in Smart Cities by universities to meet the demands of a new society with new types of digital skills, expertise and knowledge (Kamel-Boulos et al. 2015). According to this point of view, new ways of learning must be implemented with proper resources to teach in a different way these concepts in order to prepare smart citizens for Smart Cities (Wolff, Kortuem and Cavero 2015). Innovation is another important and transversal key to avoid collapse and to promote sustainability of cities, regions and their infrastructures (Kamel-Boulos et al. 2015). Due to this, innovation and problem solving competences are unique qualities of intelligence and must be enhanced at this educational level (Sierra 2013), improving entrepreneurial competences in citizens (Alonso-Gonzalez et al. 2017b), encouraging the integration of the population at risk of social exclusion (Alonso-Gonzalez et al. 2017a) and taking into account the importance of a proper educational environment within the current urban community (Peris-Ortiz et al. 2017).

5.2.5   Examples of Smart Cities All Over the World

Many cities are experimenting with ICT to improve their services and become closer to the Smart City concept, and there are countless initiatives of Smart Cities worldwide, though the great capitals are the ones that often have greater financial capacity to address the necessary inputs that provide advances to their projects (Vasquez-Ortega 2012). In this section, different successful projects implemented in cities all over the world will be presented, highlighting the good progress in the areas that have been improved in relation to the Smart City concept.

Many cities are using ICT to converge their goals with the Smart Cities ones, such as Amsterdam (Holland), which has developed its Sharing City program as an initiative to promote a collaborative economy to make the most of knowledge networks and sharing communities, using smartphone apps and other ICT. The next step is to extend the initiative to disadvantaged groups (Saunders and Baeck 2015). These kind of collaborative initiatives using smartphones are also being successfully implemented in Beijing (China) through its I Love Beijing initiative, consisting of a mobile app and an online map that city maintenance staff uses thanks to users reports concerning issues such as potholes and broken streetlights. The app grew from a successful pilot project where unemployed people were given hand–held digital devices and asked to report issues they spotted around the city. The app also includes a map of over 600 informal food markets in Beijing (Saunders and Baeck 2015). Lima (Peru) is also focusing on ICT initiatives, improving data transmission and open access to all citizens through a set of services including public investment projects in the municipality, a map of the museums in the city, and traffic fines information. (Patiño 2014). Some of these initiatives are supported by collaborative or crowdsourced initiatives. Jakarta (Indonesia) through its Smart City Plan has focused on citizen engagement rather than the IoT and Big Data, developing the Smart City Platform which consists of three crowdsourced apps: an issue reporting app, a flood map and a traffic management tool (Saunders and Baeck 2015).

Another aspect that can be observed in several cities is the free access to information and the development of an infrastructure capable of facilitating citizen access to that information. Buenos Aires (Argentina) and its network initiatives is an example, entering into the world of Smart Cities and focusing on access to information for its citizens. The city has deployed the largest network of free public access to the Internet in Latin America, which covers a large part of the metropolis and the subway network (Sierra 2013). Montevideo (Uruguay) is another example of this free information access policy related to government services, being the first city in Latin America which had open data for its citizens. As a result of the release of data, several initiatives now provide services for citizens have emerged. Some of these were developed by the city, while others have been implemented by entrepreneurs, civil society or just curious people (Patiño 2014). Along the same lines of thought, a similar initiative can be found in Burgos (Spain) with its Smart City project, developing a communications network that integrates wireless communications and fiber optics. Based on this network, Burgos has reduced its operational and management costs and developed self-provision services, giving access to free internet to all its citizens in streets, squares and public buildings, integrating municipal services like bike rental or other services related to city events (Sierra 2013). Stockholm (Sweden) also enjoys broadband connectivity through fixed and wireless next generation networks. 90% of residential buildings and 100% of the public buildings have access to these networks (Noreña-Rendon 2013; Sierra 2013).

Road traffic, city logistics and public transport are other areas that can be improved through the concept of Smart City. Washington D.C. (USA) is developing its Smart Highways project based on electric signals, sensors and a computerized management system that displays the slowest lane, which ones are in service or out of service due to accidents, measure traffic lights at intersections, and monitor traffic using a centralized security camera system. (Noreña-Rendon 2013). Marseilles (France) has put public transport services at the heart of its development as a Smart City. By the management of the public transport system, the city has established a communications network that provides both free connection for passengers and other services in order to improve the quality and safety of transport. The plan includes initiatives such as the introduction of NFC technology to give citizens access to an initial set of 22 different services (Sierra 2013). Masdar (Abu Dhabi) is another city focusing its priorities on public transport. It has developed the Personal Rapid Transit system as a computerized network to achieve public transport efficiency, based on the automated movement of a fleet of electric vehicles which feed energy from the road, so they do not need batteries and each car can accommodate three people (Noreña-Rendon 2013). Singapore (Singapore), as part of its Smart Nation Program, is developing the Singapore's Intelligent Transport System, which includes Electronic Road Pricing and sensors attached to taxis that help the government to monitor traffic conditions, reducing the number of journeys by private cars in Singapore (Sierra 2013; Saunders and Baeck 2015). London (UK) has also succeeded in its campaign to encourage citizens to use more public transport services, including the subway, buses and taxis, thanks to the improvement of public transport in different areas such as road infrastructure, quality, safety and efficiency in services provided, accompanied by measures such as tolls to reduce traffic jams and the entry of private vehicles in some areas to prioritize the movement of public transport (Noreña-Rendon 2013).

As it has been demonstrated in other sections, environmental initiatives are also a dimension to take into account in Smart Cities, Barcelona (Spain) and its LIVE project is an example of this, a smart initiative implemented which acronym means Logistics for the Implementation of Electric Vehicles. It is a project that aims to promote the development and mobility of electric vehicles in Barcelona and its metropolitan area (Noreña-Rendon 2013). There is also a pilot project that uses sensors on rubbish bins to optimize van collection routes by sending them only to full bins. The city estimates that the system could save 10% on waste disposal costs (Saunders and Baeck 2015). The city of Barcelona has set a goal of developing a standardized and replicable model of Smart City, through the design of each of the elements that comprise: service models, networks of sensors and platforms for service management communications, etc. (Sierra 2013). Genoa (Italy) is applying a similar project based on a circular economy to improve waste management, using intelligent rubbish bins as an example of a feasible waste-related project in the context of Smart Cities (Del Borghi et al. 2014). Stockholm (Sweden) and its Vision 2020 strategy is the best example of how to implement and maintain efficient Smart City models focused on the environment. This city won the Green Capital Award in 2010; as such this award is only given to cities that have significantly reduced air pollution percentages, and also setting its main goals to become one of the most accessible cities in the world, based on its urban transport system (Noreña-Rendon 2013; Sierra 2013). Another city that could be considered as a model of environmental Smart City initiatives is Vancouver (Canada), which is implementing a series of ambitious green programs to become the greenest city by 2020, focusing on an environmental model and developing specific projects as for example: Green Economy, Weather Leadership, Zero Waste, Nature Accessibility and Local Food (Vasquez-Ortega 2012).

Efficient energy management is another area that some cities are seriously taking into consideration, as for example Malaga (Spain) with its Smart Energy Management, as a world reference in the field of energy efficiency. Since 2009 the city has developed an important project which will prevent 6000 tons of CO_2 being deposited annually into the atmosphere, and a reduction of 20% in energy consumption. To this end, measures such as the introduction of electric vehicles and the power grid transformation into a smart grid have been adopted. The city has several lines of action: Smart Green (intelligent management of power storage and distribution), Smart Generation (self-generation and power storage from renewable sources) and Smart Energy Management (efficient management of end use energy) (Sierra 2013; Vasquez-Ortega 2012). Glasgow (UK) is another city with efficient energy management, implementing intelligent streetlights, a pilot project which is testing whether sensors on streetlights will save energy by allowing lights to automatically turn on and off when people walk past them at night (Saunders and Baeck 2015). Singapore (Singapore), as part of its Smart Nation Program, is also implementing an Intelligent Energy System (IES) using a two-way flow of information on the power grid, and allowing a reduction of energy consumption by around 3% (Sierra 2013; Saunders and Baeck 2015). In London (UK), the Canary Wharf group launched the Cognicity Challenge, a pilot project to apply Smart City technologies on the Canary Wharf estate, which aims to help businesses to reduce electricity costs by intelligently monitoring electricity usage (Saunders and Baeck 2015).

In the area of government and participatory democracy, Bangalore (India) has implemented the Next Bangalore initiative, which combines a website where residents can submit and debate ideas. The initiative has helped to create a vision of what residents want their area to look like, as well as keeping a record of their everyday needs and problems. Buenos Aires (Argentina) is another example of these new political trends, raising the concept of open government in different spheres of interaction with other actors as entrepreneurs, technological and academic institutions, in order to integrate them into the process of urban innovation, developing five main categories: security, education, green agenda, mobility and culture, to which they could submit projects (Patiño 2014).

There are cites that have other initiatives to improve citizens urban services and their quality of life. For example, Gijon (Spain) has one of the most advanced citizen identification services. Through a single citizen card, city residents can access various services such as free internet, bike rental, citizen virtual office, public transport pools, art center's and library services (Sierra 2013). Rio de Janeiro (Brazil) has implemented the Intelligent Operations Center that provides information of critical systems, services and infrastructure throughout the city, so that operative services have an integrated vision. As a result, there has been a 30% decrease in the response time in an emergency (Sierra 2013). Santander (Spain) and its Smart Santander project is another example of combined initiatives to accomplish a Smart City objective. The Spanish city has focused on the application of the concept of IoT and Internet of the Future (hereafter IoF), proposing an experimental research platform for the development and application of services related to a Smart City (Sierra 2013). Santander is home to one of the largest city wide sensing pilots in the world, with over 12,000 sensors collecting data on everything from parking space availability to air quality. The developed platform will be attractive to all stakeholders involved: companies, user communities, and other entities willing to use the experimental platform for the development and evaluation of new services and applications, and internet researchers who can validate their new technological developments (Sierra 2013; Saunders and Baeck 2015). Another city which combines different Smart City initiatives in different areas is Madrid (Spain), with some interesting Smart City services focused on citizens, security, environmental sustainability and mobility. Examples of Smart projects that has been implemented are Home Telecare (serving over 120,000 seniors, one of numerous services appreciated by locals), the Integrated Security and Emergency Centre of Madrid (CISEM, coordinates firefighters, police, emergency services, civil protection and traffic agents), bus fleet management (allowing continuous, instantaneous and automatic location of the 2100 buses from the central control station), and the remote control of hydraulic infrastructures associated with the Manzanares River (automatically managing dams for river regulation) (Sierra 2013).

5.3   Methodology

5.3.1   Analysis of the Current Situation in Colombia

In Latin America, 80% of the population lives in urban areas. Cities face challenges in migration, transport, health and urban planning. Unfortunately, the design of public policies of urban management in many cases are being performed individually and separately, preventing synergies in the generation of new innovation processes that could improve the lives of its citizens (Patiño 2014).

The specific situation in Colombia demonstrates that cities are increasing their development and complexity. Citizenship has requirements that need to be satisfied, and in order to build a strategy for this, and according to the results of the National Survey of Logistics, several proposals to transform cities in sustainable environments are being implemented, as for example, spaces for scientific research, technological advances applied to solve citizens' problems, and institutional initiatives, for example Colciencias (Vasquez-Ortega 2012). Through private initiatives, the citizens' quality of life in Colombia continues to evolve thanks to the hospitality industry, providing residential telephone services that have created and improved services that have brought ICT to Colombian homes, improving the quality of life through the proper use of logistical tools that promote technological development of the country towards the Smart City concept (Vasquez-Ortega 2012). Nevertheless, it must be emphasized that in Colombia there is a growing concern in relation to inefficiencies in the goods supply chain demanded by cities, because of increasing urbanization in Colombian society, this problem is the main challenge that needs to be tackled, in order to reach the maximum level of services for Colombian urban citizens (Vasquez-Ortega 2012).

Another area where Colombia has become a reference model in citizenship services is the e-government initiatives. Colombia is a leader in electronic and participatory government in Latin America and the Caribbean, according to UN reports. In this field there are some interesting projects, for example: Government Online, Governmental Intranet, the standardization of procedures and online city services, and the development of the first Online Government Services for terrestrial digital television and other initiatives within the program Vive Digital, such as Online Notaries, Online Congress, and Zero Paper initiative (Vasquez-Ortega 2012).

According to the literature revised in the current work, it has been found that there are very few academic studies related to the Smart City concept, in reference to the most important cities in Colombia. Significant research work was found for two cities, namely Medellin and Bogota, the capital of the nation. Medellin is close to be considered a Smart City, thanks to all the projects that have been implemented with the help of the cities' Mayor and numerous organizations that oversee the quality of life of the cities' population (Vasquez-Ortega 2012). Medellin is the first city in Colombia with a governmental program related to the Smart City model. The Medellin Smart City program has been implemented in four strategic initiatives: open government, citizen participation, social innovation and sustainability. These initiatives improve citizens' quality of life through access to better information, empowering tools necessary to transform their realities, finding relevant solutions to the city problems, and during the process reducing environmental impact (Sierra 2013). Mobility is one of the biggest problems in Medellin and its metropolitan area, and it has been a familiar problem not only in Colombian cities but worldwide. Understanding this phenomenon in order to find solutions to improve the quality of life of citizens and it has become one of the top priorities for many local governments (Noreña-Rendon 2013).

In the case of Bogota, the main approach towards the Smart City concept has been developed in urban mobility areas under the Mobility Master Plan. Thanks to this initiative, the city has structured the new Integrated Public Transport System (SITP), as an instrument to ensure better quality of life for its citizens, optimizing levels of service levels on journeys made in the city and integrating in the same project the TransMilenio system. This system has established itself as a world leader in mobility, with a gradual and controlled implementation that will change the history of the city, eliminating many problems suffered in the past associated with public transport and mobility (Sierra 2013).

5.3.2 Smart City Concept: Proposal of a New Definition and Dimensions Applied to Colombian Cities

According to Mosannenzadeh and Vettorato (2014), to create Smart Cities it is necessary to identify the main goals and provide a defined Smart City plan, set the main sub-systems and their relationships, and the key stakeholders involved in these plans. Then, ICT implementation should enhance the functionality of urban services and infrastructure, integrating the plans and implementing the different sub-systems through collaborative work between stakeholders who are involved in the creation of a Smart City.

With the intention to establish a strong definition and set the dimensions that could help to initiate the Smart City concept for Colombian cities and urban policies, the first task to be be performed in this section is an intensive review of the Smart City term presented by the authors cited in this paper: Vasquez-Ortega (2012), Sierra (2013), Casas-Perez (2014), Cohen and Obediente (2014), Patiño (2014), Villanueva et al. (2014), Boob (2015), Hernandez-Escobar and Perez-Hernandez (2015), Ishkineeva et al. (2015), Montiel-Casas (2015), and Rizzo (2015). As it was highlighted in the previous section, there is a strong implication for the technological dimension to achieve the objectives defined by the Smart City concept, and specifically new technologies related to ICT, but although this concept is a cornerstone of this discipline, it should be noted that other authors also add importance on problem solving capacity and sustainability of the whole project, as well as other academics who uphold the importance of the human factor and its combination with infrastructure, environment, systems and services, in order to achieve the global objectives of the Smart City concerning its citizens: productive competitiveness, efficient mobility, smart energy management, premium services, e-government, quality of life, and environmental awareness. Taking into account all of these terms and observations, they can be combined to propose a new definition that integrates all the concepts studied so far and referred to as Smart Cities: "A Smart City is a urban and metropolitan hub based on ICT and other new technologies that help citizens to interact through their personal devices, offering the best experience and mobility results, energy management, premium services, participatory democracy, health and safety, environmental impact, and any other section which could be relevant for citizens, integrating human capital, city systems, infrastructure, and its related services, in order to maximize the citizens' quality of life, education and professional career development, and personal and social happiness".

This definition is a proposal as a result of the combination of the views and studies of authors, researchers and academics cited in this work, and therefore it could be applied to the requirements of Colombian cities, so that they would be considered contemporary Smart cities. Once this new definition has been proposed, a study of the different dimensions that should be measured is mandatory. For this reason in a previous section, the studies were introduced in reference to this question and presented by Kanter and Litow (2009), Paskaleva (2011), Vasquez-Ortega (2012), Sierra (2013), Casas-Perez (2014), Cohen and Obediente (2014), and Hernandez-Escobar and Perez-Hernandez (2015). From the combination of this research made by these authors, and using the model described by Kanter and Litow (2009) from a project performed by the European Smart Cities Association as a basis, the proposed model includes six dimensions and 27 subcategories as essential to define and measure the concept of Smart City, which can be used to monitor the status of Colombian cities in their advance towards the Smart City concept:

- Smart Government (political strategies and perspectives, transparency, and community participation in decision making by online services)
- Smart Citizenship (diversity and integration, education, innovation and creativity, and participation in public life)
- Smart Infrastructure (personal welfare, housing availability, tourism and cultural infrastructure and services, health and safety)
- Smart Environment (smart buildings, sustainable urban development, sustainable resource management, pollution control, and environmental protection)
- Smart Mobility (strong ICT infrastructure, multimodal access, efficient and sustainable transport systems)
- Smart Growth (business environments, knowledge economy, innovation and competitiveness, workforce education, local and global high productivity, opportunities for entrepreneurs, and the ability to transform connections and networks)

Both Colombian cities considered in this study, Bogota and Medellin are in different early stages of implementation of all these defined dimensions. In comparison with other Smart City projects identified by authors like Vasquez-Ortega (2012), Noreña-Rendon (2013), Sierra (2013), Del Borghi et al. (2014), Patiño (2014), and

Saunders and Baeck (2015), in the case of Bogota the city is focusing its projects on urban mobility and public transport. The SITP and TransMilenio initiatives are similar to the ones developed in Marseilles (France). Citizens are also using smartphone apps like Waze to monitor the traffic flow in order to increase their efficiency in urban mobility, which is similar to Singapore (Singapore) and its Electronic Road Pricing program, and Beijing (China) and its I Love Beijing initiative. The Ciclovia program is also having a great impact on citizens' awareness, thanks to pedestrian access on main roads and streets in the city on Sundays and Bank Holidays, thus reducing traffic and pollution and increasing healthy activities like jogging, biking and roller skating. Technologies related to ICT are also being used to enhance citizens' participation with their interaction with government institutions and other services, in a similar way to Lima (Peru) and Amsterdam (Holland), although in Bogota these projects are in the early stages of implementation.

Medellin can be considered as the Colombian city closest to the Smart City concept. The infrastructure that has been developed in recent years has placed this city as one of the most advanced in terms of urban mobility and services. As it was highlighted in the previous section, Medellin's Smart City program is being implemented in four strategic stages: open government, citizen participation, social innovation and sustainability, leading the city towards advanced initiatives, similar to the ones implemented in London, Santander, Madrid, Buenos Aires or Amsterdam.

5.4 Conclusions and Future Research

Since ancient times, cities have become a recurrent ambivalence: on one hand, they have acted as a powerful site to exchange ideas and opportunities; while on the other hand, they have led to conflict and isolation. The explanation for these seemingly contradictory phenomena is complex and offers different points of view depending on the social, economic, innovative, environmental and political dimension in which the city is observed. Cities have historically acted as poles and territorial catalysts of both economic and social transformation and the majority of the most qualified, creative and entrepreneurial population of the planet is concentrated in these urban centers, but they are also a focus of social and environmental problems. Obtaining a balance between those two positive and negative outputs ultimately depends on the actions and desires of individuals and groups that populate the cities (Fernandez-Güell 2015). In this way, the Smart City concept arises trying to solve these shortcomings, having as a main goal the efficient management of resources and improvements in quality of life.

The first part of this work was an extensive review of the recent literature, in order to understand the Smart City concept as an evolution of the conventional city term. Even though, there is no consensus on the definitions, there are some elements to highlight. The first one is the relevance of technology as a key resource in the development and growth of these kinds of cities. Secondly, the importance of better and more abundant resources provided to its citizens. Thirdly, the need of optimizing the use of increasingly scarce resources, which drives the concept of sustainability and sustainable development. Lastly, the main goal is improving the quality of life in urban areas. In addition to this, the next part of the document, analyzed the different dimensions that need to be considered in the Smart City concept approach. These dimensions are described as the most important determinants to understand and measure these Smart Cities.

The effects, challenges and opportunities that Smart Cities can offer to their citizens were also introduced. Some factors to point out are the needs of proper development to ensure the existence of urban areas. One important input for the proper functioning of Smart Cities is the quality and quantity of data available at all levels. It is also important to reiterate the importance of education on overcoming the challenges of these cities. The first part of this study gave examples of different programs, projects and initiatives that cities all over the world implemented, as for example Amsterdam (Holland), Bangalore (India), Beijing (China), Buenos Aires (Argentina), Gijon (Spain), Glasgow (UK), Lima (Peru), London (UK), Madrid (Spain), Malaga (Spain), Rio de Janeiro (Brazil), Santander (Spain), Singapore (Singapore), and Vancouver (Canada), focusing on different areas such as sustainable economic growth, environmental protection, quality of life, participatory governance, social and community development, citizenship education, efficient urban mobility, tourism services, and health and safety.

The literature revised in the current work has found very few academic studies relating to the Smart City concept relating to the most important cities in Colombia. The two cities where significant research work was found were Medellin and Bogota, the capital of the nation. Medellin is the first city in Colombia with a governmental program similar to the model of Smart Cities, with its "Medellin Smart City", a program that has been implemented in four strategic approaches: open government, citizen participation, social innovation and sustainability. In the case of Bogota, the main progression towards the Smart City concept has been developed in urban mobility area through the "Mobility Master Plan". Reviewing the two Colombian cities studied, the previous aspects have been taken into account to establish a new definition of the Smart City concept and a set of six dimensions and 27 subcategories as essential to define and measure the concept of the Smart City. This model can be used to monitor the status in Colombia, in order to approximate the current valuations of Colombian cities, to qualify for the concept described as the Smart City.

Due to the lack of studies relating to the concept of Smart Cities and its relevance to Colombian cities observed in the current work, further research must be focused not only on getting more data concerning the situation in Bogota and Medellin, but also having the opportunity to examine the situation in other important cities such as Barranquilla, Cali, Bucaramanga and Cartagena, where there is no current information available. These future studies should be focused on refining the definition of the Smart City concept and establishing quantitative criteria based on the six measurement dimensions and 27 indicators defined. To further understand the phenomenon of Smart Cities in Colombia, it is necessary to first do a diagnosis of the current status of the main cities, pointing out the challenges and opportunities. In a second stage, the main goal would be to analyze the applicability of the six dimensions on solving those problems.

References

Agredo, E. A. C., et al. (2015). Pervasive NFC-based solution for the analysis of tourism data in an environment of smart cities. *Sistemas & Telematica, 13*(32), 41–60.

Alfaro-Martinez, E., & Soria-Rodriguez, M. (2012). Innovando para ciudades inteligentes. *Monográfico El Camino hacia las Smart Cities. BBVA Innovation.*, 188, *12*(3), 38–40.

Alonso-Gonzalez, A., Palacios-Chacon, L. A., Rueda-Armengot, C., & Peris-Ortiz, M. (2017a). Collaborative networks between Colombian Universities and population at risk of social exclusion: The Sergio Arboleda University experience. In M. Peris-Ortiz, F. Teulon, & D. Bonet-Fernandez (Eds.), *Social entrepreneurship in non-profit and profit activities. (pp. 65–72) theoretical and empirical landscape*. Cham: Springer. ISBN 978-3-319-50850-4.

Alonso-Gonzalez, A., Plata-Rugeles, D., Peris-Ortiz, M., & Rueda-Armengot, C. (2017b). Entrepreneurial initiatives in Colombian Universities: The Innovation, Entrepreneurship and Business Center of Sergio Arboleda University. In M. Peris-Ortiz, J. A. Gómez, J. M. Merigó-Lindahl, & C. Rueda-Armengot (Eds.), *Entrepreneurial Universities* (pp. 151–163). Cham: Springer International Publishing. ISBN: 978-3-319-47949-1.

Anusha, N., Harikrishna, B., & Swarna Latha, T. (2015). Green computing hunted: Energy utilization in the IT commerce and by domestic computers in five foremost INDIAN smart-cities. *Journal of Current Computer Science and Technology, 5*(1), 1–5.

Auvinet, C., & Lloret, A. (2015). Understanding social change through catalytic innovation: Empirical findings in Mexican social entrepreneurship. *Canadian Journal of Administrative Sciences, 32*, 238–251.

Balaji, R. S. (2013). Big data: Road to smart cities. *International Journal of Science and Research (IJSR), 4*(4), 1210–1213.

Ben Ahmed, M., et al. (2015). Dynamic traffic light control for intelligent mobility in smart cities. *Journal of Theoretical and Applied Information Technology, 73*(2), 260–268.

Benitez, L., & Ortega, M. (2015). Las TIC y la gestion de los desafios de sostenibilidad energetica de las ciudades inteligentes. *Sostenbilidad Ambiental, 395*, 88–94.

Biancalana, C., Micarelli, A., & Sansonettim, G. (2015). Personalized extended government for local public administrations. *3rd International Workshop on PErsonalization in eGOVernment and Smart Cities (PEGOV)*, pp. 26–31.

Boob, T. N. (2015). Transformation of urban development in to smart cities: The challenges. *IOSR Journal of Mechanical and Civil Engineering (IOSR-JMCE), 12*(3), 24–30.

Casas-Perez, M. L. (2014). Ciudades inteligentes y ambientes de comunicación digital. *Global Media Journal, 11*(22), 1–19.

Cohen, B., & Obediente, E. (2014). *Estudio ranking de ciudades inteligentes en Chile*. Pais Digital Foundation, Working Paper.

Dattagupta, O. (2014). Global integration and developing Indian smart cities: New hopes and challenges. *International Journal of Innovative Social Science & Humanities Research*. ISSN: 2349-187630, *1*(2), 30–42.

De Domenico, M., et al. (2015). Personalized routing for multitudes in smart cities. *EPJ Data Science, 4*(1), 1–11.

Del Borghi, A., et al. (2014). Waste management in smart cities: The application of circular economy in Genoa (Italy). *Impresa Progetto Electronic Journal of Management, 2014*(4), 1–13.

Djahel, S. et al. (2015). Toward V2I comunication technology-based solution for reducing road traffic congestion in smart cities. *Conference Paper*, 2–7.

Erkkilä, K. (2014). Espoo is a smart city through collaboration. *Interdisciplinary Studies Journal University of Applied Sciences, 3*(4), 218–226.

Fernandez Guell, J. M. (2015). Ciudades inteligentes: la mitificacion de las nuevas tecnologias como respuesta a los retos de las ciudades contemporaneas. *Economia industrial, 395*, 17–28.

Fertner, C., & Gorth, N. B. (2015). *Energy-smart cities-DK. Benchmarking the energy situation of Danish municipalities: Background Report*. Centre for Strategic Urban Research. Working Paper 23, pp. 2–19.

Graham, G., & Zhang, L. (2015). *Smart cities and digital technologies the case of bike-sharing systems*. University of Leeds Business School and Liverpool Business School, United Kingdom. Working Paper, pp. 1–10.

Hambleton, R. (2015). From smart cities to wise cities. Paper Session 3558: Digital Disruptions and Urban Governance, for the AAG Annual Meeting Chicago, Illinois, pp. 2–20.

Hernandez-Escobar, O., & Perez-Hernandez, M. P. M. (2015). *Medición de las ciudades inteligentes: una propuesta desde México*. Working Paper National Polytechnic Institute, Mexico D. F., Mexico, pp. 1–15.

Ishkineeva, G., Ishkineeva, F., & Akhmetova, S. (2015). Major approaches towards understanding smart cities concept. *Asian Social Science, 11*(5), 70–73.

Jamil, M. S., et al. (2015). Smart environment monitoring system by employing wireless: Sensor networks on vehicles for pollution free smart cities. *Humanitarian Technology: Science, Systems and Global Impact 2015, HumTech2015, 107*, 1–6.

Kamel-Boulos, M. N., Tsouros, A. D., & Holopainen, A. (2015). Social, innovative and smart cities are happy and resilient: Insights from the WHO EURO 2014 international healthy cities conference. *International Journal of Health Geographics 2015, 14*(3), 1–9.

Kanter, R. M., & Litow, S. S. (2009). Informed and interconnected: A manifesto for smarter cities. *Harvard Business School General Management Unit Working Paper, 9*(141), 1–27.

Klimek, R., & Kotulski, L. (2015). *Towards a better understanding and behavior recognition of inhabitants in smart cities: A public transport case*. AGH University of Science and Technology, Krakow, Poland. Working Paper, pp. 1–11.

Klingert, S., et al. (2015). Renewable energy-aware data centre operations for smart cities. The DC4Cities approach. *Preparation of Camera-Ready Contributions to SCITEPRESS Proceedings*, pp. 1–8.

Mancheno, D., & Teran, J. F. (2013). Ciudades inteligentes, ciudades productivas: La tercera revolución industrial, otra opción para una metrópoli diversa. Cuestiones Urbano Regionales. *Revista del Instituto de la Ciudad, 2*(2), 31–67.

Martinez-Ballesteros, L. G., Alvarez-Alvarez, O., & Markendahl, J. (2015). *Quality of Experience (QoE)-based differentiation in the smart cities context: Business Analysis*. Conference Paper, pp. 1–16.

Misra, P., et al. (2015). *An interoperable realization of smart cities with plug and play based device management*. Working paper, pp. 1–5.

Montiel-Casas, A. (2015). Ciudades felices versus smart cities. *Tag Urbanisme, 15*(2), 74–78.

Mosannenzadeh, F., & Vettorato, D. (2014). Defining smart city. A conceptual framework based on keyword analysys. TeMA journal of land use, mobility and environment, *Eighth International Conference Smart City – Planning for Energy, Transportation and Sustainability of the Urban System, Special Issue*, pp. 684–694.

Muñoz de Dios, M. D., Hernandez-Galan, J., & De la Fuente-Robles, Y. M. (2014). Social work and smart cities: Towards a new conception of accessibility in tourism destinations for the promotion of personal autonomy. *Revista Internacional de Trabajo Social y Bienestar, 14*(3), 64–68.

Nasar, S. (2011). *Grand pursuit. The story of economic genius*. New York: Simon and Schuster.

Noreña-Rendon, S. (2013). *Vigilancia tecnológica para la movilidad en Ciudades Inteligentes*. Final Thesis to fullfill the requirement for the Technological Innovation Management Degree, Pontifical Bolivarian University, Medellin, Colombia, pp. 1–78.

North, D. C. (1981). *Structure and change in economic history*. New York: Norton and Company.

North, D. C. (2005). *Understanding the process of economic change*. Princeton: Princeton University Press.

O'Connell, L. (2008). Exploring the social roots of smart growth policy adoption by cities. *Social Science Quarterly, 89*(5), 1357–1372.

Papa, E., & Lauwers, D. (2015). Smart mobility: Opportunity or threat to innovate places and cities? *Proceedings REAL CORP 2015 Tagungsband: Plan together-Right now-Overall*, pp. 543–550.

Paskaleva, K. A. (2011). The smart city: A nexus for open innovation? *Intelligent Buildings International, 3*(2011), 153–171.

Patiño, J. A. (2014). *Datos Abiertos y ciudades inteligentes en América Latina: Estudio de Casos.* Comisión Económica para América Latina y el Caribe (CEPAL), Consorcio W3C & Centro Internacional de Investigaciones para el Desarrollo (IDRC).

Peris-Ortiz, M., Alonso-Llera, J. J., & Rueda-Armengot, C. (2017). Entrepreneurship and innovation in a revolutionary educational model: École 42, included in. In *Social Entrepreneurship in Non-Profit and Profit sectors Theoretical and empirical perspectives* (Vol. 36, pp. 85–98). Cham: Springer.

Raut, S. K., & Raut, P. B. (2015). Building inclusive smart sustainable cities through virtual environment. *Proceedings REAL CORP 2015: Plan together – right now – overall*, Tagungsband, pp. 105–109.

Rizzo, F. (2015). Design and social innovation for the development of human smart cities. *Design Ecologies, 2015*(6), 1–8.

Rochet, C., & Pinot de Villechenon, F. (2015). *Urban lifecycle management: System architecture applied to the conception and monitoring of smart cities.* Working paper, pp. 1–15.

Saunders, T., & Baeck, P. (2015). *Rethinking Smart Cities from the ground up* (pp. 1–72). Nesta: Intel & UNDP., Special Issue.

Sierra, J. F. (2013) *Vigilancia tecnológica e inteligencia competitiva en ciudades inteligentes: caso salud pública.* Final Thesis to fullfill the requirement for the Technological Innovation Management Degree, Pontifical Bolivarian University, Medellin, Colombia, pp. 1–78.

Tripathi, S. (2015). Do upcoming smart cities need to provide smart distribution of higher urban economic growth? Evidence from Urban India. *Munich Personal RePEc Archive Paper No. 61527*, pp. 1–23.

Vasquez-Ortega, M. C. (2012). Ciudades inteligentes y modelos logisticos de ciudades. (Bachelor's thesis, Medellin: Universidad de Buenaventura, 2012).

Villanueva, F. J., et al. (2014). CIVITAS. Plataforma de Soporte a las Ciudades Inteligentes. In *Convocatoria de Comunicaciones y 2ª Bienal de Proyectos de Edificación y Urbanismo Sostenible (2014 Edition)*. Málaga: Greencities & sostenibilidad.

Wolff, A., Kortuem, G., & Cavero, J. (2015). Urban data games: Creating smart citizens for smart cities. *15th IEEE International Conference on Advanced Learning Technologies*, pp. 6–9.

Chapter 6
The Economy of Communion as a Social Innovation to Humanise Business

Asunción Esteso Blasco, Maria Gil-Marques, and Juan Sapena Bolufer

Abstract The purpose of this chapter is to better understand the growth of EoC, analysing this movement from the perspective of social innovation and examining the innovative activities of EoC businesses. We have found that EoC is based on solid values and principles, and has a clear objective, which is to fight for a better world, eliminating poverty. Companies inspired by human-oriented management practices are those which move to achieve this objective. We argue in this chapter that EoC is a radical social innovation, as it is social in both its ends and its means, meeting social needs and creating new social relationships and collaborations. This paper analyses three Spanish EoC companies, using a qualitative case study methodology. The study reveals that innovation appears as a result of the desire to help others, such as customers and employees. Moreover, findings show that a culture of dialogue among employees, managers and the organisation as a whole enhances risk-taking and, therefore, innovation. We conclude by highlighting the need to address the social and economic challenges faced by individuals and communities and the need for a cultural change to humanise business.

Keywords Economy of communion · Gratuitousness · Leadership · Organisational culture · Reciprocity · Social innovation · Spirituality

6.1 Introduction

The Economy of Communion started in 1991. Over 800 businesses in five continents are currently involved in this movement, which has attracted the interest of scholars and economists alike (Bruni and Héij 2011). Most EoC businesses are small and medium-sized companies, but some have more than 100 employees

A. Esteso Blasco · M. Gil-Marques (✉) · J. Sapena Bolufer
Department of Management, Faculty of Economics, Catholic University of Valencia, Valencia, Spain
e-mail: asuncion.esteso@mail.ucv.es; maria.gil@ucv.es; juan.sapena@ucv.es

© Springer International Publishing AG, part of Springer Nature 2018   89
M. Peris-Ortiz et al. (eds.), *Strategies and Best Practices in Social Innovation*,
https://doi.org/10.1007/978-3-319-89857-5_6

(Bruni and Uelmen 2006). This type of business experience dovetails with other initiatives that try to humanise the economy by searching for new relationships between the market and society, and by aiming for the Common Good (Zamagni 2012).

The Economy of Communion is built on experience. However, a vibrant intellectual ferment has accompanied the growth in EoC businesses, through graduate, Masters, and PhD theses, and scientific papers (covering its anthropology, sociology, economics, philosophy, psychology and theology).

In words of the Economy of Communion's founder, Chiara Lubich, "The EoC is a project which involves entrepreneurs, employees, managers, consumers, citizens, researchers, and economic agents committed at different levels in the promotion of a praxis and an economic culture characterised by communion, gratuitousness and reciprocity" (Lubich 1999). The project has received significant international recognition from organisations such as the UNESCO and the Council of Europe, and has been awarded various honorary doctorates by prestigious universities (Linard 2003).

The project uses a new style of economic action, i.e. a new way of conceiving and implementing business management, and labour and economic relations. Companies adopt the EoC project by applying the logic of gratuitousness and of giving as an expression of universal fraternity. EoC companies promote ethical behaviour and an organisational culture of reciprocity (Del Baldo and Baldarelli 2015).

"The Economy of Communion says to us that the market, under a very precise condition, can become an instrument which can reinforce social ties, favouring both the promotion of practices of wealth distribution through its mechanism (rather than operating outside these or against these) and the creation of an economic space in which it is possible to regenerate those values (such as trust, sympathy, benevolence) on which the very existence itself of the market ultimately depends" (Zamagni 2014: p. 6).

EoC has attracted the attention of Corporate Social Responsibility (CSR) researchers. Del Baldo and Baldarelli (2015) highlight that EoC companies are very close to CSR focusing their attention on their mission, governance and accountability models. EoC companies help to create a society that is more civil due to the fact that they are directly involved in combating poverty while being not only a productive structure but also by promoting new humanistic management.

This chapter is organised as follows. Firstly, the origins of EoC are presented. Secondly, we analyse EoC as a social innovation, explaining how this movement fights to eradicate poverty by introducing new social relationships. Thirdly, we explain the management principles of EoC businesses and the innovation that takes place in EoC companies, through the analysis of three representative Spanish EoC companies with extensive business experience. We conclude with a summary of the main conclusions, accompanied by proposals for further research.

6.2   The Origins of EoC and the Sharing of Profits

The genesis of the Economy of Communion lies in the foundation of the ecumenical and interreligious based organisation, the Focolare Movement. It is a secular organisation, approved by the Vatican, whose statutes admit adherents not only from within the Catholic Church, but also from other Christian churches, from other religions and from people simply professing goodwill with no religious belief (Abela 2014).

The Focolare Movement emphasises the ethic of mutual love, which is given its practical expression through adherents living a communion of goods, as a free and personal choice, in the manner ascribed to first-century Christians, so that none in their community are in need. Its spirituality is based on a profound belief in the unity of the human family, regardless of differences of race, nationality or religious belief (Linard 2003). The Focolare Movement operates in 182 nations, has more than 100,000 adherents and supports the right to private property.

Understanding the EoC means understanding the roots of the Focolare Movement. When Chiara Lubich was young, she was attracted to the Franciscan charism, which centres on the idea of poverty. She even took the name of Chiara instead of her original name, Sylvia Lubich, because of Chiara of Assisi. Lubich understood that the core of the message of the Gospel does not relate primarily to a series of moral directives but in the revelation of God's love, and that this perspective includes economic and social realities. During the Second World War, Chiara and her first companions wanted to solve social problems by helping poor people in the city where they lived, Trento (Italy). Accordingly, a community was formed in which everything was shared out according to the needs of each one. In these first Focolare communities, the communion of goods was the flame that kept this fraternity alive. It was a free communion of goods which did not require everyone to sell all of their possessions. Everyone contributed the extra money that they had, but the identity of the donor and the amount remained secret. It is important to note that the original name of the EoC highlights the freedom aspect: "EoC in Freedom". According to Gold (2003), Lubich and her companions discovered an economic logic in the Gospel that is unique, based on communion and the emancipation of the poor. This has been taken to a different level with the creation of EoC businesses that attempt to put this ethos into practice within capitalist economic structures.

In 1991, the EoC founder, Chiara Lubich, visited the Focolare community in San Paolo, Brazil. Just before the plane landed, as she watched Sao Paulo from above, she was struck by the marked contrast between the skyscrapers, which were surrounded by the slums where some of the Focolare members lived. Chiara Lubich explains how that vision was important for her to understand that the traditional communion of goods among members of the Focolare movement was insufficient. Some remained homeless, while others were unable to send their children to school or buy them clothes. Many of the sick could not afford medical treatment. As Lubich reflected with the Focolare community in Brazil, they began to see new possibilities and a proposal was put forward to set up businesses to increase opportunities for employment and create profits that could be donated (Bruni and Uelmen 2006).

Table 6.1 Distribution of EoC companies in the world

Continent	1992	2001	2016
Europe	132	481	463
Asia	10	40	18
Africa	0	9	84
America	99	224	246
Australia	1	15	0
Total	242	769	811

Source: EoC Central Secretariat (Rome – Italy)

In line with this view, an EoC company aims to meet three objectives: (1) creating new businesses, increasing and strengthening existing ones through productivity, employment and sustainable development, and supporting the State in helping the most vulnerable; (2) training employees and managers in the values of brotherhood and reciprocity (educational activities including conferences, workshops, seminars, courses) with a special focus on the new generations and (3) helping the poor at local and global level, giving them assistance with basic needs in emergency situations (Baldarelli 2007; Argiolas 2014).

Over the years, seven industrial parks were born: two in Brazil (Igarassu and Cotia) and one in Argentina, Croatia, Belgium, Portugal and Italy. The first industrial pole was built in Brazil (Igarassu) in 2002, a few years after the EoC was launched. The most developed industrial poles are located in South America (Brazil and Argentina) and Italy where the EoC and Focolare movement were born respectively. Others are in a start-up phase in Germany, Philippines, Brazil (Benevides) and Kenya. The EoC industrial poles do not only arise for economic reasons, concentration, productive efficiency and elasticity, but to also be a visible sign of a different way to make economy (Ferrucci 2005).

The following Table 6.1 shows the evolution of distribution of EoC companies in the world.

6.3   The EoC as a Social Innovation

The need for companies to address critical social and global issues is growing constantly. Accordingly, we see increased interest in corporate social responsibility and business ethics, as well as growing research interest in social innovation that contributes to improved wellbeing (Dawson and Daniel 2010). Social innovation has grown rapidly, spreading to all sectors of society, including non-profit, social entrepreneurship, social economy, service sector, and corporate social responsibility practices (Edwards-Schachter et al. 2012).

Social innovation is attracting the interest of researchers, practitioners, and policy makers around the world. It has grown mainly out of practice, and despite incipient and promising research in the area, there is still a need to better understand exactly what this term means (Mulgan 2012; Bock 2012).

Literature on the subject states that the aim of social innovation is to improve the wellbeing of people in society (Dawson and Daniel 2010) and emphasises the objective of catering for social needs (Goldenberg 2004). In addition, social innovations are shaped by an interest in people and communities rather than being motivated by profit or business pressures. According to this, the birth of EoC is directly related to the aim of improving social conditions for people in need through companies whose main focus is not commercial gain but a world without poverty.

We believe that two key aspects of EoC must be considered to analyse this movement from the point of view of social innovation. Firstly, the reason why it was created, i.e. the desire to eliminate poverty (Bruni and Uelmen 2006; Bruni and Héij 2011). Secondly, the core features of its originality, focusing on the basis of communion: reciprocity, gratuitousness and generativity (Zamagni 2014).

6.3.1   The Poor and Poverty in the EoC

As Dawson and Daniel (2010) state, social innovation is prompted by an interest in improving the wellbeing of people in society, with social problems being the core drivers behind the development and application of new ideas. The social innovation paradigm integrates social rationality, and combines it with conventional economic and technological criteria. Social innovation is intentional, as it aims to change to the better, at least as people perceive it. The intentionality of social innovation is what distinguishes it from social change. Social change just happens (Franz et al. 2012)

Ims and Zsolnai (2015) argue that social innovation does not involve profit as its primary goal. Instead, social, spiritual and humanitarian goals, such as minimising suffering and empowering people and communities are emphasised. According to this statement, we can consider the EoC as a social innovation since profit is not a goal. It is conceived as a way to reduce poverty.

The EoC annual report on the destination of aid explains how resources have been used, highlights the results achieved, and details the assistance provided to cater for basic needs in emergency situations (Del Baldo and Baldarelli 2015). The local Focolare Movement communities know who the people in need are. The Focolare Movement also runs an important non-governmental organisation focused on development, with over 1000 active projects called AMU (Azione per un Mondo Unito – Actions for a United World). The barriers of distrust that often exist between business and NGOs in formal partnerships have not been a problem within the EoC due to the high level of prior knowledge of the work of the Focolare in the field of NGOs and its communion of goods (Ims and Zsolnai 2015).

As we can observe, in the EoC, the poor are not an anonymous mass. There is a close relationship with them and a broad understanding of their needs. The idea is that everyone has something to give, even if giving means expressing a need or sharing experiences. In addition, many of the poor who participate in the EoC Project stop or give back the help they have been receiving as soon as they obtain minimum economic independence, as a way to live in reciprocity.

In practice, companies find different and creative ways to establish relations with people in need. Freedom is in the centre of the governance in the company and companies find the best way to follow the EoC Management Principles according to the different situations and contexts. For example, some businesses are more engaged in local development projects in the neighbourhood near the company; whilst in other companies, due to their type of business, there is no need for highly trained employees so when they hire people they assure that they are vulnerable people. Finally, other companies prefer to generate high turnover and profits because the more they earn, the more the company can share.

Therefore, new relationships are generated in the EoC model. This idea is linked to the definition put forward by Hubert (2010), who described social innovations "as new ideas (products, services and models) that simultaneously meet social needs and create new social relationships", as well as in the Guide to Social Innovation (European Commission 2013), which states that social innovations are social in both their ends and their means, defining them as new ideas that simultaneously meet social needs and create new social relationships or collaborations.

As Callebaut (2012) suggests, the EoC is a proposal that can be considered as a real innovation in the sense that Chiara Lubich did not give a traditional speech about profit-sharing within companies or contributions to charity outside companies. The EoC proposal is, in our view, a radical social innovation, according to Callebaut's (2012) arguments, as it is not only an innovation in terms of production in order to distribute profits, but also in terms of the way it takes place. The EoC has some very innovative proposals to improve society and develop new social relationships. Firstly, the engagement and active role of the middle class and entrepreneurs (as opposed to other ways to combat poverty, such as that proposed by the Theology of Liberation). Secondly, the provision of a distribution model for economic production, rather than leaving this task solely in the hands of state agencies; and thirdly, providing a charismatic role for the world of free enterprise by integrating intrinsic motivations and their potential in the economic process.

6.3.2 New Social Relationships: Generativity, Gratuitousness and Reciprocity

Following Bruni and Héij (2011), the EoC did not come about to renew businesses, but to renew social relations. The EoC project considers that sharing is more than a question of sharing profits. Although entrepreneurs offer tangible goods through the donations of profits and assume the obvious risks, giving is not confined to quantifiable items. Understanding, attention, forgiveness, talents, and ideas are also gifts to give (Bruni and Uelmen 2006). Relationships inside the company based on gratuitousness and reciprocity are the key for an EoC business.

According to Bruni and Héij (2011), the most important innovation of the EoC is that it is not an experience where there are philanthropists or a great entrepreneur who gives his leftovers to the poor, without questioning his own life, or becoming a brother or sister who is equal to the poor they are is helping. These authors consider that EoC businesses are also an economy of communion when they have no profits to give, but when they are working and produce a culture of fraternity with people in need and inside the company.

In order to explain these new relationships in EoC companies, Zamagni (2014) identified three key characteristics in the genome of the EoC model: generativity, gratuitousness and reciprocity. Firstly, generativity refers to the capacity to generate new ways of doing business, new modes of organising the productive process, and new ways of realising the specific role of entrepreneurship. Secondly, gratuitousness is related to the idea of not considering a business as a money-making machine, but as a place to give value to ideals that increase personal and collective freedom. The EoC characterises gifts as gratuitousness, which is the specific interpersonal relationship that is established between the donor and the donee. This concept is not the same as 'munus' which is what you give to somebody else free of charge. Finally, the characteristic of reciprocity is applied to all the types of stakeholders interested in the activity of the EoC firm. Gratuitousness is the condition for reciprocity that generates reciprocity.

Following Bruni and Uelmen (2006), capitalistic businesses are becoming increasingly social. Nevertheless, what is unique in the EoC is the characteristic of gratuitousness. An EoC company considers the value of the relationship with those who lack material resources. They are an occasion for reciprocity and brotherhood. In addition, EoC companies develop this business culture and governance, fostering the gratuitous gift that can permeate the entire vision of the business. For this reason, it will never be enough for an EoC company solely to share its profits.

Bruni (2008) distinguishes three types of reciprocity that operate together in EoC businesses. Firstly, reciprocity based on contracts, which is instrumental, but very important to establish economic rules and responsibilities. Secondly, reciprocity as friendship that goes beyond the duties of a formal contract, fostering cooperation and enthusiasm, such as relations with customers and employees. Thirdly, reciprocity based on agape, that is, unconditional behaviours. This is an idealistic code yet is quite real. It involves, for example, being open to forgive behaviours that standard economic logic does not generally accept. This is not very frequent but it makes life worth living and is essential to civil coexistence. Unconditional reciprocity or reciprocity based on friendship humanises the reciprocity based on contract, thus humanising the market.

According to the EoC perspective, the firm is seen as a community, not as a commodity that can be bought and sold in the market according to the conveniences of the moment. What characterises the EoC is the ability to organise the internal governance of the firm in such a way that all three characteristics (generativity, gratuitousness and reciprocity) operate jointly.

As literature on economics highlights, market systems are consistent with many cultures that are conceived as tractable patterns of behaviour or, more generally, organised systems of values. Gold (2003) states that an important aspect of the communitarian ethos of the Focolare is the building of relationships based on communion. This ethos may be called a culture of giving, and rests on a different anthropology of the human person than the one that dominates economic theory. Gold (2003) stresses that the focus of the Focolare's work does not centre on alleviating poverty per se, but on building relationships based on mutual care and solidarity.

Zamagni (2014: p. 16) states that "contrary to what it might be believed, economic phenomena have a primary interpersonal dimension. Individual behaviors are embedded in a preexisting network of social relations which cannot be thought as a mere constraint; rather, they are one of the driving factors that prompt individual goals and motivations. People's aspirations are deeply conditioned by the conventional wisdom about what makes life worth living". Argandoña (2011) states that in the EoC phenomenon, we cannot forget that strong spirituality is behind fostering and enhancing behaviour, based on Catholic social teaching.

6.4 Social Innovation in EoC Companies: Case Study Analysis

The analysis of EoC growth and theoretical and empirical studies enables us to define this movement as a radical social innovation. The novelty of the EoC project is that communion is engaged in all aspects of a firm's economic activity.

As the EoC Identity Card[1] states, those who adhere to this project commit themselves to living the values and culture of communion in the light of the charism of unity, both as individuals and in the organisations in which they work.

The Guidelines to Running an Economy of Communion Business[2] have been written based on the experience of entrepreneurs and workers, and are divided into seven areas, which include the following lines to guide action. The business is managed in a loyal and civil way, holding quality relationships with all stakeholders, including competitors, suppliers, clients, civil society and public administration. The EoC leadership style is participative. Communication is open and sincere, which favours the exchange of ideas and information at all levels of responsibility. Work has a meaning not only for professional growth, but also for spiritual and ethical development among its members, which will enhance the sharing of talent, ideas and competencies. Particular attention is devoted to the quality of relationships, promoting mutual support to become a real community.

Following these guidelines, many of the businesses have not only survived, but have thrived in the market (Bruni and Uelmen 2006). EoC businesses commit themselves to creating new wealth and jobs through creativity and innovation. Innovation can be defined following the Oslo Manual, as the "implementation of a new or

---

[1] http://www.edc-online.org/en/businesses/the-eoc-identification-card.html. Consulted on 04/09/2017.
[2] http://www.edc-online.org/en/businesses/guidelines-for-conducting-a-business.html. Consulted on 04/09/2017.

Table 6.2 Case study businesses

	Quality consultancy	Day centre	Pharmacy
Location	Madrid	Seville	Cordoba
Year founded	1994	2002	1914
Year joined	1994	2002	2006
Revenues	€1,000,000	50 users	€2,300,000
No. employees	18	18	8
Scope	National	Local	Local
No. interviews	3	4	3
People interviewed	Managing director	Managing director	Managing director
	Financial director	Governess	Pharmacist
	Consultant	Psychologist	Assistant technician

significantly improved product (or service), process or method of marketing or organizational practices in the organization, in the workplace or in external relations (OECD-EUROSTAT 2005: 33).

To understand what type of innovation takes place in EoC businesses we analysed three representative Spanish EoC companies with extensive business experience. As Cassell and Simon (2004) state, case study research is useful to understand the context and circumstances. These three companies belong to different sectors and were selected because of the learning opportunities they offer (Brown and Eisenhardt 1995).

We visited the companies to better understand their specific contexts through direct observation. The interviews were recorded after consent was given by the interviewees. Subsequent queries were solved by telephone.

The following Table 6.2 contains the most relevant data of the companies.

6.4.1 Innovation in the Quality Consultancy Case

This quality consultancy company approaches innovation broadly, aiming to evolve constantly through new products, processes and organisational innovation. They consider innovation to be fundamental, and their aim is to maintain a constant pace of change. The Managing Director explains:

"I always remember what Chiara said 'If you do not move forward, you will fall back.' In business we are very innovative. We were the first to offer a validation course on biological methods in Spain. The customer pulls you forward... that is the key, and if you can grasp this, you will be able to face challenges. The pace of internal change is constant. This is the only way to go. Let's take another example: we are one of the few companies offering inter-comparative tests on the web."

Likewise, the consultant we interviewed explained the following:

"We are continually trying to adapt to change and especially on very technical issues when there is new legislation...". "We have an internal policy that we must improve so we don't stop".

Evidence shows a constant internal rate of change, both in terms of product and internal processes, such as computer applications. For example, the Managing Director showed us Excel spreadsheets with each worker's training on them, so that when a client places an order, it is assigned to the best trained person in that field. If there is a shortage of training, then a plan is implemented. When employees have to cover for one another, this is organised using this information.

The Financial Director also talked about day-to-day innovations.

> We try to update our resources to ensure the wellbeing of our employees ... machinery, materials, furniture have been improved; the chairs have been replaced ... and we also provide training to improve processes.

All the interviewees agreed on the importance of spaces and climate for dialogue to create a positive working environment and a culture that can generate the conditions for learning and for innovation. We realised that this company's leaders sought the development of people at work and also encouraged teamwork. As the Financial Director explains:

> From time to time, all the consultants meet up and establish project monitoring, harmonisation of criteria, definition of technical assistance processes and follow-up audits. We maintain a culture of dialogue. Dialogue always helps, it is necessary and there must always be communication to move forward ... At the same time, it is difficult because if we all give our opinion ... but there must always be someone that makes the final decision. The management team is in fact the one that makes the final decisions.

There was an open-door leadership policy that fostered communication and there were informal spaces where people could get to know each other and interpersonal relationships could be strengthened. As a Consultant explains:

> The Managing Director makes you a part of the business at all times, and networks well with everyone. Every day at 11.15 we all stop for coffee together, and we talk about everything: politics, religion, soccer...

6.4.2 Innovation in the Day Centre Case

This company uses different innovations that put them at the forefront of the day centre sector, such as its computer-based cognitive stimulation programs. Most day centres do not have as broad a range of services. The centre also has an extended weekend schedule to offer a better service to families.

The day centre's psychologist explains the stimulation programmes:

> These computer-based cognitive stimulation programmes need very expensive software which is neuropsychologically validated... We have the software and an expert that can create individual sessions. Some public institutions have a budget and have the equipment, but they are underutilised because they do not have people trained to use those resources. We do not depend on subsidies, yet we are lucky to be a profitable company. It's a different economic management model.

One of the innovations in this company came from the management's desire to improve the working conditions of one of the employees. This occurred when they launched a new service, offering workshops led by the psychologist. According to the Managing Director, this was an innovation that was introduced to improve a worker's job and offer users a better service.

This constant search for innovation has also led the company to offer services such as transport and providing cover at the weekend. The Managing Director explains:

> To offer a more comprehensive service, we had to provide transportation. It has worked well. Another important innovation not offered by other day centres is providing services at the weekend.

This concern has also led to innovations at organisational level. The centre reorganised the schedules to increase working hours for part-time staff. This has relieved those who have more work and has provided extra income to those who had fewer hours. The Assistant Technician explained the organisational innovations that had brought relevant improvements at work:

> Another thing that has been improved is the way the service is given. We relieve those who have a heavier workload, and they are helped by those who have fewer hours of work; we are all happy: some because they can rest, and others because we have better pay.

The interviewees emphasised the importance of meetings in which new solutions to daily problems are found, when they give their point of view. The psychologist, for example, values not having controlling bosses and admits that he is very independent in his work. He points out the importance of the efforts that are made to find the time for dialogue. The Managing Director explained the following:

> My main function is to create those spaces where everyone feels that they are an important part of the company and can contribute their ideas, their way of seeing things... Twice a year, we have a meeting with all our workers to share our thoughts: where we are going, how to distribute profits, how they can participate, how to solve any existing conflicts … this is often the most difficult issue. We take time to see why there is an issue with this person and what has happened. This is important to overcome problems and difficulties.

For the Governess, these innovations are fruit of the climate of dialogue in the meetings. She believes that this climate of support generates creativity, new ways of doing things and it is the actual staff who are willing to take risks. This is how the Governess explained it to us:

> The truth is that when we have a meeting with the auxiliaries or with the staff, if anyone proposes an innovation we try to implement it, and the opinion of everybody is taken into account. People do not feel as though they are under pressure. Auxiliaries drive the van. Going out with a vehicle is a risk and even more so when it is full of older people. Yet they take this risk. They do not tell you this is a risk for them and stop doing it, it is rather the other way around.

6.4.3 Innovation in the Pharmacy Case

In this case, we found different types of innovations: new product lines such as orthopaedic products for sportspeople, compounding, and specialisation in homeopathy. The Managing Director emphasised the importance of their innovations in compounding and homeopathy, explaining there was a clear focus on the customer, as the effort to change came from "wanting to help the person in front of you." In this company, the most modern means available are used to provide customers with useful goods and services. As the Managing Director remarked, the search for the best solution for the patient is the driving force behind innovation. As he explains:

> The EoC gives you another vision of the business, of the person; you see the reciprocity in others, in how to improve, how to do things or how not to do things.

The innovation in sports medicine derives from the personal interest of an employee who suggested it to the Managing Director. Other innovations come from the need to adapt to new regulations. We can observe there is a context of teamwork and collaboration, promoted by a participative leadership style. The Assistant Technician's interest in good outcomes for the organisation, in keeping up-to-date, is patent, as his comments show:

> Every day there are new requirements. We all have to try to help; everyone does their bit". "For example, about a year and a half ago, we brought out a specialist orthopaedic line for sport; I did it with a couple of colleagues because we often do sport and we saw that there was a demand for it... The Managing Director is the first person to encourage us to carry out responsible innovation; we have to tell him because he's the boss, but we're always looking for areas in which we can innovate and do it.

As these interviews show, the exchange of ideas, information and trust among workers enhances talent-sharing. This climate of dialogue in the company fosters creativity and empowers workers to engage in organisational changes and improvements:

> Every year we improve in one thing. For example, it might be a physical thing, like someone said last year that we needed another refrigerator, so we bought one. Someone else suggested changes in the compounding and logos; in other words, we all contribute to these changes and we like to agree on all decisions. I think that dialogue is important in this mutual assistance. Obviously, we have arguments, but in the end we come up with solutions to them; you get friction even in families but it clears some things up that even I think are wrong and that you have to do them in another way.

6.5 Conclusions

Social innovation is spreading to all sectors of society and is attracting more and more interest from scholars, as it contributes to improve the wellbeing of people (Dawson and Daniel 2010). Social innovations are social in both their ends and their means (European Commission 2013).

The Economy of Communion searches for new relationships between markets and society, aiming for the common good. EoC businesses aim to create employment and sustainable development in order to help the most vulnerable. These companies promote training and the values of brotherhood and reciprocity.

The EoC proposal is, in our view, a radical social innovation as it is not only an innovation in terms of production in order to distribute profits, helping the poor at a local and global level, but also in terms of the way it takes place as it forges new social relationships (Callebaut 2012).

Two key aspects of the EoC must be considered to analyse this movement from the point of view of social innovation. Firstly, the reason for its creation: the desire to eliminate poverty (Bruni and Héij 2011) and secondly, the core features of its originality, focusing on the basis of communion: reciprocity, gratuitousness and generativity (Zamagni 2014).

What is unique in the EoC is the characteristic of gratuitousness. An EoC company considers the value of the relationship with those who lack material resources, as it provides the chance to put reciprocity and brotherhood into practice. In addition, EoC companies develop a business culture and governance which foster the gratuitous gift that can penetrate the entire vision of the business (Bruni and Uelmen 2006).

The EoC rests on a different anthropology of the human person than that which dominates standard economic theory (Zamagni 2014). In the EoC phenomenon, strong spirituality is behind the fostering and enhancing of organisational culture, values and behaviours based on Catholic social teaching (Argandoña 2011).

The important difference in social innovation in the EoC is not only the innovation itself, in terms of the idea of sharing profits, but also the way in which it is carried out: looking for reciprocity and communion. A striking aspect of the EoC project is that everyone involved is given equal consideration. Those who receive help are not considered as donees or beneficiaries. Rather they are regarded as active participants in the project, who are all part of the same community, and also live the culture of giving. The emphasis is not on philanthropy, but on sharing, in that each person gives and receives in equal dignity (Lubich 2001).

The Guidelines to Running an Economy of Communion Business have been written based on the experience of entrepreneurs and workers. To understand what types of innovation take place in EoC businesses, we analysed three representative Spanish EoC companies with extensive business experience. Evidence shows that in EoC companies there is a continuous effort to innovate; the aim is to better serve customers, to launch new products and services, reorganise processes and invest in technology. The desire to help others and forge relationships based on dialogue are the drivers behind innovation.

In all three cases, the fact of not having controlling bosses is highly rated, which in a way is also closely linked to the climate of trust, and the principles of fair treatment and even-handedness. This trust encourages people to overcome their fear of change and feel that they can take risks, experiment and work independently. Employees are proactive and know that their team efforts are valued and recognised. Knowing they are driven by the common good gives them strength and enables them to overcome fear. Furthermore, the fact that they enjoy their work makes them more creative.

This qualitative study has enabled us to gain greater insight into the reality of EoC companies, although it has its limitations, as it does not allow us to draw general conclusions, since the three companies selected for the case study are leading EoC businesses. Therefore, we would suggest some lines of research for the future that may broaden the scope of our study taking into account companies with less experience in the movement. Finally, we consider that it would be valuable to carry out studies in other countries such as Italy or Brazil as the EoC is a global phenomenon. This would make it possible to compare countries and have a greater variety of companies of different sizes and in different industries.

Acknowledgements We gratefully acknowledge support from the Research Grant (Management and Human Resources 0.2017- 238-001) of the Catholic University of Valencia, and from the Spanish EoC Association, and the three companies that participated in the research.

References

Abela, A. V. (2014). Appealing to the imagination: Effective and ethical marketing of religion. *Journal of Business Research, 67*(2), 50–58.

Argandoña, A. (2011). Review of new financial horizons: The emergence of an economy of communion by Lorna gold. *Journal of Markets & Morality, 14*(1), 207–210.

Argiolas, G. (2014). *Il valore dei valori*. Roma: Città Nuova.

Baldarelli, M. G. (2007). I poli industriali dell'Economia di Comunione (EdC) in una prospettiva economico-aziendale: nuove sfide nelle aggregazioni tra aziende e rivitalizzazione del rapporto fiduciario con il sistema creditizio. *Rivista Italiana di Ragioneria e di Economia aziendale, 3,* 178–191.

Bock, B. B. (2012). Social innovation and sustainability; how to disentangle the buzzword and its application in the field of agriculture and rural development. *Studies in agricultural economics (Budapest), 114*(2), 57–63.

Brown, S. L., & Eisenhardt, K. M. (1995). Product development: Past research, present findings and future directions. *The Academy of Management Review, 20*(2), 343–378.

Bruni, L. (2008). *El precio de la gratuidad*. Madrid: Ciudad Nueva.

Bruni, L., & Héjj, T. (2011). The economy of communion. In *Handbook of spirituality and business* (pp. 378–386). London: Palgrave Macmillan.

Bruni, L., & Uelmen, A. J. (2006). Religious values and corporate decision making: The economy of communion project. *Fordham Journal of Corporate & Financial Law, 11,* 645.

Callebaut, B. (2012). Economy of communion: A sociological inquiry on a contemporary charismatic inspiration in economic and social life. *Claritas: Journal of Dialogue and Culture, 1*(1), 8.

Cassell, C., & Symon, G. (Eds.). (2004). *Essential guide to qualitative methods in organizational research*. Thousans Oaks: Sage.

Dawson, P., & Daniel, L. (2010). Understanding social innovation: A provisional framework. *International Journal of Technology Management, 51*(1), 9–21.

Del Baldo, M., & Baldarelli, M. G. (2015). From weak to strong CSR: The experience of the EoC (economy of communion) industrial parks in Germany and Italy. *Uwf Umwelt Wirtschafts Forum, 23*(4), 213–226.

Edwards-Schachter, M. E., Matti, C. E., & Alcántara, E. (2012). Fostering quality of life through social innovation: A living lab methodology study case. *Review of Policy Research, 29*(6), 672–692.

European Commission. (2013). *Guide to social innovation. regional and urban policy*. Brussels: European Comission.

Ferrucci, A. (2005). La sfida dei poli produttivi. *Economia di comunione, 23*, 4–5.

Franz, H. W., Hochgerner, J., & Howaldt, J. (Eds.). (2012). *Challenge social innovation: Potentials for business, social entrepreneurship, welfare and civil society*. Berlin Heidelberg: Springer Science & Business Media.

Gold, L. (2003). The roots of the Focolare movement's economic ethic. *Journal of Markets and Morality, 6*(1), 143–159.

Goldenberg, M. (2004). *Social innovation in Canada: How the non-profit sector serves canadians-and how it can serve them better*. Canadian Policy Research Network Incorporated.

Hubert, A. (2010). Empowering people, driving change: Social innovation in the European Union. Bureau of European Policy Advisors (BEPA). Available online: http://ec.europa.eu/bepa/pdf/publications_pdf/social_innovation.pdf.

Ims, K. J., & Zsolnai, L. (2015). Social innovation and social development in Latin America, Egypt, and India. Ethical Innovation in Business and the Economy. In Georges Enderle and Patrick E. Murphy (Eds.): *Ethical Innovation in Business and the Economy*. (Eds). Edward Elgar. Cheltenham, UK. and Northampton, MA, USA. pp. 197–213.

Linard, K. T. (2003). Economy of communion: Systemic factors in the rise of a new entrepreneurship. *Systems Research and Behavioral Science, 20*(2), 163–175.

Lubich, C. (1999). *The economy of communion experience: A proposal for economic activity from the spirituality of unity*. Strasbourg: Council of Europe.

Lubich, C. (2001). *L'economia di comunione: storia e profezia*. Roma: Città nuova.

Mulgan, G. (2012). Social innovation theories: Can theory catch up with practice? In *Challenge social innovation* (pp. 19–42). Berlin Heidelberg: Springer.

Eurostat, O. E. C. D. (2005). Oslo Manual. *The Measurement of Scientific and Technological Activities. Guidelines for Collecting and Interpreting Innovation Data*. 3a. ed. París, OCDE/Eurostat. OSILAC.

Zamagni, S. (2012). *Por una economía del bien común*. Madrid: Ciudad Nueva.

Zamagni, S. (2014). The economy of communion project as a challenge to standard economic theory. *Revista Portuguesa de Filosofia, 70*, 44–60.

Chapter 7
Methodology for Analysing Electrical Scenarios as a Means of Sustainable Development in Emerging Countries

Elisa Peñalvo-López, Ángel Pérez-Navarro, Francisco J. Cárcel-Carrasco, and Carlos Devece

Abstract Electricity is one of the main driving forces for development, especially in remote areas where access to modern energy is linked to poverty. One of the main challenges of the international community is to minimize the inequality of energy services between OECD and developing countries. According to many different organizations, such as the United Nations, the World Bank or the International Energy Agency, electricity provides the necessary framework for economic, social and human progress with deep effect on productivity, health, education, climate change, food and water security, and communication services. The need for sustainability in the electrical sector forces to introduce as much as possible renewable sources in any scenario considered, covering the electrical needs of every country. The most extreme solution, that one assuming a 100% coverage of these electrical needs by renewable sources, could be impossible to apply for different reasons: reliability of the system, renewable resources availability, economic viability, and many others. A methodology that enables to deduce the realistic level of participation of renewable energies in the electrical scenario in each particular case is required. Such methodology should take into account all the factors involved and, by conciliating the different constraints imposed by each of them, find the maximum level of renewable energy possible in the system. This chapter describes the basis of this methodology to address that problem by taking into account demand, generation, level of resources and technologies.

Keywords Electrical planning · Scenarios · Sustainable development · Renewable energies · Hybrid systems

E. Peñalvo-López (✉) · Á. Pérez-Navarro · F. J. Cárcel-Carrasco · C. Devece
Universitat Politècnica de València, Valencia, Spain
e-mail: elpealpe@upvnet.upv.es; anavarro@iie.upv.es; fracarc1@csa.upv.es; cdevece@upvnet.upv.es

© Springer International Publishing AG, part of Springer Nature 2018
M. Peris-Ortiz et al. (eds.), *Strategies and Best Practices in Social Innovation*, https://doi.org/10.1007/978-3-319-89857-5_7

105

7.1 Introduction

Energy Planning (EP) analyses the alternative paths for energy evolution of a region by studying different energy scenarios in three temporal ranges: short (1–10 years), medium (10 to approximately 30 years) and long term analysis (more than 30 years). Generally, it begins examining as a reference the actual scenario, named "Business As Usual (BAU)", and its evolution for the time span considered. Then, it compares the results from other different alternative scenarios under the same time span and demand constraints. Each energy scenario involves assessing and matching in an optimal manner the energy sources and their conversion with the energy requirements of different demand sectors (commercial, industrial, residential, etc.). Although, it may seem a simple idea, it becomes a complex problem in which various decisions and criteria converge, together with the existence of complex relationships between the different actors involved in the simulation process: generation, demand, emissions, economics, and technologies (Loken 2007). Models in energy planning are important in emerging communities and in developed urban areas, since they determine the energy path and goals for the next time period. Precise modelling requires large computational resources, thus a trade-off between exactness and resources needs to be balanced. In order to approximate reality with acceptable computational resources, models are based on certain hypotheses that tackle possible scenarios and casuistry, using estimations and assumptions which may or may not become valid under initial premises but are unknown at the moment of modelling (Grubb et al. 1993).

Traditionally, remote and non-connected areas do not use energy planning in their energy analysis due to their small size. Electrification plans normally follow simple schemes, implementing simple solutions based on one technology, the most suitable one depending on the available natural resource (solar radiation, wind, type of biomass residues, etc.) (Cherni et al. 2007). These schemes are mainly referred to stand-alone systems based on photovoltaic and/or wind configurations, storing the excess of energy in batteries and using private diesel generators as backup. However, this simple approach based on stand-alone systems does not take into consideration important factors such as: energy needs of the population, potential flexibility of consumers, expected demand's growth and synergies between different renewable generation systems. This complexity invites to analyse more in detail the different variables and relationships involved in energy planning from a new perspective, considering decentralized energy modelling and customer's participation.

7.1.1 Centralized Versus Decentralized Planning

Energy planning is normally analysed at a national scale with modelling tools based on a centralised approach. In this case, improving electrical access to remote communities is pursued by initial infrastructure investments in large power plants, such as coal, natural gas, nuclear, hydroelectric, photovoltaic and wind parks, aiming to take advantage of the economy of scale. However, cost reduction of small-scale technologies, such as solar panels or small wind turbines, has encouraged distributed generation. This is particularly attractive for isolated communities with relatively low consumption and difficult accessibility to the grid since its expansion is very costly (Levin and Thomas 2007). Furthermore, modern access to electricity involves a wider range of energy mix and demand strategies, enhancing energy valorisation of local resources in a decentralized approach.

Along with this, it is recommended that energy planning introduces decentralized models considering the following aspects (Hiremath et al. 2007):

- Literature studies and projects in rural environment show that their implementation focuses only in one or two available energy resources. Decentralized energy planning should enhance models focusing on distributed strategies to increase reliability of the system.
- Exploration of the optimal matching of demand-supply paradigm with a maximum share of renewable sources.
- Consideration of decentralized energy models at a national level to assess the impact of decentralized planning in order to consider the generation of non-connected systems and the electrical demand of isolated areas in the global model.

7.1.2   Methods and Tools

Literature reviews show numerous tools for energy planning. The applicability and benefits of software tools in energy planning, which facilitate calculations and reduces processing time, is widely demonstrated (Connolly et al. 2010). Tools allow comparing different alternatives in order to assess the advantages and disadvantages of each solution, assisting in the evaluation of different energy planning scenarios in a feasible time frame. In 2010, Connolly et al. (2010) published a review of 37 computer tools for analysing the integration of renewable energy into various energy systems. A list of the revised tools is presented at the table below (Table 7.1).

Among all the tools, it should be highlighted the use of EnergyPLAN and LEAP as user friendly software for detailed analysis of national energy systems.

EnergyPLAN (Lund 2009) is a computer tool developed by the Department of Development and Planning at Aalborg University (Denmark). It provides hourly simulation of complete regional or national energy systems including electricity, individual and district heating/cooling, industry and transportation. It facilitates the design and evaluation of sustainable energy systems using a mix of renewable and fossil energy sources Lund (2007). General inputs are demands, renewable energy sources, energy plant capacities, costs and a number of optional regulation strategies emphasizing import/export and excess of electricity production. Outputs include energy balances and resulting annual production, fuel consumption, import/

Table 7.1 Tools for analysing renewable energies in energy systems

Tools for renewable energy analysis	
AEOLIUS: power-plant dispatch simulation tool	BALMOREL: open source electricity and district heating tool
BCHP Screening Tool: assesses CHP* in buildings	COMPOSE: techno-economic single-project assessments
E4cast: tool for energy projection, production, and trade	EMCAS: creates techno-economic models of the electricity sector
EMINENT: early stage technologies assessment	EMPS: electricity systems with thermal/hydro generators
EnergyPLAN: user friendly analysis of national energy-systems	energyPRO: techno-economic single-project assessments
ENPEP-BALANCE: market-based energy-system tool	GTMax: simulates electricity generation and flows
H2RES: energy balancing models for Island energy-systems	HOMER: techno-economic optimisation for stand-alone systems
HYDROGEMS: renewable and H2 stand-alone systems	IKARUS: bottom-up cost-optimisation tool for national systems
INFORSE: energy balancing models for national energy-systems	Invert: simulates promotion schemes for renewable energy
LEAP: user friendly analysis for national energy-systems	MARKAL/TIMES: energy–economic tools for national energy-systems
MESAP PlaNet: linear network models of national energy-systems	MESSAGE: national or global energy-systems in medium/long-term
MiniCAM: simulates long-term, large-scale global changes	NEMS: simulates the US energy market
ORCED: simulates regional electricity-dispatch	PERSEUS: family of energy and material flow tools
PRIMES: a market equilibrium tool for energy supply and demand	ProdRisk: optimises operation of hydro power
RAMSES: simulates the electricity and district heating sector	RETScreen: renewable analysis for electricity/heat in any size system
SimREN: bottom-up supply and demand for national energy-systems	SIVAEL: electricity and district heating sector tool
STREAM: overview of national energy-systems to create scenarios	TRNSYS16: modular structured models for community energy-systems
UniSyD3.0: national energy-systems scenario tool	WASP: identifies the least-cost expansion of power-plants
WILMAR Planning Tool: increasing wind in national energy-systems	

CHP*: combined heat and power

exports and total costs including income from electricity exchange (Neven et al. 2008). EnergyPlan has been implemented in numerous scientific publications, analysing different scenarios, such as Jayakrishnan et al. (2011) who presented in 2008 a comparative analysis of hourly and dynamic power balancing models for validating future energy scenarios based on a feasible technology mix for a higher share of wind power. EnergyPLAN optimizes the operation of a given system during a year rather than tools which optimize the investment and Operation & Maintenance costs, reducing any procedures which would increase the calculation time.

LEAP, (Long range Energy Alternatives Planning system) is a widely-used software tool for energy policy analysis and climate change mitigation assessment. It was developed in 1980 in USA and is currently maintained by the Stockholm Environment Institute (Heaps 2016). It is an integrated modelling tool used to evaluate energy consumption, production and resource extraction in all sectors of an economy in a certain scenario. LEAP has been implemented in many regions with published results, such as California (Ghanadan and Koomey 2005), Venezuela (Bautista 2012), Korea (Jun et al. 2010; Shin et al. 2005), Bangkok (Phdungsilp 2010), Thailand (Wangjiraniran et al. 2011) and Lebanon (Dagher and Ruble 2011), among others. On the demand-side, LEAP implements the bottom-up approach in the definition of energy consumption at the different sectors and top-down macroeconomic modelling. On the supply side, it provides a technology database for energy generation modelling and capacity expansion planning, but it does not support optimisation.

7.2   Simulation Tool

This chapter introduces a simulation tool for energy scenarios developed for evaluating an energy context. The tool checks if the hybrid systems have the potential to cover in a sustainable manner the electrical requirements of a particular area.

The tools mentioned in the previous section estimate the behaviour of a particular renewable energy system but without the possibility to determine in a direct way the optimal HRES configuration to be installed. As mentioned, the two most remarkable software programs, EnergyPLAN and LEAP have an application range reduced to national or regional levels. EnergyPLAN is more oriented to the system operation instead of the design or economic optimisation of investments, while LEAP does not currently support optimization modelling and it focuses on different modelling methodologies: on the demand-side these range from bottom-up, end-use accounting techniques to top-down macroeconomic modelling. On the supply side, it provides a range of accounting and simulation methodologies for modelling electricity generation and capacity expansion planning.

The methodology presented in this chapter is SIMESEN ("Simulación de EscenariosEnergéticos"—Simulation of Energy Scenarios), a tool that allows determining the evolution in a short, medium and long term of a particular energy scenario using as starting point the energy demand and the primary energy availability; then it deduces the role that renewable energies could play to enable a sustainable scenario within a predetermined timeframe.

Table 7.2 SIMESEN variables and relationships

Variable	Definition
$P(t)$	Population
$GDP\ (t)$	Gross domestic product
$TEP(t)$	Total primary energy
$EP(t)$	Evolution of the primary energy demand for each source [$i = 1$ (coal); $i = 2$ (oil); $i = 3$ (natural gas); $i = 4$ (renewable); $i = 5$ (nuclear); $i = 6$ (electricity generation)]
$DA(t)$	Evolution of the final energy demand from each sector [$j = 1$ (transport); $j = 2$ (industrial); $j = 3$ (residential); $j = 4$ (services); $j = 5$ (agricultural and fishing); $j = 6$ (electricity generation)]
$TDA(t)$	Evolution of total final energy demand from each sector
$TEF(t)$	Evolution of total final energy consumption
$DR(i,j,t)$	Evolution of the percentage of each energy source (i) in the demand of a particular sector (j)
$TEM(t)$	Evolution of total CO_2 emissions
$EM(i,j,t)$	Evolution of the CO_2 emissions due to the use of a particular source of energy (i) in a demand sector (j)
$SEM(t)$	Evolution of the total CO_2 emissions from the sector j
$CEM(i,j)$	Emission coefficients due to the energy source (i) used in each sector (j)
$R(j,t)$	Growth rate evolution for the energy demand in the sector (j) and for the population ($j = 7$) and the GDP in $j = 8$.

7.2.1   Simulation Model

SIMESEN is based on a linear model that relates the demand with possible contributions of each primary energy source and electricity. The use of linear models to tackle complex problems is usual in energy modelling (Connolly et al. 2010). It provides the evolution of each of these contributions and their associated CO_2 eq. emissions in order to analyse a series of energy variables.

The following variables are taken into consideration in SIMESEN (Table 7.2):

The evolution of the independent variables, which are assumed to be the energy demand of each sector, can be defined by predetermined mathematical laws. In this type of analysis annual rhythms of variation are often used, for which it is defined vector $R(j,t)$. The relationship between the different variables is implemented according to the methodology presented by Peñalvo-López et al. (2017). The degree of compliance with the sustainability objectives is quantified by analysing the evolution of the following indicators, selected among those most frequently used in the literature:

- External dependence on the primary energy supply
- Share of renewable energies in total energy consumption
- Energy intensity, defines as the ratio energy consumption/gross domestic product, as a measure of energy saving and efficiency
- Total amount of CO_2 emitted by the energy sector

SOCIOLOGIC DATA				
YEAR	DATA FROM: GEOGRAPHIC AREA	POPULATION Million of inhabitants	GPD M€ cte of 2010	Annual CO2 Mt
2.014	RDC	74,88	52.200	4,660

Fig. 7.1 SIMESEN sociological data

7.2.2 Code Structure

The tool presented in this paper, called SIMESEN, was developed at the Institute for Energy Engineering of Universitat Politècnica de València in 2010 based on the methodology presented by Peñalvo-López et al. (2017). It uses a centralized approach to analyse different energy alternatives towards a sustainable energy transition of an area, a region or a country. It explores the impact of sustainable solutions in the energy roadmap of a country or region. The tool compares two macro-level energy scenarios: Business As Usual (BAU) and HRES (Hybrid Renewable Energy Systems), an exploratory energy scenario based on renewable energies. It compares the evolution of the actual energy context of the region with a scenario based on distributed power generation based on renewables. The HRES scenario explores the impact of increasing the contribution of hybrid renewable power plants in a country or region (Hurtado et al. 2015; Peñalvo-López et al. 2017). SIMESEN allows analysing two alternative paths in order to identify the key factors and quantify the contribution of renewable sources for reaching a sustainable objective.

SIMESEN is composed by three independent modules: Input data, calculation engine and results.

The first module corresponds to data input, which include a first screen with the data on population, GDP, energy demand, and CO_2 production rates of the analysed community (Fig. 7.1).

Input data for consumption includes primary and final energies required by each demand sector from each resource (Fig. 7.2).

Finally, data from CO_2 emissions associated to the use of each type of energy in every demand segment, including electricity, is collected in the final screen of this module (Fig. 7.3).

This module calculates the time variation rates of each indicated variable by means of a first subroutine. In this process it is determined the evolution of each parameter in the temporal range for which data is available, then future data is extrapolated using a linear regression approach to determine the expected growth rates for each of these variables. In addition, it is defined the scenario to be simulated. This is carried out by calculating the percentages in which each primary source and electricity contribute to cover the demand of each economic sector.

The second module is a calculation engine that estimates the evolution of the energy consumption and CO_2 emissions for the energy scenario defined in the input module, using the variables and relationships detailed in Peñalvo-López et al.

CONSUMPTION DATA

DRC   VER

PRIMARY ENERGY (ktep)						
SECTOR	Coal	Oil	Natural Gas	Renewable	Nuclear	Total
Total Primary Energy	0	1.532	0	27.089	0	28.713
Import-Export	92					

FINAL ENERGY (ktep)						
SECTOR	Industry	Transport	Services	Residential	Agriculture and Fishing	Total
Total Final Energy	3.370	1.490	69	16.580	0	21.509

CONTRIBUTION (ktep)							
SECTOR	Electricity	Coal	Oil	Natural Gas	Renewable	Nuclear	Total
Industry	373	0	39	0	2.958	0	3.370
Transport	0	0	1.490	0	0	0	1.490
Commercial/Services	69	0	0	0	0	0	69
Residential	237	0	3	0	16.340	0	16.580
Agriculture/Fishing	0	0	0	0	0	0	0
Electricity Gen.	119	0	0	0	759	0	878

Efficiency of Elecric Generation   77,34%   SOURCE: IEA 2014

Fig. 7.2 SIMESEN consumption data

CO_2 COEFFICIENT PER TYPE OF ENERGY AND SECTOR

CO_2 Production (MtonCO$_2$/Mtep)						
SECTOR	Electricity	Carbon	Oil	Natural Gas	Renewable	Nuclear
Industry	0,0	4,5	3,1	2,4	0,0	0,0
Transport	0,0	0,0	2,0	1,0	0,0	0,0
Commercial/Services	0,0	4,5	3,1	2,4	0,0	0,0
Domestic	0,0	4,5	3,1	2,4	0,0	0,0
Agriculture/Fishing	0,0	4,5	3,1	2,4	0,0	0,0
Electric Generation	3,5	6,2	4,8	2,4	0,0	0,0

(Electricity in "Electric Generation" corresponds to import-export, and the estimation of the average CO2 emission in origen)

Fig. 7.3 SIMESEN CO_2 coefficients

(2017).This module evaluates the sustainability indicators resulting in the HRES scenario and calculates the degree of improvement with regards to the BAU (Business As Usual), assuming that no qualitative changes are introduced in the evolution of the energy system, maintaining constant the initial values defined in the input data and the contribution percentage from each energy source to the demand segments.

The evolution of the sustainable indicators for both considered scenarios (BAU and HRES) are calculated in this module. Sustainable evaluation of the scenarios is based on the following main indicators:

- Percentage of external dependence in primary energy supply.
- Percentage of renewable energy in overall energy consumption.

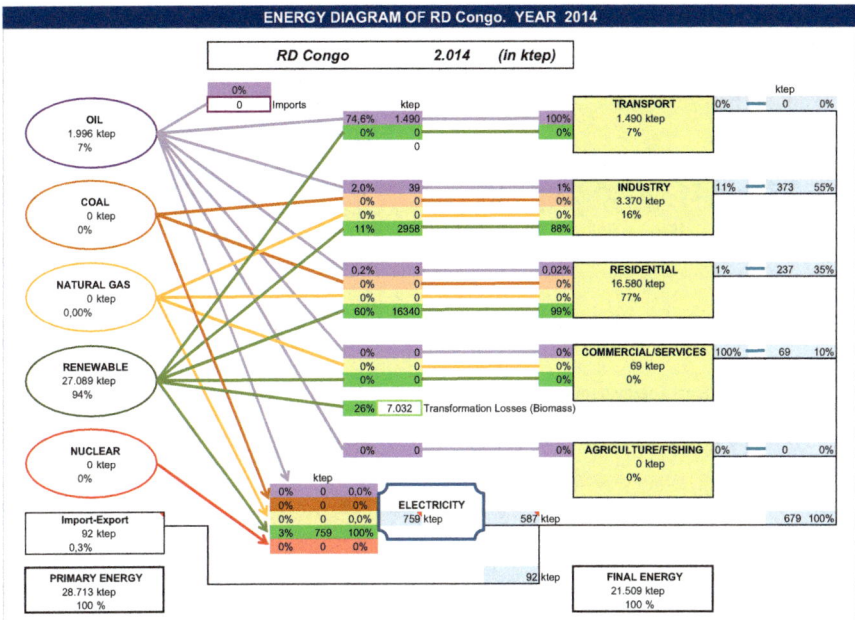

Fig. 7.4 SIMESEN. Example of General Overview Output

- Energy intensity, defined as the ratio between energy consumption and gross domestic product. The evolution of this parameter is considered as an indicator of the improvement in energy saving and efficiency.
- Total amount of CO_2 emissions from each energy sector.

Finally, HRES scenario provides the required renewable contribution to achieve a sustainable energy transition. Then, it is assessed whether such scenario is feasible with the available renewable resources in the area under study. In case renewable sources are limited, SIMESEN tool allows iterating until a compatible scenario with those available renewable resources is obtained.

The third module is dedicated to SIMESEN outputs and presentation of the results, both graphically and numerically.

The first output screen shows a diagram with the initial energy context of the region in year zero. This is the initial point used for the calculation (Fig. 7.4).

The second output screen displays the evolution of the energy consumption, both primary and final, for the various primary energy sources and the different demand segments. Also, it displays the evolution of the CO_2 emissions. Resulting graphs compare the results from BAU and HRES scenario (Figs. 7.5, 7.6, and 7.7).

The third screen presents the comparison of the sustainability indicators between both scenarios (BAU and Sustainable) (Fig. 7.8).

Finally, the SIMESEN tool provides the numerical outputs of the sustainable parameters (Table 7.3).

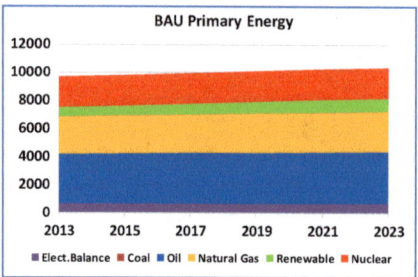
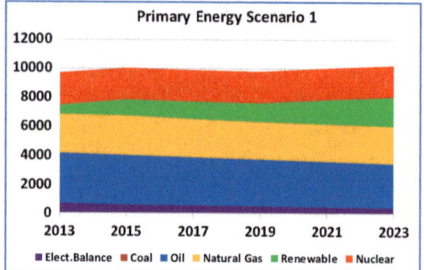

Fig. 7.5 SIMESEN. Example of primary energy

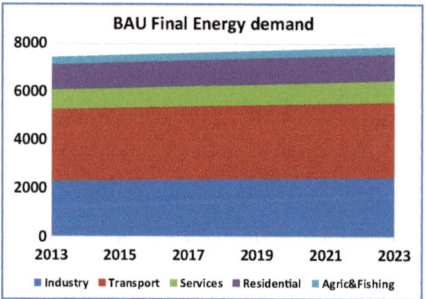
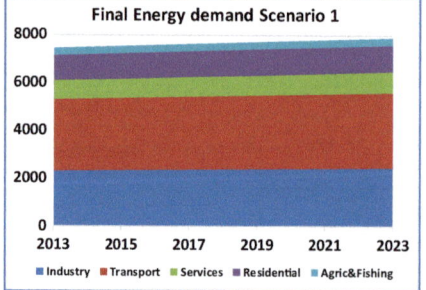

Fig. 7.6 SIMESEN. Example of final demand

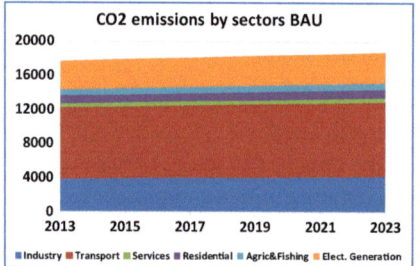
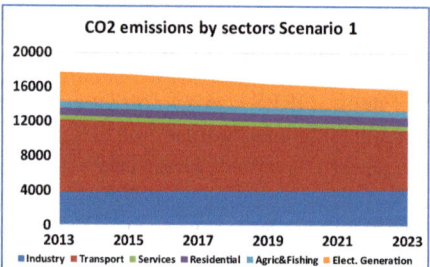

Fig. 7.7 SIMESEN. Example of CO_2 emissions

7.3 Conclusions

In the present study, the authors present SIMESEN, a practical methodology to enhance sustainability in the energy sector. SIMESEN methodology analyses different energy scenarios to increase the electrification rate while maintaining the commitment with climate change and CO_2 eq. emissions reduction. This methodology allows identifying the best energy path to achieve a sustainable roadmap for

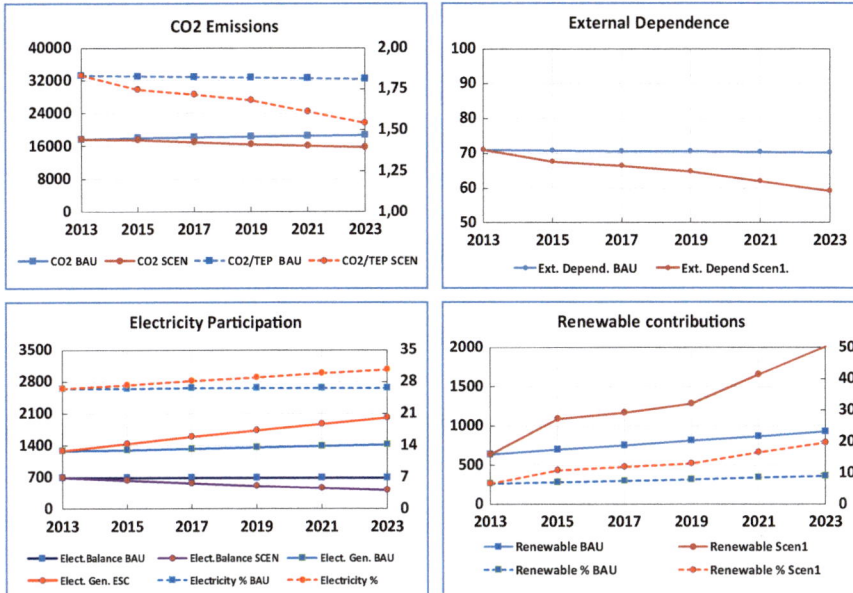

Fig. 7.8 SIMESEN. Example of indicators

developing countries. SIMESEN tool condenses a considerable amount of data, reducing the sustainability complexity to a manageable amount of meaningful information.

Results extracted from SIMESEN tool allow a realistic assessment of the renewable participation in a specific region or country, demonstrating that sustainable energy development of countries with low electrification rates based on HRES is possible and should be accompanied by national and regional energy directives. Integrating energy policies that promote the use of distributed HRES systems may reduce external dependency from fossil fuels, while increasing the electrification rate in the country, thus alleviating poverty, increasing electricity per capita and minimising CO_2 per kWh consumed.

As a summary, enhancing HRES in remote communities provides energy access to isolated areas, promoting the economic development of these communities without contributing to climate change.

Future research focus on integrating a multi-criteria decision analysis in order to support the decision making process. Despite SIMESEN tool processes a considerable amount of data and provides valuable information, there are important aspects that may be also considered, such as changing environmental regulations, variations in energy prices and technology improvements.

Table 7.3 SIMESEN. Example of simulation results

Indicators	Units	Scenario	BAU	RD Congo			
		2014	2015	2020	2025	2030	2035
Population	Million	74.9	77.2	89.9	104.6	121.8	141.8
GDPppp	M€$_{2010}$	52.200.000	52.412.599	53.488.650	54.586.794	55.707.483	56.851.180
Consumption of electricity	TWh	7.9	8.0	8.7	9.5	10.4	11.3
CO$_2$ emissions	Mt	4.53	4.85	6.82	9.64	13.68	19.45
Primary energy (EP)	ktep	28.713	29.520	33.978	39.265	45.586	53.214
EP generated	ktep	20.057	20.558	23.264	26.344	29.852	33.848
Import-export	ktep	92	94	102	111	121	132
Generated electricity	ktep	587	597	648	706	771	843
Exterior dependency	%	30.15	30.36	31.53	32.91	34.51	36.39
GDPppp/capita	M€$_{2010}$/inhab	0.70	0.68	0.60	0.52	0.46	0.40
TEP/capita	tep/hab	0.383	0.382	0.378	0.375	0.374	0.375
TEP/GDPppp	tep/M€$_{2010}$	0.55	0.56	0.64	0.72	0.82	0.94
Electricity/capita	kWh/inhab	0.11	0.10	0.10	0.09	0.09	0.08
CO$_2$/TEP	t/tep	0.16	0.16	0.20	0.25	0.30	0.37
CO$_2$/GDPppp	t/M€$_{2010}$	0.09	0.09	0.13	0.18	0.25	0.34
CO$_2$/capita	t/inhab	0.060	0.063	0.076	0.092	0.112	0.137
Fraction ER in EP*	%	69.9	69.6	68.5	67.1	65.5	63.6
Fraction ER in EE*	%	86.5	86.5	86.5	86.5	86.5	86.5

Fraction ER in EP and EE*: % of renewable energies contribution to primary energy and electrical generation

References

Bautista, S. (2012). A sustainable scenario for Venezuelan power generation sector in 2050 and its costs. *Energy Policy, 44*, 331–340.

Cherni, J., Dayner, I., Henao, F., Jaramillo, P., & Smith, R. (2007). Energy supply for sustainable rural livelihoods. A multi-criteria decision support. *Energy Policy, 35*(3), 1493–1502.

Connolly, D., Lund, H., Mathiesen, B., & Leahy, M. (2010). A review of computer tools for analysing the integration of renewable energy into various energy systems. *Applied Energy, 87*(4), 1059–1082.

Dagher, L., & Ruble, I. (2011). Modeling Lebanon's electricity sector: Alternative scenarios and their implications. *Energy, 36*(7), 4315–4326.

Ghanadan, R., & Koomey, J. G. (2005). Using energy scenarios to explore alternative energy pathways in California. *Energy Policy, 33*, 1117–1142.

Grubb, M., Edmonds, J., Ten Brink, P., & Morrison, M. (1993). The cost of limiting fossil-fuel CO2 emissions: A survey and analysis. *Annual Review of Energy and the Environment, 18*(1), 397–478.

Heaps, C. G. (2016). *Long-range energy alternatives planning (LEAP) system*. [Software version: 2015.0.23] Stockholm Environment Institute. Somerville. https://www.energycommunity.org

Hiremath, R. B., Shikha, S., & Ravindranath, N. H. (2007). Decentralized energy planning; modeling and application – A review. *Renewable and Sustainable Energy Reviews, 11*(5), 729–752.

Hurtado, E., Peñalvo-López, E., Pérez-Navarro, A., Vargas, C., & Alfonso, D. (2015). Optimization of a hybrid renewable system for high feasibility application in non-connected zones. *Applied Energy, 155*, 308–314.

Jayakrishnan, R. P., Heussen, K., & Østergaard, P. A. (2011). Comparative analysis of hourly and dynamic power balancing models for validating future energy scenarios. *Energy, 36*, 3233–3243.

Jun, S., Lee, S., Park, J.-W., Jeong, S.-J., & Shin, H.-C. (2010). The assessment of renewable energy planning on CO2 abatement in South Korea. *Renewable Energy, 35*(2), 471–477.

Levin, T., & Thomas, V. M. (2007). Least-cost network evaluation of centralized and decentralized contributions to global electrification. *Energy Policy, 41*, 286–302.

Loken, E. (2007). Use of multicriteria decision analysis methods for energy planning problems. *Renewable and Sustainable Energy Reviews, 11*, 1584–1595.

Lund, H. (2007). Renewable energy strategies for sustainable development. *Energy, 32*(6), 912–919.

Lund, H. (2009). *Renewable energy systems – The choice and modeling of 100% renewable solutions*. Oxford: Elsevier Science Publishing Company. ISBN:9780123750280.

Neven, D., Goran, K., & Carvalho, M. G. (2008). RenewIslands methodology for sustainable energy and resource planning for islands. *Renewable and Sustainable Energy Reviews, 12*(4), 1032–1062.

Peñalvo-López, E., Cárcel-Carrasco, F. J., Devece, C., & Morcillo, A. I. (2017). A methodology for analysing sustainability in energy scenarios. *Sustainability, 9*, 1590. https://doi.org/10.3390/su9091590.

Phdungsilp, A. (2010). Integrated energy and carbon modeling with a decision support system: Policy scenarios for low-carbon city development in Bangkok. *Energy Policy, 38*(9), 4808–4817.

Shin, H. C., Park, J. W., Kim, H. S., & Shin, E. S. (2005). Environmental and economic assessment of landfill gas electricity generation in Korea using LEAP model. *Energy Policy, 33*, 1261–1270.

Wangjiraniran, W., Vivanpatarakij, S., & Nidhiritdhikrai, R. (2011). Impact of economic restructuring on the energy system in Thailand. *Energy Procedia, 9*, 25–34.

Chapter 8
State Legitimacy in France as a Determinant of Competitiveness and Social Innovation

Alicia Blanco-González, Camilo Prado-Román, and Francisco Díez-Martín

Abstract The state legitimacy is the degree of citizen support to their state and a key of competitiveness and economical and social development. This research analyzes the level of state legitimacy across the belongingness to groups of population because the citizens can give different legitimacy scores to the State. It introduces the state legitimacy in France and its segmentation variables such as nationality, age, religion or political ideology. Source data for this study is derived from the last round of European Social Survey (ESS) for France in 2014. With a sample of 1.917 citizens it is proved that political ideology, age, political interest or affective state determine different scores in the state legitimacy. These results are relevant for government since it can establish which are the most sensitive groups and develop effective social politics and communication campaigns. The objective of the state is obtaining the trust within its institutions and citizen satisfaction, and besides an analysis depending on the membership group offers detailed information. Moreover, the management of the legitimacy guarantees the stability and quality of the institutions that is a precursor to social innovation.

Keywords State legitimacy · Social innovation · France · Competitiveness

8.1 Introduction

State legitimacy is the degree of support of its citizens for the operation and exercise of political power (Beetham 1991; Easton 1975; Gilley 2006). States with low legitimacy spend most of their efforts on staying in power rather than on effectively managing their institutions. This makes them more vulnerable to citizen unrest and economic turbulence (Baum and Oliver 1991; Gilley 2012).

A. Blanco-González (✉) · C. Prado-Román · F. Díez-Martín
Department of Business Administration, Faculty of Social Sciences and Law,
Rey Juan Carlos University, Madrid, Spain
e-mail: alicia.blanco@urjc.es; camilo.prado.roman@urjc.es; francisco.diez@urjc.es

© Springer International Publishing AG, part of Springer Nature 2018   119
M. Peris-Ortiz et al. (eds.), *Strategies and Best Practices in Social Innovation*,
https://doi.org/10.1007/978-3-319-89857-5_8

The components of legitimacy (for example, political support, institutional trust, or involvement in public events) are key elements for the social, political, and economic equilibrium in a country, the strength of the economy, and the competitiveness and growth of the state. The analysis of the state legitimacy permits to establish effective political strategies, develop efficient social politics and social innovation, and apply relevant communication actions. In this sense, a government with this information could have a more robust intelligence system and could approve more accurate politics.

From the perspective of Institutional Theory, States as institutions must find competitive advantages (Porter 2002) and adjust to the social and economic demands of its environment (Blanco-González et al. 2015; Díez-Martín et al. 2013) in order to survive and gain access to necessary resources. Institutions need to create an impression of legitimacy to receive support from their stakeholders and be competitive (Cruz-Suárez et al. 2014; Grigoli and Mills 2014).

Moreover, it is necessary to consider the differences among social groups because there are social, economic and demographic disparities in global population. The academic literature is replete with techniques that incorporate a number of segment-defining characteristics, including attitude, behavior, demographic, geographic, and psychographic. Although this literature has applied, adopted and extended many of these techniques to the field of elections and voting (Baines 1999; Baines et al. 2002, 2003; Newman 1994, 1999; O'Shaughnessy 1987; Phillips et al. 2010; Reid 1988; Schiffman et al. 2002; Smith and Hirst 2001; Smith and Saunders 1990; Yorke and Meehan 1986), it has not been applied in the research of legitimacy in general or state legitimacy in particular. Baines et al. (2003) determine that affect voter decision making and choice entails a segmentation approach. They describe what issues, positions and traits are important to a given segment of voters and identify the determinants for it.

The objective of this research is to measure a state legitimacy based on the specific characteristics of social groups, in this case France. In this line, we first define the concept of state legitimacy. After that, we explain the sample used and methodology. We then present the results broken down by segments. Finally, we explain how to interpret the results and how it can influence the stability of the country and become an effective indicator for policy-making.

8.2 State Legitimacy

State legitimacy is a basic concept that refers to how different uses of power influence its conscious acceptance by its constituents (Beetham 1991; Easton 1975; Gilley 2006). It is a determinant factor for a country's structure, stability, quality and operations. Countries must dedicate their resources to effective governance and not to maintain the control. The countries without state legitimacy present lower levels of social support and are more sensitives to social instability or economic crisis (Blanco-González et al. 2017; Gilley 2006).

Fig. 8.1 State legitimacy.
(*Source:* Own elaboration)

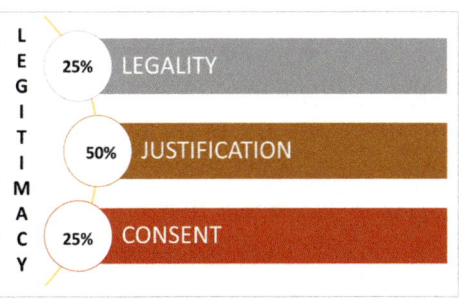

This research is based on the state context because the state is the basic institutional and ideological structure of a political community (Gilley 2006). A state's stability is guaranteed by citizen participation and good governance (Muller et al. 1982; Lillbacka 1999), but is "threatened" by a lack of trust in their institutions. Aspects such as corruption, citizen participation, trust in the law, weaken legitimacy (Blanco-González et al. 2016).

In this sense, there is a necessary distinction between the legitimacy of the state as an institution and other political sciences concepts like democratic legitimacy, effectiveness, or satisfaction. This research studies how much the state as an institution is socially accepted; but not how much social or other type of support exists for democracy (Dahl 1971; Easton 1975; Gunther et al. 1995; Inglehart 1997; Linz 1988; Torcal and Montero 2006; among others).

The concept of state legitimacy is analyzed from three dimensions (Beetham 1991; Blanco-González et al. 2016; Gilley 2006): legality, normative justifiability, and expressed consent (Fig. 8.1).

Firstly, within the dimension of legality or acceptance of legal authority, the state exercises its political power in concordance with its citizen's views on laws, rules, and customs. These are important because they are generally applied and predictable. Rules create predictability in social life, which is in itself a moral good. An example of this dimension is how citizens perceive corruption and the rule of law or the actions followed by the police.

Secondly, the dimension of normative justifiability looks at shared principles in a specific society: its ideas and values. Citizens react to the moral reasons given by the state to act in a certain way. Legitimacy arises from the degree of synchrony with the shared moral values in the discourse of its citizens (Nevitte and Kanji 2002). In other words, there is a set of shared beliefs that intermediate power relationships (Beetham 1991). The notion of moral congruency between state and society is the basis of the literature on comparative politics and sociology (for example, Nevitte and Kanji 2002). Some indicators of this dimension are trust in political leadership or opinions on the effectiveness of political institutions.

Thirdly, dimension of consent or political support provide a complementary explanation for state legitimacy, citizen support and participation that does not have a normative root as the two previous dimensions. At any given time, a citizen can only evaluate the legality or justification of a small fraction of the entire system

Fig. 8.2 Segmentation of state legitimacy. (*Source:* Own elaboration)

regulated by political power. To fill this legitimacy gap, "acts of expressed consent" are those positive actions that express the acknowledgment by a citizen that the state possesses overarching political authority and that he or she must follow the resulting decisions. Examples of acts of expressed consent would be voter turnout, level of participation in associations, or membership in political parties.

Legitimacy can be lost, maintained, or acquired. For this reason, institutions should actively manage it (Suchman 1995; Deeds et al. 2004). Various academic studies have analyzed how certain actions can help obtain, or lose, legitimacy (for example, Phillips et al. 2004). Their findings confirm Suchman's (1995), who noted that oftentimes the best course of action is simply to adjust to what the environment is asking for. This admits degrees; it is a thermometer or a metric of the situation (Walzer 2002) and can have varying degrees of intensity (Gur 1971).

It is necessary to quantify the differences in state legitimacy among social groups. The academic literature has identified a number of segments and its characteristics (attitude, behavior, benefit, demographic, geographic, and psychographic). The segmentation in political markets has been previously outlined (O'Shaughnessy 1987; Reid 1988). Much of the academic literature on market segmentation has been analyzed from a product marketing perspective, including political markets, which have been segmented using geographic, behavioral, psychographic and demographic methods (Smith and Saunders 1990). For example, Baines et al. (2003), suggested that developing political messages that affect voter decision making and choice entails a segmentation approach that not only describes what issues, positions, and traits are important to a given segment of voters, but that also identifies the reasons for it.

Although this literature has applied, adopted, and extended many of these techniques to the field of elections and voting (Baines 1999; Baines et al. 2002, 2003; Newman 1994, 1999; O'Shaughnessy 1987; Phillips et al. 2010; Reid 1988; Schiffman et al. 2002; Smith and Hirst 2001; Smith and Saunders 1990; Yorke and Meehan 1986), it has not been applied in the research of state legitimacy (Fig. 8.2).

8.3 Sample and Methodology

To measure the state legitimacy, we have followed the guidelines used by other well-regarded indexes in high impact publications, such as the University of Michigan Consumer Sentiment Index (MCSI). This index measures consumer attitudes on the business climate, personal finance, and spending (Vosen and Schmidt. 2011). Another index we studied, the Consumer Confidence Index (CCI), is designed to measure overall consumer confidence, relative financial health, and purchasing power of the average US consumer (Kwan and Cotsomitis 2006; Tsalikis and Seaton 2007). It achieves this by providing a score between 0 and 1 that is modified by positive, negative, and neutral indicators; allowing us to analyze change over time (Prado-Román et al. 2016).

Every 2 years, the Standing Committee for the Social Sciences (SCSS) of the European Science Foundation leads the European Social Survey (ESS). This represents an effort to measure change in the attitudes, beliefs, and behavior patterns of the various populations in Europe, improve the quality of quantitative measures, and establish a set of solid social indicators to evaluate well-being in European countries.

To quantify state legitimacy we have adapted the indicators proposed Prado-Román et al. (2016) and Gilley (2006). It is possible to use the results of social surveys to build a state legitimacy measure as they contain indicators of social and political nature (Gilley 2012; Grimes 2008; Hetcher 2009; Rothstein 2010).

We have collected the bi-annual ESS data for Spain in 2014 and select 20 items (identified in Table 8.1) that measure legitimacy by referring to citizen's acceptance, trust, an public participation in the countries analyzed (2 items for legality, 8 for normative justifiability, and 10 or expressed consent).

Some additional data homogenization is necessary to allow us to compare the different measures. As shown in Table 8.1, the scales of the items in the ESS are not homogeneous. Some of them receive values between 1 and 10, others between 1 and 2, and some data cleansing was also necessary. Scales are converted to 0–100 by applying base 10 logarithms (0 = minimum legitimacy; 100 = maximum legitimacy), and variables on the 1–2 scale are re-coded by reversing the values (2 = no legitimacy; 1 = full legitimacy). Following these transformations, we weight, calculate the average values and attribute the value of each dimension to the building of a weighted state legitimacy. This allows us to compare items and obtain a robust index (Hair et al. 2009).

Common-sense segmentation requires the researcher to first choose the variables of interest, and then to classify this segments in accordance with those variables (Pulido-Fernández and Sánchez-Rivero 2010). The choice of these variables is based on European Social Survey indicators and proposals found in the literature for similar cases (Baines et al. 2003, among others).

With respect to the segmentation criteria, there are basically five types of variables (Table 8.2): religion, political orientation, discrimination group, citizenship and demographics.

Table 8.1 State legitimacy items

Dimensions	Item
Legality	*Trust in the legal system*
	Trust in justice
Justification	*Satisfaction with your country's democracy*
	Satisfaction with your country's economic situation
	Sate of education in your country
	Satisfaction with your country' government
	Trust in parliament
	Trust in political parties
	Trust in politicians
	State of health services
Consent	*Participation in an election in the last 12 months*
	Boycotted a product in the last 12 months
	Feeling of closeness with a specific political party
	Contact with public administration in the last 12 months
	Member of a political party
	Participated in a lawful public demonstration in the last 12 months
	Signed a petition in the last 12 months
	Voted during the last general elections
	Worked in an organization or association in the last 12 months
	Worked in a political party or action group in the last 12 months

Source: Own elaboration by Prado-Román et al. (2017) and European Social Survey (2014)

Table 8.2 Segmentation variables

Segmentation criteria	Item
Age	*ED. age of the respondent*
Gender	*GEN. Gender*
Type locality	*LOC. Type locality*
Level of education	*EST. highest level of education*
Main activity	*LAB. Main activity in the last 7 days*
Religion	*REL. Belongs to a particular religion or denomination*
Citizenship	*CIUD. Country citizen*
Discrimination	*DISC. Member of a group discriminated against in this country*
Affective state	*AFEC. Satisfaction with your life*
	AFEC. Level of happiness
National Identity	*IDENT. Feeling of closeness to your country*
Political ideology	*IDEOL. Close to some political party*
	IDEOL. Location on left-right scale
Political interest	*INTPOL. Level of political interest*
Political representation	*REPR. The political system allows people to have a voice in what the government does*
	REPR. The political system allows people to influence politics
	REPR. Politicians care about what people think

Source: Own elaboration

Table 8.3 Anova analysis

Type	FRANCE
ED. age	0.031***
GEN. Gender	*0.826*
LOC. Type locality	*0.183*
EST. level of education	0.000***
LAB. Main activity	*0.123*
REL. Religion	*0.268*
CIUD. Citizenship	*0.145*
DISC. Discrimination	0.000***
AFEC. Affective state	0.000***
IDENT. National Identity	0.000***
IDEOL. Political ideology	0.000***
INTPOL. Political interest	0.000***
REPR. Political representation	0.000***

*** $p > 0.001$

8.4   Results

Anova analysis for the variable of state legitimacy showed differences with regard to the following variables (Table 8.3). If the level of significance is less than 0.05, it means that there are differences which depend of the segmentation criteria.

To build the specific state legitimacy, those segmentation variables which were tested as significant in Anova analysis have been selected. These variables have an influence in the state legitimacy: age, level of education, discrimination, affective state, national identity and variables related with political attitude.

The legitimacy score according to the segment of membership shows disparate results that identify groups more sensitive to the actions of the State. Table 8.4 identifies the disaggregated results and identifies the strength of this variation. When legitimacy varies less than 5% is considered to be stable, when the index varies between 6% and 10% is incorporated an arrow up or down depending on the increase or decrease. When legitimacy varies between 11% and 25% is incorporated a double arrow. And when the index varies more than 25% is a segment of greater sensitivity, is identified with a triple arrow.

The measurement of legitimacy according to the age ranges shows that the French population less than 21 years of age gives a greater value to the legitimacy of the French State (62.7 vs 55.3) with a moderate upward variation. Likewise, the variations generated by the level of studies are moderate. The higher the educational level the greater the legitimacy, being a lower tertiary level that suffers a greater variation (+ 11%). Also, those individuals who feel discriminated against criminalize the actions of States (−14%), and that those who feel totally unsatisfied transmit their negativity to legitimacy (−35%).

Table 8.4 Results of specific state legitimacy Vs global state legitimacy

Variables	Items	France		
	Legitimacy	*55.3*	*Variation*	
ED. age	**< 21**	*62.7*	**13%**	↑↑
	21–30	*57.9*	5%	↑
	31–40	*55.2*	0%	≈
	41–50	*54.1*	−2%	↓
	51–60	*53.2*	−4%	↓
	61–70	*54.4*	−2%	↓
	> 71	*56.1*	1%	↑
EST. level of education	Less than lower second.	52.7	−5%	↓
	Lower secondary	55.8	1%	↑
	Lower tier upper second.	52.1	−6%	↓
	Upper tier upper second.	55.9	1%	↑
	Advanced vocational	54.9	−1%	↓
	Lower tertiary education	**61.4**	**11%**	↑↑
	Higher tertiary education	59.7	8%	↑
DISC. Discrimination	Yes	47.4	−14%	↓↓
	No	56.6	2%	↑
AFEC. Affective state	**Extremely dissatisfied**	**36.0**	**−35%**	↓↓↓
	Dissatisfied	50.3	−9%	↓
	Neutral	53.5	−3%	↓
	Satisfied	58.4	6%	↑
	Extremely satisfied	60.2	9%	↑
IDENT. National Identity	Very close	56.0	1%	↑
	Close	56.2	2%	↑
	Not very close	**45.8**	**−17%**	↓↓
	Not close at all	**24.3**	**−56%**	↓↓↓
IDEOL. Political ideology	Left	49.8	−10%	↓
	Left - moderate	58.4	5%	↑
	Neutral	56.0	1%	↑
	Right - moderate	55.6	0%	≈
	Right	**48.8**	**−12%**	↓↓
INTPOL. Political interest	Very close	56.0	1%	↑
	Quite close	56.8	3%	↑
	Not close	54.3	−2%	↓
	Not at all close	50.9	−8%	↓
REPR. Political representation	**Strongly disagree**	**42.5**	**−23%**	↓↓
	Disagree	57.3	4%	↑
	Neutral	**65.8**	**19%**	↑↑
	Agree	**69.9**	**26%**	↑↑↑
	Strongly agree	**64.8**	**17%**	↑↑

If we analyze the variables of a political type, the results of the legitimacy broken down by groups indicate that those who do not feel close to the state strongly penalize legitimacy (−56%) and those who feel represented by their politicians reward legitimacy (+ 26%).

8.5 Implications and Discussion

Legitimacy impacts a country's competitiveness and growth. Institutions, same as States, must find competitive advantages and adjust to the social and economic demands of its environment in order to survive and gain access to necessary resources (Blanco-González et al. 2017; Díez-Martín et al. 2010). Institutions need to create an impression of sustainability and legitimacy so they will receive support from their stakeholders and be competitive (Cruz-Suárez et al. 2014; Grigoli and Mills 2014). Achieving this source of competitive advantage is the main reason states must pay attention to their legitimacy (Blanco-González et al. 2015; Díez-Martín et al. 2016).

This study establishes that a state legitimacy in France is 55.3 in a scale 0–100. A score which shows a moderate acceptance (higher that 50). The French government needs to reinforce this score if it wants permanent and solid institutions. In this sense, the social innovation is a way to strengthen this legitimacy. After that, this research adapted the state legitimacy to the particularities of the French population clusters. This specific information reflects more detailed information inside the country and permits to establish effective political strategies, develop efficient social politics, and apply relevant communication actions.

The empirical study evidences the link between state legitimacy and age, level of education, discrimination, affective state and political variables (national identity, political interest, political ideology and political representation). Also, it proves that gender, type locality, main activity, religion or citizenship don't have any influence in state legitimacy.

With respect to the different variables, there are three level of influence. Firstly, the critical variables, which generate variations higher than 25%, are: affective state (satisfaction with the life and level of happiness), national identity (feeling of closeness to the country) and political representation (politicians care about what people think). Secondly, the variables with positive influence, which generate positive variations between 11% and 25%, are: age and level of education. Thirdly, the variables with negative influence, which generate negative variations between 11% and 25%, are: discrimination (member of a group discriminated against in the country) and political ideology (close to some political party and location on left-right scale).

The results of the research confirm that legitimacy can serve as a tool to measure government effectiveness, anticipate political, social, or economic difficulties for states, and impact a country's competitiveness. In general, governments need not only to increase citizen satisfaction by ensuring the rule of law and political, educational, and healthcare systems; but they also need to encourage social innovation. By this way, it measures specific legitimacy, the trust to the state as a whole will be increased, the economic system will be more stable, and investors will be attracted.

Finally, there are certain limitations to the current study. It would be necessary to analyze the correlation between legitimacy and political, social, and economical variables, as well as to increase the sample, or compare these results to other countries.

References

Baines, P. R. (1999). Voter segmentation and candidate positioning. In B. I. Newman (Ed.), *Handbook of political marketing* (pp. 73–86). Thousand Oaks: Sage.

Baines, P. R., Harris, P., & Lewis, B. R. (2002). The political marketing planning process: Improving image and message in strategic target areas. *Marketing Intelligence & Planning, 20*(1), 6–14.

Baines, P. R., Worcester, R. M., Jarrett, D., & Mortimore, R. (2003). Market segmentation and product differentiation in political campaigns: A technical feature perspective. *Journal of Marketing Management, 19*(1/2), 223–249.

Baum, J. A. C., & Oliver, C. (1991). Institutional linkages and organizational mortality. *Administrative Science Quarterly, 36*(2), 187–218.

Beetham, D. (1991). *The legitimation of power*. London: Macmillan.

Blanco-González, A., Díez-Martín, F., & Prado-Román, A. (2015). Entrepreneurship, global competitiveness and legitimacy. In *New challenges in entrepreneurship and finance* (pp. 57–69). Cham: Springer International Publishing.

Blanco-González, A., Prado-Román, C., & Díez-Martín, F. (2017). Building a European legitimacy index. *American Behavioral Scientist, 61*(5), 509–525.

Cruz-Suarez, A., Prado-Román, C., & Díez-Martín, F. (2014). Por qué se institucionalizan las organizaciones. *Revista Europea de Dirección y Economía de la Empresa, 23*(1), 22–30.

Dahl, R. A. (1971). *Polyarchy. Participation and opposition*. New Haven: Yale University Press.

Deeds, D. L., Mang, P. Y., & Frandsen, M. L. (2004). The influence of firms' and industries' legitimacy on the flow of capital into high-technology ventures. *Strategic Organization., 2*(1), 9–34.

Díez-Martín, F., Blanco-González, A., & Prado-Román, C. (2010). Legitimidad como factor clave del éxito organizativo. *Investigaciones Europeas de Dirección y Economía de la Empresa, 16*(3), 127–143.

Díez-Martín, F., Prado-Román, C., & Blanco-González, A. (2013). Beyond legitimacy: Legitimacy types and organizational success. *Management Decision, 51*(10), 1954–1969.

Díez-Martín, F., Blanco-González, A., & Prado-Román, C. (2016). Explaining nation-wide differences in entrepreneurial activity: A legitimacy perspective. *International Entrepreneurship and Management Journal, 12*, 1–24.

Easton, D. (1975). A reassessment of the concept of political support. *British Journal of Political Science, 55*, 435–457.

European Social Survey (2014). Round 7. www.europeansocialsurvey.org (Last Access june 2017).

Gilley, B. (2006). The meaning and measure of state legitimacy: Results for 72 countries. *European Journal of Political Research, 45*(3), 499–525.

Gilley, B. (2012). State legitimacy: An updated dataset for 52 countries. *European Journal of Political Research, 51*(5), 693–699.

Grigoli, F., & Mills, Z. (2014). Institutions and public investment: An empirical analysis. *Economics of Governance, 15*(2), 131–153.

Grimes, M. (2008). Consent, political trust and compliance: Rejoinder to Kaina's remarks on "organizing consent". *European Journal of Political Research, 47*(4), 522–535.

Gunther, R., Diamandouros, P., & Phle, P. H. (1995). *The politics of democratic consolidation: Southern Europe in comparative perspective*. Baltimore: The Johns Hopkins University Press.

Gur, T. (1971). *Why men rebel. Princeton*. New Jersy: Princeton University Press.

Hair, J. F., Black, W. C., Babin, B. J., & Anderson, R. E. (2009). *Multivariate data analysis: A global perspective* (7th ed.). Upper Saddle River: Prentice Hall.

Hechter, M. (2009). Legitimacy in modern world. *American Behavioral Scientist 53*(3), 279–288.

Inglehart, R. (1997). *Modernization and postmodernization: Cultural, economic and political change in 43 societies*. Princeton: Princeton University Press.

Kwan, A. C. C., & Cotsomitis, J. A. (2006). The usefulness of consumer confidence in forecasting household spending in Canada: A national and regional analysis. *Economic Inquiry, 44*(1), 185–197.

Lillbacka, R. (1999). *The legitimacy of the political system: The case of Finland*. Abo: Abo Akademi University Press.

Linz, J. J. (1988). *Legitimacy of democracy and the socioeconomic system*. Boulder: Westview Press.

Muller, E. N., Jukam, T. O., & Seligson, M. A. (1982). Diffuse political support and antisystem political behaviour. *American Journal of Political Science, 26*(2), 240–265.

Nevitte, N., & Kanji, M. (2002). Authority orientations and political support: A cross-national analysis of satisfaction with governments and democracy. *International Studies in Sociology and Social Anthropology, 1*, 157–182.

Newman, B. I. (1994). *The Marketing of the President: Political marketing as campaign strategy*. Thousand Oaks: Sage.

Newman, B. I. (1999). *The mass Marketing of Politics: Democracy in an age of manufactured images*. Thousand Oaks: Sage.

O'Shaughnessy, N. J. (1987). America's political market. *European Journal of Marketing, 21*(4), 60–66.

Phillips, N., Lawrence, T. B., & Hardy, C. (2004). Discourse and institutions. *Academy of Management Review, 29*(4), 635–652.

Phillips, J. M., Reynolds, T. J., & Reynods, K. (2010). Decision-based voter segmentation: An application for campaign massage development. *European Journal of Marketing, 44*(3/4), 310–330.

Porter, M. E. (2002). *Enhancing the microeconomic foundations of prosperity: The current competitiveness index in world economic forum, the global competitiveness report 2001–2002* (pp. 2–26). Oxford: UK.

Prado-Román, C., Blanco-González, A., Díez-Martín, F., & Payne, G. (2016). Building the index of state legitimacy in Baltic and Nordic countries. *Esic Market Economics and Business Journal, 47*(3), 37–45.

Pulido-Fernández, J. I., & Sánchez-Rivero, M. (2010). Attitudes of the cultural tourist: A latent segmentation approach. *Journal of Cultural Economics, 34*(2), 111–129.

Reid, D. M. (1988). Marketing the political product. *European Journal of Marketing, 22*(9), 34–47.

Rothstein, B. (2010). Happiness and the welfare state. *Social Research, 77*, 441–468.

Schiffman, L. G., Sherman, E., & Kirpalani, N. (2002). Trusting souls: A segmentation of the voting public. *Psychology and Marketing, 19*(12), 993–1007.

Smith, G., & Hirst, A. (2001). Strategic political segmentation: A new approach for a new era of political marketing. *European Journal of Marketing, 35*(9/10), 1058–1073.

Smith, G., & Saunders, J. (1990). The application of marketing to British politics. *Journal of Marketing Management, 5*(3), 295–306.

Suchman, M. (1995). Managing legitimacy: Strategic and institutional approaches. *Academy of Management Review, 20*(3), 571–610.

Torcal, M., & Montero, J. R. (2006). *Political disaffection in contemporary democracies: Social capital, institutions and politics*. London/New York: Routledge.

Tsalikis, J., & Seaton, B. (2007). Business ethics index: USA 2006. *Journal of Business Ethics, 72*(2), 163–175.

Vosen, S., & Schmidt, T. (2011). Forecasting private consumption: Survey-based indicators vs. Google trends. *Journal of Forecasting, 30*(6), 565–578.

Walzer, M. (2002). The argument about humanitarian intervention. *Dissent, 49*, 29–37.

Yorke, D. A., & Meehan, S. A. (1986). ACORN in the political marketplace. *European Journal of Marketing, 20*(8), 63–76.

Chapter 9
Developing Sustainability Awareness in Higher Education

Rui Pedro Lopes, Cristina Mesquita, María de la Cruz del Río-Rama, and José Álvarez-García

Abstract Sustainable development is, currently, a major concern by most of the world's nations. Since the report Our Future, by the World Commission on Environment and Development in 1987, the pattern of resources usage has been driven by the concern of meeting the "needs of the present without compromising the ability of future generations to meet their own needs". This definition established the basis for the holistic and joint preservation of the natural world, considering economic, social and environmental factors. According to the United Nations, education is fundamental for achieving sustainable development. Beyond education for environment protection, the consumers' and the producers' attitudes has to change towards social awareness in a long term. Higher education institutions have the responsibility, and even gain from it, to implement projects and practices that foster sustainable development as well as contribute to the development of sustainability thinking among their students. The development of these competences should also be part of the curriculum of higher education degrees, which describe the training intentionality in the curricular unit forms. These are rigorously focused around the scientific area of the program, but they also include transversal skills, that contribute to empower the student with a broader set of knowledge and abilities. This study analyses three dimensions of sustainability: the teaching curricula, the scientific production and the policies and attitudes regarding the infrastructures. The first, because of their large quantity, are analyzed through the textual content of the curricular unit forms, using text mining tools and techniques, to get an overall idea of the intentional development of sustainability thinking in a higher education

R. P. Lopes · C. Mesquita
Polytechnic Institute of Bragança, Bragança, Portugal
e-mail: rlopes@ipb.pt; cmmgp@ipb.pt

M. de la C. del Río-Rama (✉)
Department of Business Organisation and Marketing, University of Vigo, Ourense, Spain
e-mail: delrio@uvigo.es

J. Álvarez-García
Department of Financial Economics and Accounting, University of Extremadura,
Cáceres, Extremadura, Spain
e-mail: pepealvarez@unex.es

institution. The second uses the same approach to assess the areas and orientation of the scientific production, available in the institutional repository. Finally, the infrastructures component, which includes energy efficiency and waste management, is analyzed through the assessment of the policies and projects implemented in this area. Although there are sustainability concerns in the institution, mainly associated to the scientific and specific component of each area, there is no holistic and transversal strategy, with a balance between the economic, social and environmental spheres of sustainability. There are still challenges that higher education institutions must face, to stimulate the sustainability awareness among their students.

Keywords Higher education · Sustainability thinking · Sustainable development · Text mining · Student development

9.1 Sustainable Development

Sustainable development is, currently, a major concern by most of the world's nations. Since the report Our Common Future, by the World Commission on Environment and Development (Brundtland Comission) (1987), the pattern of resources usage has been driven by the concern of meeting the "needs of the present without compromising the ability of future generations to meet their own needs" (Sect. 9.1, para. 1). This definition emphasizes the multilateralism and interdependency of the nations in the pursuit of sustainable development beyond environmental issues. In fact, the report connects economy and social equity to the environmental issues, highlighting that "even the narrow notion of physical sustainability implies a concern for social equity between generations, a concern that must logically be extended to equity within each generation" (Sect. 9.6, para. 3). This statement implies the necessity for developing a social awareness that transforms the relation of the man with the world.

Sustainability establishes the basis for the holistic and joint conservation of the natural world, considering economic, social and environmental factors (Emanuel et al. 2011). Sustainability results from the blending process of these three spheres, that should not be regarded separately (Fig. 9.1). Although each one of them focus in an important aspect, all of these should be considered integrated, such as natural resources use, pollution, water, land and waste management, with societal aspects, such as health, population, education or security, and with the economic factors, such as profit, cost savings or growth. Each of these three spheres has similar importance in creating and maintaining stability and balance.

More recently, the United Nations (2015) restates the integrative perspective that highlights the balance between the three dimensions. The 17th Sustainable Development Goals document presents five fundamental aspects that should be considered to achieve 169 targets: people, planet, prosperity, peace and partnership.

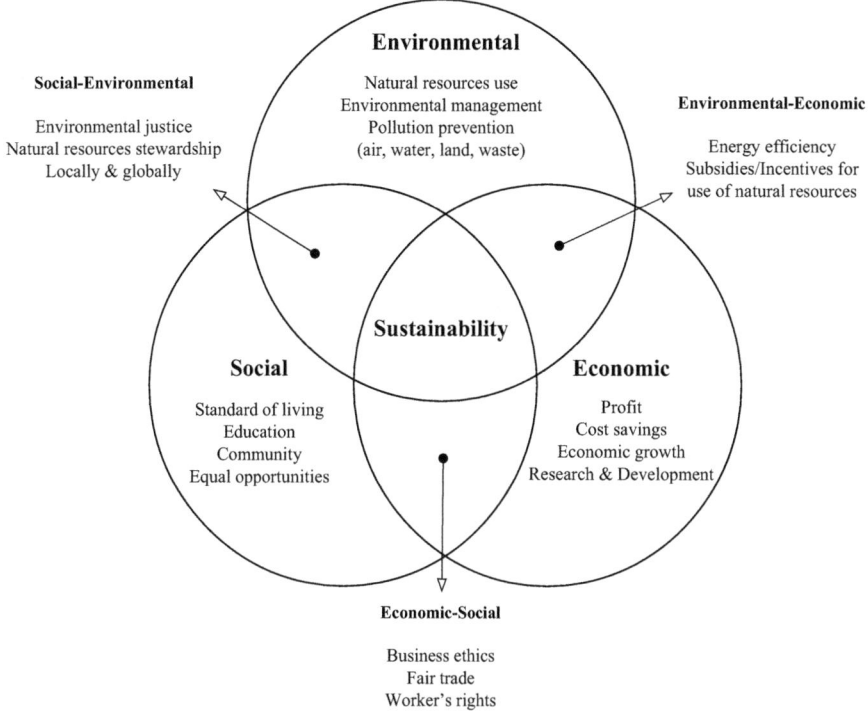

Environmental
Natural resources use
Environmental management
Pollution prevention
(air, water, land, waste)

Social-Environmental

Environmental justice
Natural resources stewardship
Locally & globally

Environmental-Economic

Energy efficiency
Subsidies/Incentives for
use of natural resources

Sustainability

Social

Standard of living
Education
Community
Equal opportunities

Economic

Profit
Cost savings
Economic growth
Research & Development

Economic-Social

Business ethics
Fair trade
Worker's rights

Fig. 9.1 The three spheres of sustainability. (Emanuel et al. 2011. *Source:* Authors)

In this sense, it is necessary to adopt some strategies that follow these guidelines towards building the sustainability awareness:

- Education as a right for all: an informed population can make choices and decide in a responsible way.
- Science and technology: research can lead to the creation of integrative projects that contribute to the development of enterprises, organizations, communities in the respect for the environment and the populations' rights.
- Promote equity and equal opportunities for all.
- Value the communities and their cultural and natural heritage.
- Respect for the human rights and promote gender equality and the empowerment of women and men.
- Protection of the planet and its natural resources.
- End poverty and hunger everywhere.
- Promote partnership and collaboration with the participation of all countries, all stakeholders, and all people.
- Ensure prosperous and fulfilling lives for human beings.

Everyone should contribute to pursue these goals. The United Nations assumes this commitment in several areas of intervention. In order to respond to these challenges, it is important to develop new ideas based on the design of new products, services and intervention models adjusted to social needs and, on the other hand, that ensure the capacity of societies to act (Bureau of European Policy Advisers 2011). The promotion of sustainable development is related to the concept of social innovation, since sustainable development needs socially adjusted and ethically situated ideas and interventions, so that it can be achieved. Considering this, in the next section we will reflect on the notion and purposes of social innovation, as an indispensable way to ensure social transformation.

9.2 Social Innovation for Sustainability

The concerns of the modern world have been targeting new and more effective answers to the issues that have been threatening our lives and our way of living. The climate is changing, the evolution of society has introduced new epidemic and chronical diseases and the gap between rich and poor have been increasing. Reducing the carbon footprint, keeping people healthy and with universal access to healthcare, and eradicating poverty are questions of the utmost importance that we have to tackle urgently (Murray et al. 2010). These are further stressed by migration and highly diverse communities, which put pressure on community cohesion and place additional demands on local services. Moreover, a rapidly ageing population is increasingly demanding on health and healthcare services. The growing personal budget has been facing difficulties by the austerity many countries face in crises periods (TEPSIE 2014).

This question has placed social innovation as an intentional means of social transformation, based on ethically situated purposes that aim to promote the equity of social justice and citizen participation. This perspective requires reflection on the concept of social innovation that has often been used in different contexts in ambiguous definitions, often confusing it with other forms of innovation and without considered the criteria that characterize the social dimension.

The perception of the ambiguous use of the term and the need to make it explicit has led to reflection, which has its most recent expression in the Vienna Declaration, where it is assumed that social innovation should be considered as an urgent alternative to technology-oriented innovation, since it has not had the desired impact in solving the problems mentioned (Franz et al. 2011).

In a global and social economy, the answers to these questions are not compatible with traditional organizations and models. The rising cost is an issue, with more money being necessary for treating diseases, controlling pollution and supporting assistance programs. Old models are not able of coping with these challenges. Society have to innovate in the way to deal with this issue.

The Vienna Declaration reflects the major societal challenges identified by the European 2020 strategy, which affirms the importance of social innovation to overcome the problems of unemployment, climate change, education, poverty and social exclusion. In this sense, social innovation interconnects the foundations and principles (the ethically situated intentions) with actions and interventions and the effects and the final results of that same intervention. This study assumes that social innovation describes "new solutions to social challenges that have the intent and effect of equality, justice and empowerment" (Anderson et al. 2014, p. 26). This suggests that a social innovation activity must be new, address a social challenge, and contribute to create equality, justice and empowerment, with the final effect on the social change and in the well-being of people's lives.

In this perspective, social innovation leads us to the idea of awareness (*conscientização*, using the words of Freire) that allows the person integrated in its natural and social context, to reflect about himself and about the word, and by becoming involved in it and with others, he/she performs actions (Freire 1981). Regarding this there is no awareness outside praxis, outside the theoretical-practical unity and reflection and action. Praxis is always animated by values and systems of thought. Praxis is understood as an indissoluble unity between man's action and reflection on the world, emphasizing man's ability to act upon the world and to transform it (Freire 1979).

When facing these difficulties, ordinary people, in their own localities, can respond in a creative and innovative way to the pressing challenges that they experiencing. Consumer cooperatives, exchange and social currency networks, free universities, and others, are some examples that are born in such difficulties through cooperation and will.

Considering this perspective, higher education institutions assume a fundamental role in preparing their students to react positively under such circumstances. They should be prepared to understand and to develop empathy with the others. They should be creative and participative, request and accept help and have energy to propose solutions and to create alternatives. They should have the confidence and awareness to improve the lives of the more vulnerable communities. This is transversal to all the scientific areas.

The main question of this study is to check if higher education institutions are, intentionally, developing sustainability awareness in their students, in the curricula of the programs, the infrastructures, the policies and the attitudes they encourage.

9.3 Sustainable Development in Higher Education

According to the United Nations (2012), education is fundamental for the sustainable development (Wals 2012). Since 2005, this organization recognizes that education institutions are fundamental partners in pursuing the sustainability goals. The document Decade of Education for Sustainable Development (DESD) (UNESCO 2005), assumes the main goal as the integration of "the principles, values, and practices of sustainable development into all aspects of education and learning" (p. 6). Regarding this, it is necessary to develop efforts to "encourage changes in behavior that will create a more sustainable future in terms of environmental integrity, economic viability, and a just society for present and future generations" (p. 6). This perspective goes beyond the environmental protection, focusing in the way individuals and communities behave and interact with the Earth.

This declaration creates a challenge to the HEI, under the recognition that these institutions have a main role in producing and transferring knowledge. HEI are considered fundamental partners to develop knowledge necessary to the sustainable development and, also, for preparing current and future generations to use this knowledge on their work and on their lives. Moreover, it is assumed that HEI have a profound responsibility in the promotion of awareness, knowledge, skills and values, necessary to the development of a fairest and sustainable future.

HEI are challenged to promote action policies and strategies focused on the teaching-learning methodologies, the research area and purpose, the infrastructures, the management of people and resources, the acquisition and discard of goods, the curriculum that, within the communities, are considered as opportunities for sustainable development. Only an integrative approach, grouping several dimensions, can foster the development of a holistic perspective of sustainability (Fig. 9.2).

The Johnston report (2010) analyses 15 HEI, to study and understand strategies that constitute opportunities for the promotion of sustainable development. Several instruments were used, to diversify the collected data, which included the contributions by students, staff and community.

One of the main conclusions of the study is related to the assumed perspective for sustainability. In the 15 case studies, sustainability is assumed in very specific terms. All demonstrate a strong focus in environmental sustainability, without a significant focus on the social responsibility, associated to the students and staff well-being, and on the relations with the community and on the economic issues. The study shows that it is necessary to create and adopt a strategy that integrates sustainable development in all the functions and areas of HEI.

Considering the specificity of programs and scientific areas, the development of an integrated perspective of sustainability in the curriculum is a challenge for HEI. It is important because it should provide students a more explicit sustainability

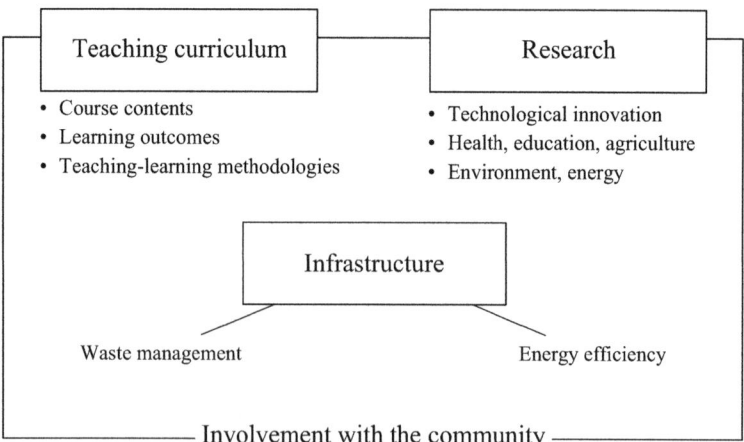

Fig. 9.2 Sustainability in Higher Education. (*Source:* Authors)

perspective, able to broaden the student's ideas regarding this issue. In this sense, the different study areas should highlight their interdependency, supporting the students in the development of more realistic views of the world. This line of work implies that HEI create teaching and learning methodologies that include analyzing, synthesizing, evaluating, questioning and reflecting in addition to the know, understand and apply, to favor the development of critical thinking, supported in the economic, social and environmental reality.

The development of sustainability awareness does not depend on the study area, but it is an integral part of each subject. The notion of sustainability goes beyond the subject scientific perspective, broadening the curriculum with environmental, social and economic issues.

If, on one hand, educating for sustainability can be focused on the specific knowledge of the area, approaching questions such as financial sustainability, waste, biodiversity, etc., in seminars or practical activities, on the other hand, it can also be focused on "learning towards change".

Sustainability awareness requires developing complex level thinking. In this sense, curricula should reflect this intentionality in the curricular units' forms. These, in addition to the main scientific area content, should also highlight this type of knowledge.

Considering this conceptualization, this study analyzes how the learning outcomes described in the curricular units' forms, of a higher education institution, assume the development of complex order thinking. For that, and because of the huge number of curricular units, text mining tools were used, to interpret the explicit intentionality for sustainability awareness in the students.

9.4 Methodology

The study presented in the article assumes an exploratory approach that intends to verify the sign of intentional development of sustainability awareness in three dimensions: the curricula of a higher education institution programs, both as specific and as transversal competence, the scientific production and the infrastructures. This was performed through the analysis of the curricular units' content, complemented with the analysis of the content of the scientific repository in the institution and the projects that contribute to energy efficiency and waste management in the infrastructure management.

It was performed in a Portuguese public higher education institution with 1st and 2nd cycle programs in a wide area of knowledge and technology. It is a medium to high size institution, with over 7000 students and 500 teachers, representing a diverse environment of subjects, scientific areas and pedagogical methodologies. In total, the educational offer includes 43 degrees and 38 masters, grouped in seven areas:

- Arts, communication and multimedia (6 degrees +0 master programs),
- Agriculture sciences and natural resources (4 degrees +4 master programs),

- Education and teacher training (3 degrees +8 master programs),
- Business sciences and law (8 degrees +7 master programs),
- Health and social protection (7 degrees +9 master programs),
- Technologies (13 degrees +9 master programs),
- Tourism, sports and leisure (2 degrees +1 master programs).

We started by collecting all the curricular units' forms (CUFs) in a single relational database, to simplify the access, analysis and correlation of information. We then pre-processed the information, by removing repeated forms, building a dictionary of terms, eliminating irrelevant words and minimizing the number of different words, through reduction of inflectional form of the words. The content of the scientific repository was also accessed through automatic procedures, using the Application Programming Application exported by the platform.

After this initial step, we performed a histogram of unigrams (terms composed of a single word) and bigrams (terms with two consecutive words). Then, a comparative relevance analysis was made, through the Term Frequency/Inverse Document Frequency (TF-IDF) numerical statistic index (Paik 2013), in both the teaching-learning methodologies and in the learning outcomes fields, to assess the most frequent terms and the most relevant terms for each area. Based on these terms, we proceeded to check for the existence of specific terms that are associated to sustainability categories, such as "environment", "social" and "economic", with the context in which they appear (the previous and the following words). The definition of terms was performed with the terms collected in the literature, in particular the reports of the United Nations and others (Buckler et al. 2014; Emanuel et al. 2011; Lartey 2015; Lotz-Sisitka 2014; United Nations 2012, 2015; World Commission on Environment and Development 1987). The terms were grouped according to the sustainability sphere they belong to (Table 9.1).

Concerning the teaching-learning methodologies, we did an analysis of the most frequent methodologies per scientific area. This allowed us to verify if there are differences in the methodologies and if this contributes to the sustainability awareness of the teaching-learning process. Due to number of different CUFs and the huge amount of text to process, we used text mining techniques and the Apache UIMA framework.

9.4.1   Text Mining

The way we work and live has been shaped by the advances of technology and, with it, by the ubiquity of data. We carry, with us, devices that are constantly used to produce data, when we take a photograph, write a message, post in a social network, and consume data. The omnipresent devices make it easy to save things previously discarded. Our decisions, holiday pictures, documents, supermarket choices, walking tours are all registered and uploaded for future reference to the huge information

Table 9.1 List of terms associated to each sustainability sphere

Environment	Social	Economic
green	self-investment	economic
clean	culture	growth
carbon	ethics	viability
energy	equality	regional
environmental	equity	asymmetries
water	social	financial
food	responsibility	money
forest	generation	employment
sustainability	future	business
climate	human	salary
natural	justice	bank
resources	population	accounting
biodiversity	poverty	market
warming	desertification	stock
pollution	consumption	management
recycle	development	industry
reuse	well-being	development
nature	innovation	trade
renewal	creativity	investment
	initiative	

Source: Authors

repository in clouds everywhere. The generation of data is growing much faster than our capacity to understand it.

Text is a particular format of data. Text organizes letters in words and words in phrases, conveying information that can be stored, transmitted and read. Huge amounts of text can be difficult to interpret and understand. In this context, patterns can also arise from the analysis of text, through the use of similar tools and algorithms. These involve information retrieval, lexical analysis, pattern recognition, tagging, natural language processing and many others. Just like with generic data, text mining allows highlighting useful information in huge amounts of text.

In the simplest form, text mining depends on determining the vocabulary of terms. Text is split in tokens, eventually dropping symbols, accentuation or other characters. Moreover, some extremely common words may be of little value and can also be excluded from the analysis (stop words removal). After extracting the relevant tokens, they can be normalized, through the substitution of different words by a common term (for example, normalizing the words John and JOHN to john or car and automobile to car).

Finally, words can also be replaced by a base form, to reduce the diversity but maintaining their meaning. As an example, verb tenses can be replaced by the infinitive form (replacing am, was, is by be, for example) or removing the ends of words (replacing different and differentiation by differ, for example).

9.4.2 Curricular Units

Higher education degrees are defined around a specific study plan, describing the curricular units (CUs) and all the associated details. The CUs are structured in scientific areas that contribute, in a given percentage, to the study plan. Usually, the most representative scientific area is also the main program area. For example, an informatics degree can have 7 areas, such as automation and robotics (4%), computer engineering (35%), computing sciences (25%), information systems (10%), mathematics (20%), physics (3%) and signal processing (3%).

The structure and purpose of the CUs are described in a specific form, the curricular unit form (CUF), which contains the identification of the unit (name, degree, year of study, field of study, lecturers' name, and others) and the details of the learning process (learning outcomes, contents, teaching and learning methods, assessment methodology and bibliography). The CUF is of the responsibility of the lecturer and is scientifically reviewed by the department director and regulated by the program director. The later focus, specially, in the teaching and learning methods, the content and the assessment methodology. The CUFs are finally reviewed by the pedagogical council president and the faculty director. This process ensures the articulation between the horizontal and vertical subjects on the scientific and pedagogical aspects of students training, as well as enforcing the institution's policies.

The institution has a total of 3302 curricular units in the 43 degrees and 38 master programs. All the CUFs are available online, in the ECTS guide web site (http://www.ipb.pt/go/d770), in PDF format. The web site is structured in a hierarchy, starting with the cycle of study (degree or master), followed by the list of programs and, finally, the list of CUs in each program. In the analysis, we only considered higher education study cycles (bachelor and master). The forms were retrieved and the information was stored in a relational database, to provide more flexibility and speed in the analysis process. The fields were stored in a single table, with 21 columns (Table 9.2).

The CU information was pre-processed and indexed and duplicate rows removed, to reduce the bias. After removal, 1556 CUFs remained: arts, communication and multimedia (165), agrarian sciences and natural resources (151), education and teacher training (172), business sciences and law (217), health and social protection (300), technologies (482) and tourism, sports and leisure (69).

The fields RESULTADOS_APRENDIZAGEM, and METODOS_ENSINO where processed according to the following workflow:

1. The text was split into sentences and, within each sentence, into tokens (words)
2. Words were removed according to the following stop list: a, an, and, are, as, at, be, but, by, for, if, in, into, is, it, no, not, of, on, or, such, that, the, their, then, there, these, they, this, to, was, will, with
3. Words were changed, to reduce the inflectional forms, using the Porter Stemming Algorithm (Porter 1997)
4. Two word sets (bi-grams) were built and their frequency assessed

Table 9.2 Structure of the database holding the curricular units forms

Column name	Description
COD_ESCOLA	the code of the school
COD_CURSO	the code of the program
N_PLANO	the code of the program revision
N_DISCIPLINA	the code of the subject
N_OPCAO	flag to check if the subject is optional
CONTEUDO_ID	the code of the content
SUB_CONTUDO_NUM	the code of the content details
ANO_LECT	the year of study
ANO_CURRICULAR	the curricular year
ESCOLA	the name of the school
AREA_CIENT	the scientific area
UNIDADE_CURRICULAR	the name of the curricular unit
OPCAO	the name of the option
CICLO	the degree type (BSc, MSc)
CURSO	the name of the program
RAMO	in case of optional curricular path, the path's name
RESULTADOS_APREND	the learning outcomes
CONTEUDO_UC	the summary of the curricular unit content
METODOS_ENSINO	the teaching-learning methodologies
CONTEUDO_DETALHADO	the detailed content – main part
SUB_CONTEUDO_DETALHADO	the additional detailed content

Source: Authors

5. A list of words was built and their context extracted
6. The weight of sustainability sphere was measured in each scientific area

After the pre-processing, we started analyzing the text.

9.5   Analysis and Discussion

The three spheres of sustainability, economic, social and environmental, were analyzed in three dimensions: the teaching curricula, the scientific production and the policies and attitudes regarding the infrastructures. The first was based on the curricular units' forms textual content, that was processed using text mining to uncover patters about the way the higher education institution stimulate the development of sustainability awareness. The second dimension is related to the scientific production available in the institution's scientific repository. The analysis was performed on the abstract field of the metadata, through a similar technical approach. In the third dimension, the policies and attitudes relative to the infrastructures and energy consumption were assess through the projects that were implemented and that contributed to the improvement of the energy efficiency and better resource usage.

9.5.1   Teaching Curricula: Course Contents, Learning Outcomes, Teaching and Learning Methodologies

In higher education, the development of sustainability awareness includes both the programs' content and the teaching and learning methodologies, necessary to develop relational, communication and problem solving skills, as well as critical and self-critical abilities, appreciation of diversity and multiculturalism, and ethical commitment towards the others (Mesquita et al. 2016). It is well known that, active methodologies, such as role playing, cooperative workgroup, project-based learning, experiential-based learning, critical discussion, brainstorming, or case-study discussion, among others, stimulate the participation of students, contributing to develop the skills essential to foster social commitment and sustainability awareness.

Based in this, we analyzed the teaching and learning methodologies field of the CUF (METODOS_ENSINO) by first calculating the frequency of stems (reduction to the root form) to assess the main teaching-learning methodologies in each area. These were used to build the table of the most important words in each area and they were sorted descending with the TF-IDF value (Table 9.3). As explained above, this approach highlight the words that are most frequent in each area are rare in the other areas. For example, words such as articles (a, an, the, …) or prepositions (on, at, in, …) are very frequent in all areas, so they are not valued by the TF-IDF measure. On the other hand, specific and specialized words have higher value, thus a higher importance. For example, words such as sport or tourism are highly valued in the tourism, sports and leisure area.

The words used by the teachers in each teaching and learning methodology values the specific and technical component of the curricular unit. For example, sport, matlab, learner, repertoire, irrig or pharmacolog are terms used in the areas that reveal specific subjects or tools. There are some exceptions, such as real-life, learn that reveal some concern with the methodology in addition to the content.

With the full words (without any form of reduction), we built a heat map of the normalized term frequency to the scientific area, to identify possible patterns (Fig. 9.3). We selected the 35 more-frequent combination of words to analyze their distribution through the areas.

Among the listed 35 teaching and learning methodologies, most of them reflect demonstrative and theoretical-practical methodologies, traditionally used in higher education for the students to learn the content. Some active methodologies are also used, although it is not possible to assess if their mention in the CUF is reflected into teaching practices. This idea is further clarified below, in the analysis of the learning outcomes.

The scientific area of the Technologies, since it has more programs and, consequently, more curricular units (482), show more diversity of teaching-learning methodologies. It also shows more expression of practical classes and theoretical classes/concepts. This is expected, since HEI still follow the traditional, academic, model of teaching (Mesquita et al. 2014). Considering all areas, the most common

Table 9.3 Most important words in the teaching and learning field of each area

Business sciences and law	Tourism, sports and leisure	Technologies	Education and teacher training	Arts, communication and multimedia	Agrarian sciences and natural res.	Health and social protection
real-lif	sport	non-presenti	learner	audit	irrig	pharmacolog
onli	galileo	receiv	traine	sound	livestock	imag
doing	tourism	ongo	cycl	repertoir	speci	dietitian
learn	text/scientif	matlab	theoretical/illustr	music	would	patient
legal	common	mathemat	stream	piec	feed	adequaci
incorpor	submiss	non-presenci	1st	percept	farm	clinic
version	equal	engin	day-to-day	psycholog	plant	consult
problem/cas	hotel	preferenti	item	composit	close	nurs
none	free	learnig	expository-interrog	prioriti	live	versus
thesis/project/ internship	evolut	teacher-ori	partial	advis	nutrient	pharmacodynam

Source: Authors

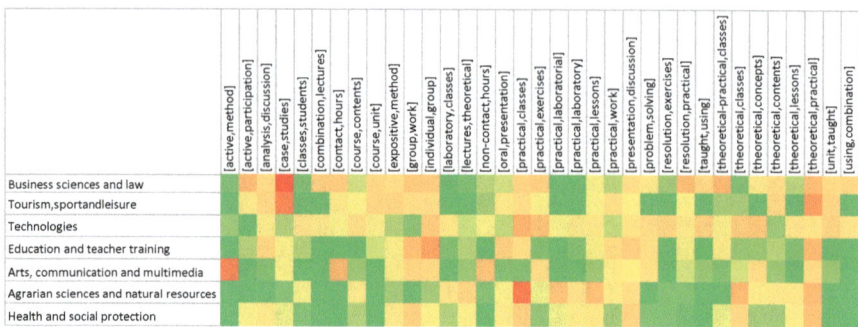

Fig. 9.3 Heat map of the scientific area to the most common bigrams (colder colors mean less evidence and warmer colors mean more evidence). (*Source:* Authors)

methodology refers to theoretical-practical classes, which is usually based on exercises and demonstrative strategies. It is interesting to realize that programs from the business sciences and tourism (with a considerable weight of the business sciences area) refer case studies as pedagogical strategy. In addition, the scientific area of the arts, communication and multimedia value active methodologies.

Learning outcomes specify what learners will be able to do as a result of a learning activity. The statement should contain three elements, describing who is to perform, what action they are to take and the result that must come from their action. Learning outcomes should also refer to an observable and measurable performance, so action verbs are used to describe what students should be able to do at the end of the session, course or degree program (Mesquita et al. 2016).

Considering that the learning process is based on growing complexity levels, from the simplest to the most complex knowledge and activities, it is supposed that, in higher education, the learning outcomes reflect the most complex level. This means that it is necessary to know a specific subject to understand it and apply it. Higher education should contribute to the development of deeper knowledge and ways to understand it, through the stimulation of the capacity to analyze, synthetize and evaluate all the developed knowledge. However, to create awareness, it is important that students make use of higher-order thinking skills, that result from the reflection and discussion of subjects, the design and implementation of projects, problem solving with creativity, or the questioning to generate new ideas.

According to this, it is expected to see action verbs to appear in this field, such as understand, know, use, and others (Table 9.4). The analysis of this field was initially performed by counting the whole words (first two columns), the stem (second two columns) and associated word (last two columns).

The context of the verb is more easily understood in the last columns. [understand, importance], [knowledge, about], [know, how] specifies clearly what the students should demonstrate. However, it is still common to see terms such as [basic, concepts], [oral, written] and others, that are not easily assessed.

Regarding the data, the most frequent verbs refer to basic knowledge, in the domain of the know and apply. This may suggest that the professional profile to be

Table 9.4 Frequency of words, stems and bi-grams in all the curricular units' forms

Word	Count	Stem	Count	Bi-gram	Count
Understand	2204	understand	3562	[basic, concepts]	203
different	1466	know	2234	[understand, importance]	180
Know	1257	use	2129	[knowledge, about]	164
knowledge	1193	develop	1696	[different, types]	159
Identify	1079	differ	1588	[know, how]	147
understand	927	identifi	1556	[most, common]	139
concepts	861	appli	1478	[know, main]	137
management	805	process	1266	[understand, basic]	124
use	770	knowledg	1244	[apply, knowledge]	122
main	760	system	1191	[recognize, importance]	113
importance	757	concept	1128	[know, understand]	112
apply	734	manag	1101	[acquire, knowledge]	107
know	716	educ	1025	[understand, apply]	92
problems	713	relat	988	[identify, main]	92
its	713	import	854	[know, different]	90
basic	712	problem	843	[teaching, learning]	87
systems	709	basic	807	[oral, written]	84
development	699	organ	799	[understand, role]	83
techniques	679	main	769	[environmental, education]	80
methods	622	interpret	767	[know, apply]	79

Source: Authors

developed in all areas is technical and specialized. There is no evidence that there is a concern with the development of higher-order thinking skills that would be valuable for the sustainability awareness.

If we relate this results with the analysis of the teaching and learning methodologies, it is possible to understand that using active methodologies may not be meaningful to the development of higher-order thinking skills, but to a learning process of academic and curricular knowledge related to the specific study areas instead. In this sense, the strategies may not contribute for the development of metacognitive skills, because they are used only as a content learning method and not an integrative process that connects the purposes, the means and the ends.

Each area is characterized by a scientific affinity between subjects. In information retrieval and text mining, the TF-IDF weighting factor measures the importance of a word in a document in relation to a collection of documents or a corpus. To minimize the word diversity, the stem form was used, allowing different suffixes to be attached (Table 9.5).

The most important words for each class are, almost exclusively, directly related to the main scientific area. For example, tax, budgetary, sale, and others are common in the business sciences and law and rare in the other areas. Tourist, destin, hotel stems are common in the tourism, sport and leisure area. Technologies use theorem, thermodynam, surface, robot, and education and teacher training value diversifi, teacher, physical-motor or planet. Arts, communication and multimedia

Table 9.5 Most important words by area

Business sciences and law	Tourism, sport and leisure	Technologies	Education and teacher training	Arts, communication and multimd.	Agr. sciences and natural res.	Health and social protection
tax	tourist	theorem	diversifi	music	forest	dietet
budgetari	destin	thermodynam	teacher	camera	veterinari	nurs
taxat	hotel	surfac	physical-motor	blender	farm	gerontolog
sale	chines	robot	planet	paint	aromat	psychotherapeut
corpor	tourism	ordinari	school	orff	crop	sexual
insur	sport	reactor	literari	video	breed	pharmaci
credit	itinerari	polym	classroom	print	orchard	therapi
bank	upper-intermedi	kinemat	preschool	semiot	exot	dietitian
auditor	galileo	momentum	didact	discov	irrig	epidemiologist
expenditur	tour	elast	pre-school	shot	forestri	geriatr
logist	entertain	reinforc	music	adob	weak	dosag
municip	travel	thermal	intergener	graphic	veget	pathophysiolog
international/glob	accommod	discret	phonet	repertoir	milk	pregnant
despit	racket	wastewat	substanti	western	cultivar	dietari
fiscal	volleybal	optimum	childhood	expand	tree	elder
hedg	handbal	hydraul	socio-educ	theatr	soil	epidemiolog
rem	attract	static	subtitl	utensil	oil	therapeut

Source: Authors

Table 9.6 Context of the sustainability associated terms

Business sciences and law	[human, resources, management][work, environment][common, population, parameters]
Tourism, sports and leisure	[short, social, relationships][chinese, culture, contemporary] [techniques, human, resource]
Technologies	[common, population, parameters][work, energy, conservation] [mechanical, energy, impulse]
Education and teacher training	[professional, development, ongoing][importance, biodiversity, our][quantitative, nature, develop]
Arts, communication and multimedia	[historical, social, economic][social, economic, cultural][urban, culture]
Agrarian sciences and natural resources	[analyze, economic, financial][techniques, food, reproductive] [plant, development]
Health and social protection	[chemical, energy, reducing][professional, development, various][transformation, energy, carbohydrates]

Source: Authors

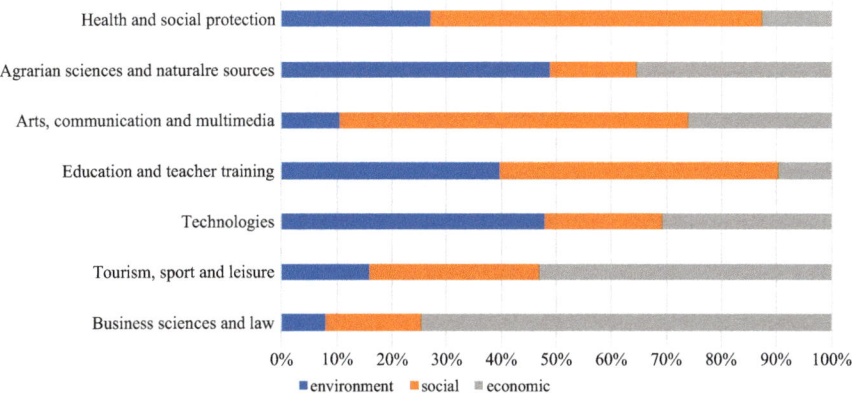

Fig. 9.4 Weight of sustainability spheres in the learning outcomes of each area. (*Source:* Authors)

rely on specific tools and techniques such as music, camera, blender or paint, and agrarian sciences and natural resources refer forest, veterinari, farm, aromat or crop. Finally, the health and social protection refer dietet, nurs, gerontolog or psychotherapeut.

Using the word set from Table 9.1, which define some terms associated with the three spheres of sustainability, we scanned the learning outcomes field for their existence and the context they appear in. It is interesting to see that the context reveal that the words are used for referencing resources and approaches related to the specific area (Table 9.6). In other words, each area is specific and contained, without integrating transversal issues.

Counting the frequency of words in each area, it is possible to get a chart of sphere distribution per area (Fig. 9.4). The expression of each sphere is logically associated to the area. Health and social protection have a larger percentage of the

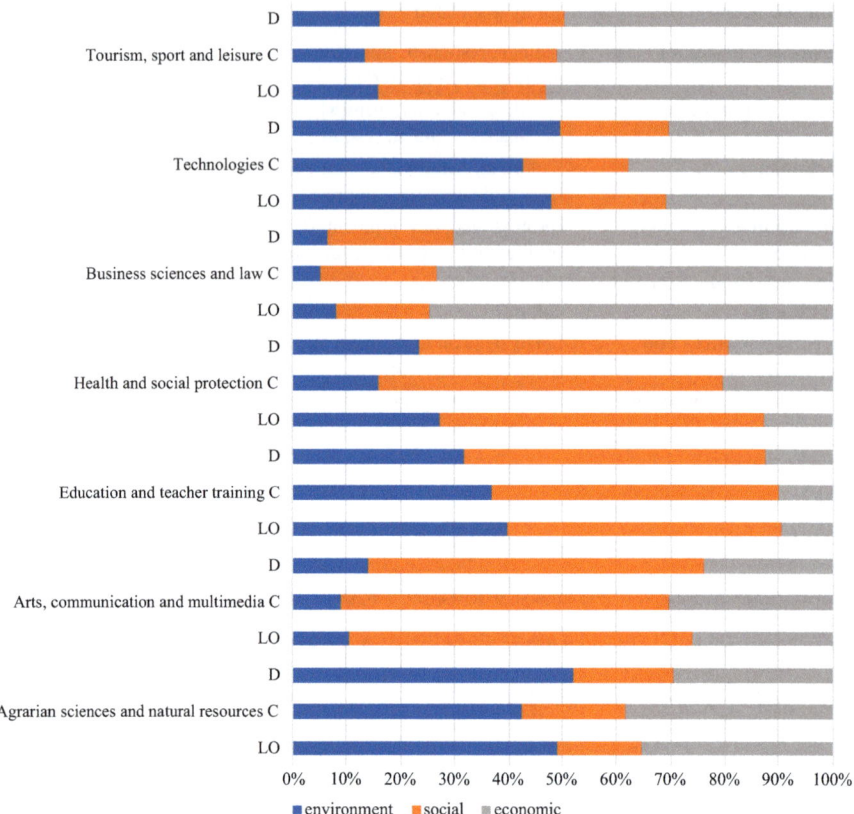

Fig. 9.5 Weight of sustainability spheres in the learning outcomes (LO), content (C) and detailed content (D) of each area. (*Source:* Authors)

social sphere, followed by environmental and, finally, economic. Agrarian sciences and natural resources value the environmental and economic spheres, and the arts, communication and multimedia have a larger percentage of the social sphere. Education and teacher training balances the environmental and social component, with the technologies area demonstrating more weight of the environmental and economic. Finally, tourism, sport and leisure have a larger component of the economic, and business sciences and law have almost 75% of the weight in the economic sphere.

Following a similar approach for the content and detailed content of the CUFs, the weight of each sphere does not change much (Fig. 9.5). Regardless of the field of the CUF, the economic, social and environmental weight in each area is similar and consistent.

These results show that there is a concern with sustainability within the expertize of each area. This means that the environment sphere is more evident in related areas, such as agrarian sciences and natural resources and technologies, because of the association with energy efficiency and usage. The social sphere is strongly observed in the areas of arts, communication and multimedia, education and teacher training and health and social protection. Finally, the economic sphere appears with higher relevance, in the business sciences and law and in the tourism, sports and leisure areas.

9.5.2   Research: Social, Technological and Environmental Innovation

Beyond the teaching curriculum, sustainability awareness is also developed through the research results, and activities and attitudes before the infrastructure, such as buildings and energy consumption (Fig. 9.2). The first is available in scientific repositories, where institutions keep the students, teachers and researchers' scientific production. The items are structured in communities and collections, and include projects, articles, thesis and documents of cultural expression and dissemination. In the context of this work, we analyzed the content of 10,350 documents retrieved from the scientific repository.

Each document is characterized by metadata, which includes the authors, title, date and abstract, among others. The documents were sorted and grouped according to scientific affinity in seven areas, as above. The abstract field was analyzed using the same methodology as above and the weight of each sustainability sphere was measured according to the word set already defined (Fig. 9.6).

The data does not allow assessing the impact of the scientific results and products on the economy and on the community well-being. However, it provides a measure of the specificity of subjects. This is closely related to the dynamics of the teaching and research staff. Although the distribution closely resembles the teaching curricula in each area, there are some differences, particularly in the tourism, sports and leisure, revealing a larger social component.

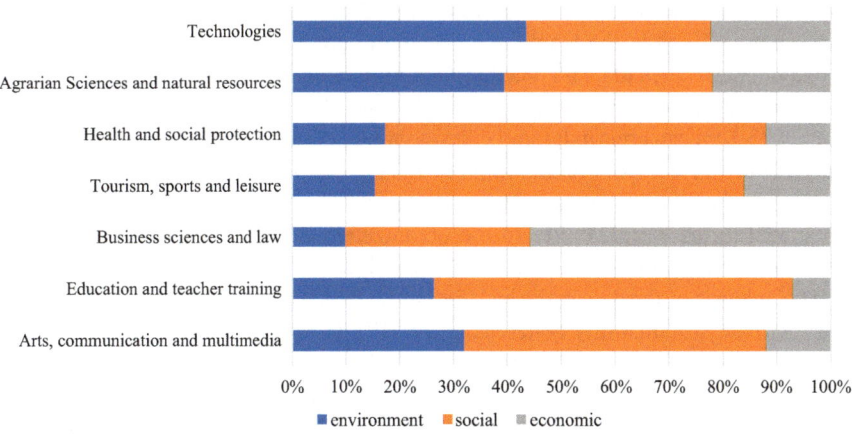

Fig. 9.6 Weight of sustainability spheres in the scientific production. (*Source:* Authors)

9.5.3   Infrastructure: Energy Efficiency and Waste Management

In relation to the infrastructures, in which we include the energy efficiency and waste management, there has been several projects and initiatives such as the Diversidad Bioconstructiva Transfronteriza, Edificación Bioclimática y su adaptación a la Arquitectura y Urbanismo Moderno (BIOURB), financed by the POCTEP (2007–2013), which made possible to update the buildings with better materials and better isolation, contributing to reduce the energy consumption. Another example is the project Acción integrada para la promoción e implantación de eficiencia energética y energías renovables como factor de competitividad (PROBIOENER), which allowed to install renewal energy production in the campus, based on solar panels (for electricity and water heating), wind generators and hydric. Another project provided financing for further optimizing the buildings, financed by the Portuguese government (Despacho n.° 11261-A/2009). In addition, the institution has been investing in temperature sensor and actuators that provide an up to date and rigorous control on the temperature and energy consumption. Moreover, almost all the administrative procedures are based on online tools and platforms, such as student academic records and requests, classifications, e-learning and assessment, and others, contributing to reduce the paper and other consumables consumption.

The implementation of this kind of initiatives has an indirect impact on the community, fostering discussion and reflection on the benefits of the respect by the natural resources and the others.

9.6   Conclusions

The main considerations of this study are related to the strategies assumed by higher education institutions for the development of sustainability awareness in three dimensions. The first, the teaching curriculum, allow us understand how the program, courses curricula and teaching-learning methodologies contribute to the development of sustainability awareness. Second, the research by students, teacher and researchers can contribute to the development of new ideas or new ways of acting that may have impact on the improvement of the well-being and quality of life of the population and the respect by the environment. Third, the infrastructures, associated to the sustainability of the organization in terms of energy efficiency, resources consumption and the articulation with the local communities.

The analysis of the data resulting from these dimensions allows us to understand that there are sustainability concerns in the HEI. However, the results reveal compartmentalized teaching actions. The holistic perspective required by the concept of sustainability adopted in this study is still far from being achieved.

The CUF analysis reveal that there is no balance between the three sustainability spheres (economic, social, environmental) in any area, although all of them include contents related to sustainability development. The development of sustainability awareness, as a metacognitive process, that allows the student to become aware of himself and of his relation with the social and environmental mean that surrounds him, also seems to be a future challenge. This conclusion comes from the analysis of the professional profiles described in the learning outcomes, whose verbs highlight the technical and specialized component to the detriment of the training transversality that incorporates the technician and the person as a social agent.

The scientific production is focused on specific issues; thus, it is expected that there is an unbalance between the economic, social and environmental spheres. The main contribution of this activity is the impact in the optimization of processes, product innovation and development, cultural and knowledge dissemination, which can all have a positive impact in the population's well-being and in the social and economic development. In this study, this impact was not possible to assess. However, it should be relevant further studies, of qualitative nature, that may emerge, from the scientific production and other sources of data (focus group, interviews, questionnaires, …) that stresses the impact of that research on the way of living of the community, well-being of people and on the environment.

Regarding the infrastructure sustainability, the institution has been adopting policies and projects that contribute to energy efficiency and building optimization. This has been indirectly contributing to make people aware of the importance and respect by the resources consumption.

This study suggests that it is still a challenge the promotion of actions, policies and strategies that enable a holistic approach of sustainability. Teaching curricula, regardless of the program, should provide an integrative perspective of the professional profile, the person and the society needs, within an ethical compromise. For that, it is important to adopt practices that foster the development of higher-order thinking. In relation to the research, it is important that this aspect is promoted and disseminated, contributing to social innovation, as a new solution for the social challenges that have the intent and effect of equity, justice and empowerment. The sustainability of higher education institutions is also associated to the well-being of the students and staff, with a rational use of resources and energy consumption.

References

Anderson, T., Curtis, A., & Wittig, C. (2014). *Definition and theory in social innovation*. Krems: Danube University. Retrieved from https://www.zsi.at/object/publication/3641/attach/ZSI_DP_33_2015.pdf

Buckler, C., Creech, H., & Unesco. (2014). *Shaping the future we want: UN decade of education for sustainable development (2005–2014): Final report*. Retrieved from http://unesdoc.unesco.org/images/0023/002301/230171e.pdf

Bureau of European Policy Advisers. (2011). *Empowering people, driving change: Social innovation in the European Union*. Luxembourg: Publications Office of the European Union.

Emanuel, W., Dickens, C., Hunter, J., & Dawson, M. E., Jr. (2011). Clarifying societies' need for understanding sustainable systems. *Journal of Applied Global Research, 2*(4), 29–39.

Franz, H.-W., Hochgerner, J., Howaldt, J., & Schindler-Daniels, A. (2011). *Vienna declaration: The most relevant topics in social innovation research.* Presented at the challenge social innovation, Vienna. Retrieved from http://www.net4society.eu/_media/Vienna-Declaration_final_10Nov2011.pdf

Freire, P. (1979). *Conscientização: Teoria e Prática da Libertação.* São Paulo: Cortez & Moraes.

Freire, P. (1981). *Educação e mudança.* Paz e Terra.

Johnston, A. (2010). *Higher education for sustainable development (HE4SD).* OECD, Europe.

Lartey, A. (2015). End hunger, achieve food security and improved nutrition and promote sustainable agriculture. *UN Chronicle, 51*(4), 6–8.

Lotz-Sisitka, H. (2014). *Conference report.* Presented at the world conference on education for sustainable development. Aichi-Nagoya: UNESCO. Retrieved from http://unesdoc.unesco.org/images/0023/002328/232888E.pdf

Mesquita, C., Lopes, R. P., García, J. Á., & Rama, M. d. l. C. d. R. (2014). Pedagogical innovation in higher education: Teachers' perceptions. In M. Peris-Ortiz, F. J. Garrigós-Simón, & I. Gil Pechuán (Eds.), *Innovation and teaching technologies* (pp. 51–60). Springer International Publishing. Retrieved from. https://doi.org/10.1007/978-3-319-04825-3_6.

Mesquita, C., Lopes, R. P., & Bredis, K. (2016). Entrepreneurship in higher education as a horizontal competence. In M. Peris-Ortiz, J. A. Gómez, F. Vélez-Torres, & C. Rueda-Armengot (Eds.), *Education tools for entrepreneurship* (pp. 223–241). Cham, Springer International Publishing. https://doi.org/10.1007/978-3-319-24657-4_17.

Murray, R., Caulier-Grice, J., & Mulgan, G. (2010). *The open book of social innovation.* National Endowment for Science, Technology and the Art London. Retrieved from http://kwasnicki.prawo.uni.wroc.pl/pliki/Social_Innovator_020310.pdf

Paik, J. H. (2013). A novel TF-IDF weighting scheme for effective ranking. In *Proceedings of the 36th international ACM SIGIR conference on research and development in information retrieval* (pp. 343–352). New York: ACM. https://doi.org/10.1145/2484028.2484070.

Porter, M. F. (1997). *An algorithm for suffix stripping* (pp. 313–316). San Francisco, CA, USA: Morgan Kaufmann.

TEPSIE. (2014). *Social innovation theory and research: A guide for researchers* (TEPSIE deliverable no. 1.4). Brussels: Seventh Framework Programme. Retrieved from http://www.tepsie.eu/images/documents/research_report_final_web.pdf

UNESCO. (2005). *United Nations decade of education for sustainable development (DESD): International implementation scheme* (No. ED/DESD/2005/PI/01). Paris: UNESCO.

United Nations. (2012). *The future we want.* United Nations. Retrieved from http://www.sd-network.eu/quarterly%20reports/report%20files/pdf/2012-June-The_Rio+20_Conference_2012.pdf

United Nations. (2015). *Transforming our world: The 2030 agenda for sustainable development* (17th sustainable development goals no. A/RES/70/1). United Nations. Retrieved from http://dept.sophia.ac.jp/econ/data/61-01.pdf

Wals, A. E. (2012). *Shaping the education of tomorrow: 2012 full-length report on the UN decade of education for sustainable development.* Unesco. Retrieved from http://library.wur.nl/WebQuery/wurpubs/fulltext/246667

World Commission on Environment and Development (Ed.). (1987). *Our common future.* Oxford, UK/New York: Oxford University Press.

Chapter 10
Corporate Universities as a New Paradigm and Source of Social Innovation, Sustainability, Technology and Education in the XXI Century

Antonio Alonso-Gonzalez, Marta Peris-Ortiz, and Lorena A. Palacios Chacon

Abstract In recent years, Corporate Universities have become a critical element in the development of human capital inside companies, institutions and organizations, promoting strategies based on knowledge management as an essential factor to achieve social innovation and sustainable competitive advantages aligned with the strategy. Therefore it is essential for these institutions to reach the highest levels of efficiency and excellence in company processes and structures and to achieve planned corporate goals and objectives. In this work an extensive and thorough review of the current literature was carried out in relation to the concept, in order to analyse the latest trends in Corporate Universities. A comparative evaluation with traditional university aspects was performed, identifying their own differentiators, for example the impact on social innovation, the development of sustainable competitive advantages, the influence on the company's internal environment, the importance of cultural and technological factors, and the relationship with the organizations strategy, which are important factors in its successful development and interconnection within the company processes. The information obtained from the aforementioned literature review, in combination with the experience gained by the team of consultants and researchers at the PRIME Business School, Sergio Arboleda University, Bogota, Colombia, allowed to present proposed in general terms a new implementation model of Corporate University. This new model is based on five distinct phases, and with minor adaptations could be to any sector in an organization.

A. Alonso-Gonzalez (✉)
EIAM—PRIME Business School, Universidad Sergio Arboleda, Bogotá, Colombia
e-mail: antonio.alonso@usa.edu.co

M. Peris-Ortiz
Departamento de Organización de Empresas, Universitat Politècnica de Valencia, Valencia, Spain
e-mail: mperis@doe.upv.es

L. A. Palacios Chacon
Escuela de Negocios, Universidad del Norte, Barranquilla, Colombia
e-mail: lorenapalacios@uninorte.edu.co

© Springer International Publishing AG, part of Springer Nature 2018
M. Peris-Ortiz et al. (eds.), *Strategies and Best Practices in Social Innovation*,
https://doi.org/10.1007/978-3-319-89857-5_10

153

The study shows that through this Corporate University model, an organization could gain differentiators to increase social innovation, in time gain sustainable competitive advantages, and a desirable alignment with the objectives and strategic goals of the organization.

Keywords Dynamic capabilities · Human capital · Innovation · Knowledge management · Social innovation · Sustainable development

10.1 Introduction

Economic development in any society is defined by the study of the different structures and their interrelationships: institutions, technology, population and ideology, able to improve economic performance if the process of economic growth is understood, which varies from economy to economy (North 1981, 2005). In this context, it is important to emphasize the links between the economic development and different discoveries, inventions, innovations and technological developments, that made possible qualitative and quantitative changes in the progress of the different societies (Nasar 2011). From this wide range of mentioned structures, the present study aims to focus on the role that Corporate Universities are developing from the point of view of social innovation, sustainability, technology and education, strengthening further studies that have been initiated in this field, by Alonso-Gonzalez et al. (2017).

Since the origins of the term in the middle of the last century, the Corporate University concept has evolved, conditioned by new demands of an increasingly dynamic and changing market, a rising flexibility required in our current globalized world and newly available technologies that changed the focus, scope and growth horizons of any company. In recent years, Corporate Universities have become a critical element in the development of the human capital among the organizations, promoting strategies based on knowledge management as a crucial differentiator to achieve sustainable competitive advantages and help companies to achieve their corporate goals and objectives over time.

In the first part of this paper, an extensive and broad analysis of the literature relating to the concept of Corporate University was conducted in order to determine the current conditions of greater relevance in the implementation and development of this process on existing organizations, focusing primarily on factors related to educational and teaching systems, technological application tools and dissemination of knowledge techniques, and new developments and innovations observed in the field of corporate management knowledge, based on Corporate Universities.

The second part of this document proposes a new model of development and implementation of Corporate University that can be applied to any company, focusing on five fundamental and distinct phases. The first one, called Initial Diagnosis, establishes the foundations for the project, proposing a thorough analysis in order to understand and assimilate the strategy of the organization, its strategical business units, strategic assets and hidden assets, current situation in training and pedagogical methodologies, testing the expectations of internal customers and audiences in relation to the project. In the second phase, called Educational Programs Development, it is necessary to establish the procedures to identify, canalize and formalize information needs for each of the existing roles, families and subfamilies, as well as the integration of this information in the construction of the curricula, that makes up the various training programs, these structures are built under a rigid, modular or flexible curriculum model. The third phase, called Generation of Processes and Structure, serves to raise the strategy that will take place for the Corporate University, according to the information obtained in the first and second phases, in order to build a governance structure, process mapping and governing policies documents and procedures for a proper operation, as well as the training structure and the different schools which form part of the Corporate University. The fourth phase corresponds to the Development and Implementation of LMS (Learning Management System), which corresponds to the integration of all processes made in previous phases in the LMS technology, as an essential tool for the proper functioning and governance of the Corporate University. Finally, the fifth phase corresponds to the Awareness and Release stage, in which the project will be offered to an internal public, proceeding to raise awareness, curiosity and high expectations. However, from the beginning of the project, these initiatives and recommendations must be implemented.

The application of this new model of development and implementation of Corporate University has been successfully applied and validated on the ground by a team of consultants from PRIME Business School at Sergio Arboleda University, Bogota, Colombia, during several projects with well-known Colombian companies, for example Suramericana, Postobon and Terpel, as a way to achieve social innovation, sustainability, technology and education development within these companies.

10.2 Theoretical Background

10.2.1 Irruption of the Corporate University Term

Recognized authors in the area like Meister (1998) allow us to establish the source of Corporate University term, fixing it in 1955 with the release of General Electric's Crotonville, although its boom began to occur in late 80s. According to the author, the main motivation of these companies to implement this new Corporate University processes began with the lack of confidence in conventional Higher Education Institutions when training their staff and employees, developing internal tools to strengthen and gain control and ownership over the learning process and redirect them to the objectives and business strategies of the organization with a vision aimed at the market.

Over time, organizations saw the Corporate University concept not only as a tool to transmit internal knowledge, but also as a process to ensure a company's survival in the long term. Nowadays, large companies such as Sun Microsystems, First Union Corporation, General Motors, General Electric, Motorola, Xerox, Saturn, and the Bank of Montreal, are using Corporate Universities as an umbrella for effective cost management concerning the educational function of its employees, as a tool to achieve their strategic objectives and goals, and as a means to develop sustainable competitive advantages in time and inimitable by their competitors. In this line, Almeida and Levy (2011) explain that the organization must provide itself with the unique competences that result in competitive advantage, and one method to achieve this is through training of internal resources in a systematic and objective way. The same thought is defended by authors like Vizcaya-Piñeros and Uribe-Atehortua (2014), arguing that nowadays knowledge can be considered as a source of competitive advantage for an organization in the long term, and through strategies such as the Corporate University, that can be generated, incorporated and transferred within all levels of the organization, as a tool to leverage business objectives. Giulio (2011) emphasizes that Corporate University concretizes the central role assumed by core competences within the firm by catalyzing the demands for change, both exogenous and endogenous and thus supporting the firm in the pursuit of a sustainable competitive advantage.

10.2.2 From Traditional Universities to Corporate Universities

There are several open debates relating to the new paradigms opened in higher education curriculum reform that are highlighting the emergence of the Corporate University term and evaluating the insistence of business interests, relating to universities that are preparing workers by teaching transferrable skills instead of the disciplines (Progler 2010). In the words of Viltard (2013), the emergence of Corporate University concept could be explained from its origins understanding the overall context in which the traditional or classical university is developed, characterized by facts and advances of all kinds that the traditional university has not always incorporated, as well as other advances related to technology and the possibilities offered to an increasingly broad and avid public target. There are other disadvantages that traditional university have, for example, the influence of political power and the difficulty in connecting to the problems faced by the business environment, that have helped private organizations to implement non-traditional educational alternatives, as in the case of Corporate University.

According to Viltard (2014), the term of Corporate Training is a boundless reign. Business Schools of Traditional Universities, Traditional Corporate Training Departments, independent professors, specialists and Corporate Universities are offering programs to a vast community of busy professionals and company employees. From the origins of the term in the second half of the last century, the concept of Corporate University has constantly evolved, conditioned by the new demands of an increasingly dynamic and changing market competition, induced by the adoption of new technologies in our globalized world and consequently a change in focus, scope and horizons of growth within companies. It is clear that Corporate Universities are on the rise in developed countries and there is a clear value of these processes for corporations in the contemporary knowledge-driven economy (Li and Alagaraja 2007).

Traditional universities must rethink their traditional, organizational, philosophical and operational tenants to align more closely with real world needs, reaching out and inviting employers to be integral and equal partners in the educational process, particularly in aligning the curriculum that has practical, experiential and real world relevance for companies. The path of engagement must be reciprocal rather than the unidirectional model of the past, which always led to the university (Van Rooijen 2009). The innate differences between a university and corporation and the reality of continuous change requires an ability to quickly address opportunities and conflicts as they arise (Roth and Magee 2002).

Thus, it could be suggested that the Corporate University and traditional universities should focus on finding their points of contribution and meeting with the aim of developing the necessary skills and abilities that enable social development and sustained growth: traditional university in the development of theoretical and conceptual elements that are based on field research, useful for society and organizations, and Corporate University in practical applications that improve the specific skills of each individual. From the influences of globalization, these competencies and skills include, knowledge and experience concerning: strategy, marketing, adaptability, change management, multicultural sensitivity, ability to work in international teams, language skills, international finance, communication and international negotiations (Viltard 2013). Corporate Universities have adopted the language and rituals of traditional universities such as granting degrees, graduation ceremonies, registrar's offices, and course catalogs. The proliferation of nomenclature of academic learning will continue to be used by Corporate Universities as partnering continues (Wills 2001).

It is also interesting to highlight the words of Meister (1998) about the concept of university relating to its differentiation between the academic and corporate sense. While the classical or traditional university term is associated with ideas involving a physical campus, deans and faculties, the Corporate University version of the term is very different and innovative. In fact, many Corporate Universities lack a physical location, replacing it with an intangible learning process throughout every employee's career, increasing performance and production efficiency at work. It is also true, however, that some Corporate Universities have physical locations that could be identified as campus, but they do not use this infrastructure as a place of learning, but a global space sharing outstanding methods, developing skills in their employees at all levels when necessary, transmitting knowledge and core competencies to achieve excellence in their current work, or preparing employee's for the future requirements of new jobs that organization's will need to cover.

Complementing the last statements, and in reference to the collaboration between both entities, Allen (2002) defends that traditional or classical universities and

Corporate Universities may have some relationship or even a high degree of cooperation. This symbiosis between both entities could be understood if the author defines the four types of Corporate University: firstly dedicated entirely to training, secondly dedicated to training and executive education, thirdly homologate training for academic credits, and finally homologate training for official and formal qualifications. In the last two cases it is when a Corporate University should seek an alliance with a traditional university to build structures that allow validation of studies for its employees, corresponding to the official approval for credits or degrees. It is therefore a win-win relationship for both actors: the Corporate University receives a formalized training for its employees, which consequently leads to a higher level of motivation, and also take advantage of this intangible qualified resource. The traditional university will gain an important ally, which will not only generate economic resources through enrollment, but will also give direct feedback from current market requirements to enable more flexible learning methodologies and improve their educational portfolio.

10.2.3   Corporate University as a Core Process in the Organization

Almeida and Levy (2011) explains that companies are actually more aligned through their objectives and goals on creating and obtaining internal knowledge, giving special attention to the management of people and organizational development. Castellani (2009) argues that Corporate Universities do not include universities or business schools, being entities that are directly controlled by the companies which generated them and which only exist in the function of their own strategic aims.

The dilemma of how to maximize this impact in terms of results derived from the implementation of a Corporate University, can reside from the conception and development of the process in the company. Firstly, it is necessary to discuss the desirability of associating the Corporate University with the area of Human Resources, or to integrate it directly as a separate area, directly related to the management of the organization. In the words of Grenzer (2006), it is not so important where the process is located, the important issue is that Corporate University must be understood as an executive arm of a modern company's short, medium and long term strategy, and to achieve this, the process must fit perfectly within the company, be accepted within the culture of the organization, be seen as a tool that can have a direct positive effect on operating and management results, and improve efficiency in company leaders and decision makers. Following this line of thought, Alfaro-Guevara (2012) defends that there cannot be a successful Corporate University model, if there are no direct strategies to generate cultural changes, and encouraging members of organization to participate. Li and Alagaraja (2007) affirm that Corporate Universities are creating and facilitating a learning culture that will develop the capabilities of the organization and its employees.

At this moment, the question would be how the Corporate University could help companies to become more competitive entities and a source of social innovation, sustainability, technology and education within the company. Auvinet and Lloret (2015) concluded that the most successful organizations in implementing innovations are hybrid organizations, dedicated to the primary sector, focused on the middle and lower socioeconomic levels, and guided by resource generation such as grants, scholarships, and volunteer or intellectual capital, which initially makes the environment unattractive for competitors to establish themselves. However, in words of Sinha and Kaul (2013), every industry is concerned about the short life of their knowledge, causing them to constantly retool their schools, and therefore Corporate Universities have become a solution for this need as employees can learn job related tools and perform the assigned job better, obtaining skills and degrees which have added value, and making them more marketable and highly competitive. By fulfilling these needs in employees, Corporate Universities have become a growing segment of the adult education market, and organizations have an advantage in terms of retaining workforce and achieving their mission of developing programs which are in synch with the broad business strategy and designed to convey corporate culture. By integrating an action learning approach, Corporate Universities can meet the educational needs of employees which otherwise might not be available to them, or if available may be very expensive. It is important to highlight a study developed by Zolfo and Mann (2007), which sets out a recurring theme observed in the participants: the importance of gaining knowledge and how it could be applied to the organization, reflecting employees' responses on their commitment to the organizations and their enthusiasm for utilizing their education to benefit their companies.

However, it is not enough for an organization to build knowledge and add it to the processes and products to create value. It is necessary to manage this knowledge, transforming it into a collective product that is built, shared, updated and consolidated among its members, there exists two major pillars that play a definitive role in this process: a learning structure based on development and extension of formal knowledge, that is consolidated by what is known as a Corporate University, and the indispensable support of the information and communications technology, which becomes a basic component to achieve this management, by building virtual flexible learning tools, independent of time and place (Alfaro-Guevara 2012). Nikolov (2009) develops an analysis of his work, specifically the importance of Information and Communication Technologies, and Mallard and Eneau (2013) also explore this paradigm, namely the implication and influence of designers and trainers in learning methodologies.

Another important question that must be overcome is the common idea shared by some departments or areas of the company that consider Corporate University as a cost, not an investment. One way to deal with these wrong perceptions is to establish a close relationship with the various business units and provide them with added value in the form of knowledge management, training and learning methodologies, and other products and services brought by the Corporate University. This is vital for the employee, due to opportunities for professional development and career planning and information that could be made available to them. Roth and Magee (2002) argue that companies could benefit from different alliances through their access to the specialized knowledge of the faculty. It is too expensive for a corporation to hire or develop the depth of expertise that top research university have. Through alliances they can share costs through faculty members and support research in areas of specific interest to them. Research conducted in corporate settings provides fresh perspectives, demonstrates the application of new ideas and gives valuable feedback. Ryan (2013) also agrees with this idea of executive education partnerships and the opportunities of mutual benefit for universities and corporations.

Corporate Universities have become a central place for the host organizations to collect accumulated business knowledge, because of their centralized organizational expertise, and to maintain employees' motivation and to ensure the host organization's constant supply of human resources. These processes also serve as an employees' career development center in conjunction with the skill building and knowledge management functions (Wang et al. 2008). According to Li and Alagaraja (2007), Corporate Universities will continue to grow if they are able to demonstrate an added value in terms of promoting learning culture within the organization, providing effective cost solutions through partnerships, agreements and outsourcing, using available technologies to offer virtual solutions to employees, and supporting organizational strategies by developing innovative and competitive competencies for the organization.

10.3   Methodology

According to Vizcaya-Piñeros and Uribe-Atehortua (2014), there is no single or ideal model of Corporate University, since it responds to the particular needs of each organization and whose processes are developed to give continuity to the strategy. However, Corporate University processes must be seen as a living entity within the organization and should be considered as a sustainable strategy over time, so planning and development are key elements to generate this value and to achieve long-term competitive advantages. Prince and Beaver (2001) reason that a Corporate University charged with leading and managing knowledge and learning initiatives from an organization needs to be at the very heart of the enterprise and its decision making, and to be successful in strategic change it has to be proactive, innovative and professionally managed.

In respect of the implementation of a Corporate University process, Vizcaya-Piñeros and Uribe-Atehortua (2014) affirm that it must be preceded by a deep consideration of key elements such as: clear understanding of the organization's learning model, identification of skills and competencies to be developed in the short, medium and long term to generate competitive advantages in the organization, as well as the definition of the internally generated appropriate knowledge, that can be transferred immediately and the knowledge which is not available, must therefore be imported from external sources.

At Sergio Arboleda University, in PRIME Business School, its Applied Research and Consultancy areas have spent years conducting extensive and detailed reviews and intensive analysis of literature and case studies related to the concept of Corporate University, in order to determine the current conditions of greater relevance in the implementation and development of this process in existing organizations, focusing primarily on factors related to the innovations observed in fields of education, training and learning systems, technology applications and dissemination tools, new developments on intangible assets, and the corporate knowledge management based on the concept of Corporate University. This work has considerable potential to be applied to these new models of development and implementation of the Corporate University, specifically large Colombian companies that are aware of the importance of this new paradigm. A team of consultants at the PRIME Business School have achieved considerable success in several projects relating to important national companies, for example Suramericana, Postobon and Terpel.

10.4   Results

From the experience acquired by our consultants, and taking into account the extensive and thorough review of the current literature relating to this concept; a new model of development and implementation of the Corporate University in any company, regardless of industry, size and country of origin, has been proposed, focusing on five fundamental and distinct phases.

In the first stage, called Initial Diagnosis, the project basis is for the implementation of the Corporate University, by formulation and thorough analysis, accompanied by a necessary data collection, in order to understand and assimilate corporate fundamentals of the organization, strategic business units, strategic assets, hidden assets, current situation in terms of processes, methodologies and training tools, learning methodologies, testing and stablishing a consensus on expectations of internal customers and other public organizations interested in generating results from this project.

With reference to Fig. 10.1, in the Initial Diagnosis stage it is important to emphasize the dimension of data collection that must be done and the directly applied methodologies to obtain the necessary results. Among these methodologies, the most important are the surveys and focus groups that are applied to internal audiences, interviews and expert opinions, directed at more specific publics groups, and workshops designed to be performed by managers and executives of the company. All of these tools must be supported by an extensive collection of documentation and reports, in order to complement and validate research results, and orientate them to get information related to the fundamentals of the company, strategic alignment, infrastructure and processes, human resources characteristics, strategic and hidden assets, Information and Communication Technologies used in the company, and any aspects relating to the training and learning processes.

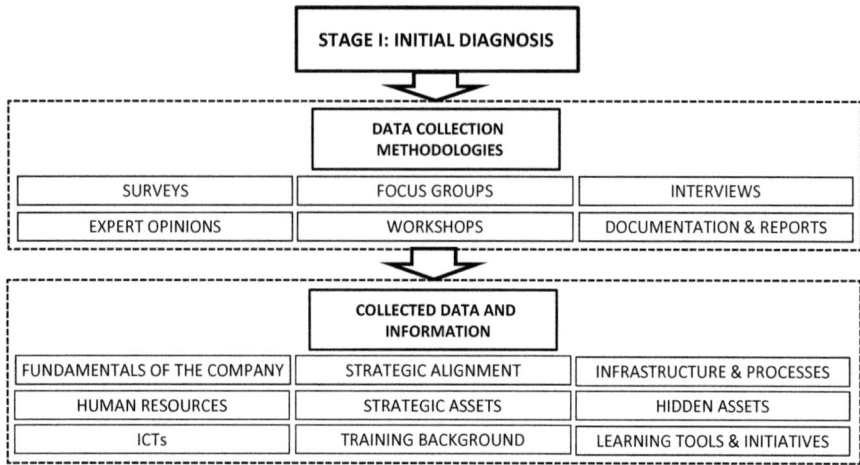

Fig. 10.1 Stage I Initial Diagnosis of the Corporate University. (*Source:* Compiled by authors)

In the second stage, called Educational Programs Development, the necessary procedures must be defined in order to identify, channel and formalize all training needs and the information for each of the functions, families and subfamilies of existing positions and roles in the organization. It is also necessary to integrate this data in the construction of curricula that constitutes the various training programs. It is important to highlight that all these structures could be built under a rigid or a flexible and modular scheme of these curricula.

As described in Fig. 10.2, in the second phase called Educational Programs Development, it is important to highlight the three different sub-phases identified: in the first one it is necessary to perform the role and position analysis, defining for each of the positions the area of school to which it belongs, the different families and subfamilies identified from the organization chart, and the learning needs required by all of these positions. Once this has been completed, the next step is the curricula development, involving the description of the target audiences, the ideal learning methodologies and knowledge transmission channels, and the internal and external resources that will be required in order to transfer this knowledge. Finally, the curricula implementation must be set, by defining the subjects that will be transversal for some or all of the described positions, stablishing the career planning that will be shown to employees, and the different indicator systems that will help to measure and monitor the impact of the system within the organization. It is important to achieve educational programs, methodologies and techniques which encourage the transmission of knowledge and contents of the curriculum, based on new skills and competences models, which primarily give the student concepts rather than contents, which are beneficial to enhance creativity and innovation skills within the company, in relation to the studies presented by Alonso-Gonzalez et al. (2016). Peris-Ortiz et al. (2017) also explain that appropriate environments could enhance the academic experience in reference to the educational methodology and techniques, thus explaining how education could work in the twenty-first century.

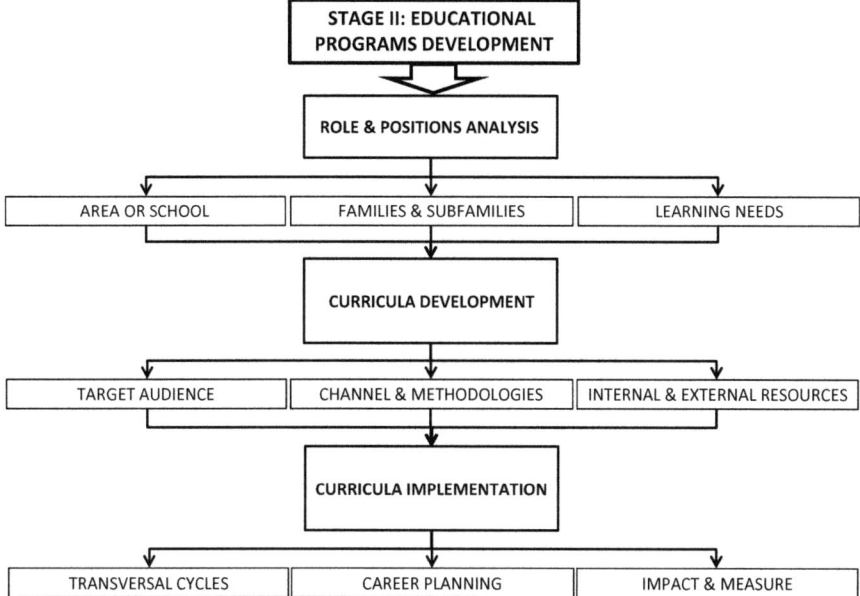

Fig. 10.2 Stage II Educational Programs Development of the Corporate University. (*Source:* Compiled by authors)

The third phase, called Generation of Processes and Structure, serves to raise the framework that will take place in the development of the Corporate University as a new process within the organization, in line with the information obtained in the first phase and in order to build its governance structure, draw the corresponding process mapping, develop regulations, documents and procedures necessary for efficient operation, and set the foundations for the division of the training areas and different schools or areas that will be part of this incipient Corporate University.

With reference to Fig. 10.3, in the Generation of Corporate University Processes and Structures stage, the Corporate University framework is established within the organization, defining the governance structures that will lead and dictate the designs originated from this area, in accordance with the board members strategic alignments of the company. This governance structure is supported by three main factors: infrastructure and personnel resources, necessary for the correct implementation and development of the project, the process planning which will describe all the interconnections and relations of the internal units and processes of the Corporate University, and the different areas or schools in which the university is divided. All of the above described aspects concerning this phase must be collected, organized and presented in a manual or document, where these units and connections between the different areas of the Corporate University are clearly identified and detailed, taking into account not to contradict external laws or internal regulations of the company.

Fig. 10.3 Stage III
Generation of Corporate
University Processes and
Structures. (*Source:*
Compiled by authors)

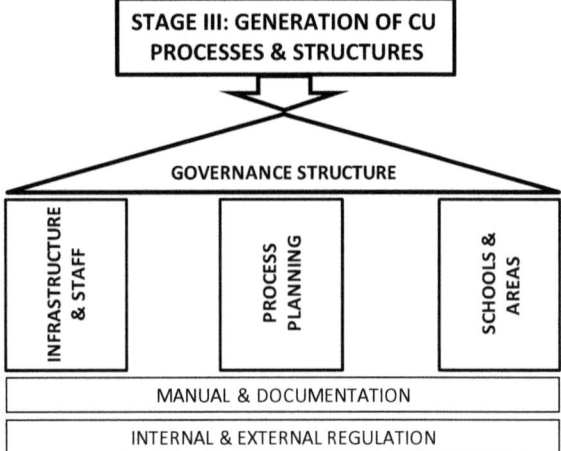

The fourth phase corresponds to the Development and Implementation of LMS (Learning Management System), and in this stage it is crucial to integrate all processes and structures developed in the previous phases described on the LMS software, this tool is an essential technological development for the correct functioning, interaction and governance of the Corporate University in the organization. In order to perform this, great care should be taken in respect of the different existing offers in the market and the convenience and additional services offered by the suppliers and providers, to finally select the proposal that best suits the needs of the Corporate University of the organization.

With reference to Fig. 10.4, the fourth stage is performed, namely the Development and Implementation of the Learning Management System – LMS, the most important thing to note at this point, is a strict and extensive process of selection, regarding the platform and software provider that will serve as an interactive tool for the employees of the organization, that will be under the umbrella of the Corporate University process. In this selection process, the first stage, you must collect the requirements and needs identified in stage I (Initial Diagnosis), II (Educational Programs Development) and III (Generation of Corporate University Processes and Structures), as well as consider any other factors that should be taken into account, in order to perfectly define the specifications that the system must fulfill in order to completely satisfy the expectations and demanding performance of services offered by the Corporate University. Another considerations that must be taken into account concerning the supplier's selection are referred to aspects inherent to the provider, (for example, its service and support capacity, warranty terms, or the business reputation, that could be checked by referrals or showing previous developments from other projects), and the specifications offered by the software itself (relating to the optimization possibilities, the cost of future tailor-made extensions, the budget available to invest in the LMS and the implementation deadlines offered by the provider to develop, implement and release the software of the project). The last issue to consider in this IV stage is the implementation of the LMS, there are some

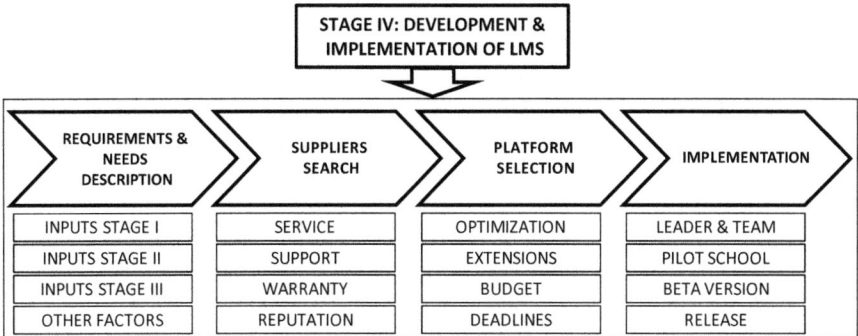

Fig. 10.4 Stage IV Development and implementation of the Learning Management System - LMS. (*Source:* Compiled by authors)

recommendations that should be followed, for example the designation of a leader and team responsible for this work, and starting the process with a pilot school and a beta version to test the system before the final release.

Finally, on the fifth phase, the Awareness and Release stage takes place, in which the project will be released and all internal audiences (and external, depending on the scope of the project) will be informed, providing its features and implications. This stage can be started in parallel with the previous ones mentioned above, to generate curiosity and high expectations among members of the organization. The company must therefore choose very carefully the channels and media that best suit its needs to expand this initiative and create a positive reaction, to deal with the change resistance phenomenon that is always present in the implementation of transversal projects.

The fifth stage is called Awareness and Release of the Corporate University and is shown in Fig. 10.5. It should be recommended an implementation in parallel with the four other phases described above, due to the importance of socializing in order to create awareness and notify the internal audiences of the company concerning the project, that is being developed and implemented, as ultimately the people in the organization will be the users and beneficiaries of the process. The most important tool in relation to this stage of awareness and release is the Communications Plan, namely a document that explains the strategy that will be used to socialize, inform and transmit the fundamentals of the project among the people in the company. As described in Fig. 10.5, this Communications Plans has different sub-steps that should fit within the four previous defined stages of the Corporate University development and implementation process. As mentioned in the project, an expectations campaign must be developed consisting of the issuance of messages and the collection of opinions from the various people within the company to have a bidirectional flow of communication in order to begin the process of raising awareness and advise them of the importance, scope and purpose of the project and how it will change training processes in the company. Once the second stage (Educational Programs Development) of the implementation process has started, it is important to define

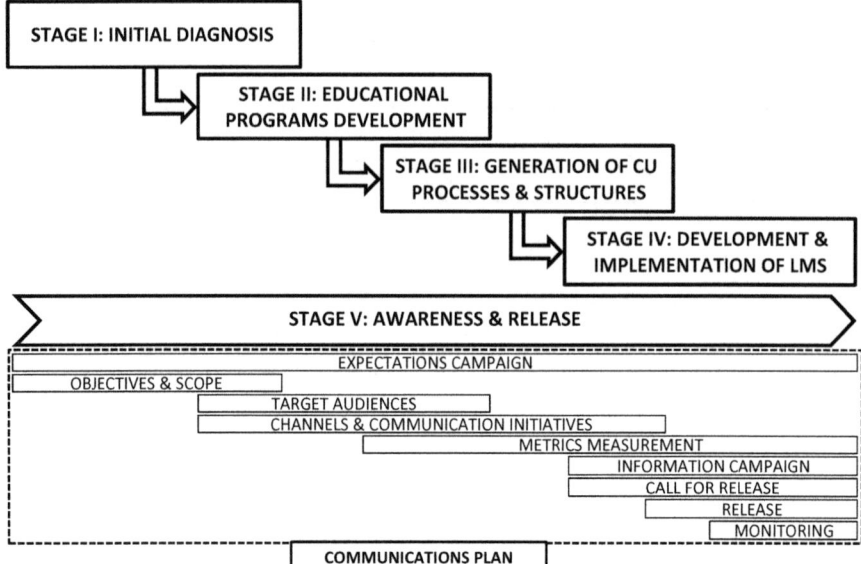

Fig. 10.5 Stage V Awareness and Release of the Corporate University. (*Source:* Compiled by authors)

the target audiences that should be suitable for selection in order to create a more effective and direct communication of the particularities of the project, implicitly the selection of the best channels of communication and specific initiatives that better fit the target audiences. Once these elements have been defined, the different metrics and measures that will be monitored must be established in order to evaluate the impact obtained from the various communication initiatives and delivered messages. The last section of this Communications Plan initiates the fourth stage (Development and Implementation of the Learning Management System – LMS), where it is important to set the official opening date and start of the Corporate University, and perform an intensive information campaign due to the proximity of the release, it is intended that the expectations regarding the project will be maximized. For the opening event, it is important to highlight that the LMS should have been tested extensively to avoid any failure or error in its presentation. It is also recommended that the event must be conducted in a professional manner, involving all people within the company: members of the board, managers, executives, employees, special guests and speakers should participate in this occasion. The event will change the way the company understands the value of human capital, knowledge management and the importance of intangible assets.

The different five stages identified and defined above, imply that senior management of the company is convinced of the benefits that Corporate University has in the development of human capital inside the organization. It is also important to highlight that the Human Resources Department is the most important executing entity, because managers are the decision makers and they know how far the process will be developed to reach the company's objectives and goals, and how this process will be aligned with the strategy. Therefore, Corporate University development involves the initial investment of a significant amount of human and financial resources to position the project, but eventually self-sustainability is achieved by offering Corporate University services, not only to internal clients, but also to external clients as suppliers and final customers, who can identify the value of these products and pay to enroll for specific training, learning programs and tailor-made solutions. Castellani (2009) explains that in recent years, Corporate University processes have tended to become profit centers and extend their activity towards the external market by exploiting the pay for service logic.

Corporate Universities offer a curriculum designed to support major initiatives changes, aligning staff development with business goals and linking the return on investment associated with training initiatives. These processes help to create conditions for strategic agility and innovation in a knowledge economy. In addition to this, it must be said that successful Corporate Universities have executive support, appropriate technologies to assure and measure transfer and retention of knowledge and skills, and a well-documented organizational plan for execution, being able to show measurable improvements to the bottom line in shareholder return, productivity, and customer satisfaction (McAteer and Pino 2011). Masannat (2014) supports the idea that it is necessary to measure the effectiveness of a Corporate University, being crucial for its credibility and in order to identify areas of improvement. Each Corporate University must create its own measurement system connected to the company's goals.

10.5 Conclusions and Future Research

Nowadays there are only few large companies that do not have a Corporate University in a physical or virtual infrastructure yet. This fact is an acknowledgment of the importance that companies have given to this process in terms of induction, training, learning and continuous improvement in its human capital resources and processes, promoting and adapting the development of this structure not only at national level but also at multinational and global levels. It should also be noted that many of these structures have become autonomous, independent and self-sustaining units within the organization, which not only provides intangible invaluable services to internal customers of the organization, but also offer interesting high value-added processes to external providers, customers and other interested people, as a way to improve efficiency beyond the value chain and set a goal of excellence in the value network.

At Sergio Arboleda University, faculty of consultants and researchers in the PRIME Business School are developing new methodologies and approaches to deal with and succeed in the development of these new educational paradigms, that will definitely change the way that current graduate education and transmission of knowledge are integrated with todays and tomorrows globalized business needs, thus fulfilling the task of meeting the concerns of our customers, developing new partnerships with companies willing to maximize the impact of their educational processes and aligning them with their commitments and strategic goals, and without leaving behind the transmission of our differentiating seal based on Integrity, Humanism and Excellency.

In this paper a new methodology has been proposed for the implementation and development of a Corporate University for any company regardless of its core activity, size or country, as a source to achieve social innovation, sustainability, technology and education development in the XXI century corporations, focusing on five fundamental and distinct phases: Initial Diagnosis, Educational Programs Development, Generation of Processes and Structure, Development and Implementation of LMS (Learning Management System), and Awareness and Release. The model was derived and presented from the considerable experience acquired by our consultants, and taking into account the extensive and thorough review of the current literature related to the concept.

As for future lines of research, further studies will be performed in order to ensure methodologies, tools and initiatives that allow the Corporate University process to become an autonomous, independent and self-sustaining process within the organization.

References

Alfaro-Guevara, L. A. (2012). *La Universidad Virtual Corporativa en México: Un modelo de desarrollo de competencias y capital intelectual mediante espacios de gestión del conocimiento*. Working Paper, Universidad del Valle, Mexico.

Allen, M. (2002). *The corporate university handbook: Designing, managing and growing a successful program*. New York: American Management Association, AMACOM.

Almeida, T., & Levy, A. (2011). *Challenges of corporate university implementation and management*. Working Paper, Universidade Federal Fluminense, Brazil.

Alonso-Gonzalez, A., Diaz-Morales, A., & Peris-Ortiz, M. (2016). Enhancement of entrepreneurship in Colombian universities: Competence approach plus personalized advice (CAPPA) model. In M. Peris-Ortiz, J. A. Gómez, F. y. Vélez-Torres, & C. Rueda-Armengot (Eds.), *Education tools for entrepreneurship* (pp. 101–112). Cham: Springer International Publishing. ISBN: 978-3-319-24655-0.

Alonso-Gonzalez, A., Peris-Ortiz, M., & Mauri-Castello, J. (2017). Collaborative networks between corporate universities, customers, and SMEs: Integrating strategy towards value creation. In M. Peris-Ortiz & J. J. Ferreira (Eds.), *Cooperative and networking strategies in small business* (pp. 197–205). Cham: Springer International Publishing. ISBN: 978-3-319-44509-0.

Auvinet, C., & Lloret, A. (2015). Understanding social change through catalytic innovation: Empirical findings in Mexican social entrepreneurship. *Canadian Journal of Administrative Sciences, 32,* 238–251.

Castellani, P. (2009). Corporate University and the company's competitiveness: The case of Lidl Italia. *Sinergie rivista di studi e ricerche, 80*(09), 177–191.

Genzer, J. W. (2006). *Developing and implementing a corporate university*. Amherst: Human Resources Development Press.

Giulio, P. (2011). The Corporate University Phenomenon and the Competences" pipeline": The role of innovation and institutional change. *Journal of US-China Public Administration, 8*(9), 1004–1015.

Li, J., & Alagaraja, M. (2007). Emerging HRD issues: A conceptual framework for corporate University in the context of Chinese organizations. Paper Presented at the Academy of Human Resource Development International Research Conference in the Americas (Indianapolis, IN, Feb 2007) (ERIC Document Reproduction Service No. ED504354).

Mallard, S., & Eneau, J. (2013). Training managers: A case study of a French corporate university. In *Changing configurations of adult education in transitional times-The 7th European research conference of the triennial European research conference-ESREA*. (CD-Rom). Humboldt Universität.

Masannat, J. (2014). *How should we measure the effectiveness of our corporate university programs?* Ithaca, New York: Cornell University ILR School, Student Works.

McAteer, P., & Pino, M. (2011). *The business case for creating a corporate university*. VP Research Corporate University Xchange.

Meister, J. C. (1998). *Corporate universities: Lessons in building a world-class work force.* New York: McGraw-Hill.

Nasar, S. (2011). *Grand pursuit. The story of economic genius.* New York: Simon and Schuster.

Nikolov, R. (2009). Towards university 2.0: A space where academic education meets corporate training. *Education, Training and Lifelong Learning, 1*, 1–9.

North, D. C. (1981). *Structure and change in economic history.* New York: Norton and Company.

North, D. C. (2005). *Understanding the process of economic change.* Princeton: Princeton University Press.

Peris-Ortiz, M., Alonso-Llera, J. J., & Rueda-Armengot, C. (2017). *Entrepreneurship and innovation in a revolutionary educational model: École 42, included in Social Entrepreneurship in Non-Profit and Profit sectors. Theoretical and empirical perspectives* (Vol. 36, pp. 85–98). Cham: Springer.

Prince, C., & Beaver, G. (2001). The rise and rise of the corporate university: The emerging corporate learning agenda. *The International Journal of Management Education, 1*(3), 17–26.

Progler, J. (2010). Curriculum reform in the corporate university: From the disciplines to transferrable skills. *Social Systems Studies, 21*, 95–113.

Roth, G., & Magee, C. (2002). *Corporate-university alliances and engineering systems research.* Massachusetts Institute of Technology, Engineering Division, Working Paper Series.

Ryan, L. (2013). The growing role of executive education in university-corporate partnerships. *Journal of Executive Education, 6*(1), 5.

Sinha, A., & Kaul, N. (2013). Corporate university: Glorified training departments or more? *Journal of Resources Development and Management, 1*(13), 49–53.

Van Rooijen, M. (2009). Transforming 21st century corporate-university engagement: From work-integrated learning (WIL) to learning-integrated work (LIW). *Journal of Cooperative Education and Internships, 45*(1), 5–10.

Viltard, L. A. (2013). Universidad Corporativa (UC) Una explicación de su existencia. *Palermo Business Review, 13*(10), 73–100.

Viltard, L. A. (2014). Are corporate universities (CU) possible in emerging countries? Arcor University (AU). *Independent Journal of Management & Production, 5*(3), 581.

Vizcaya-Piñeros, P., & Uribe-Atehortua, E. J. (2014). *Aportes de la Universidad Corporativa a la ventaja competitiva de las organizaciones en Colombia.* Colombia: Universidad de Medellín.

Wang, G. G., Sun, J. Y., Li, J. J., & Qiao, X. (2008). Exploring the corporate university phenomenon. Paper presented at the Academy of Human Resource Development International Research Conference in the Americas (Panama City, FL, Feb 20–24 2008) (ERIC Document Reproduction Service No. ED501627).

Wills, K. V. (2001) From the classroom to the cubicle: Reading the rhetoric of the emerging corporate university. *Annual Meeting of the International Reading Association.*

Zolfo, E., & Mann, D. (2007). Global competition and learning organizations: Goals and motivations of corporate leaders and employees who participate in Corporate/University Partnerships. In *Forum on public policy online* (Vol. 2007, No. 1, p. n1). Urbana: Oxford Round Table.

Chapter 11
Finland's Centennial Anniversary 2017: The First 100 Years of Finnish Social Innovations That Work for Gender Equality

Ismo Koponen and Lea Isopoussu-Koponen

Abstract In this chapter we examine such Finnish social innovations that affect any individual citizen's life from cradle to coffin. In a wider perspective, these innovations have paved our nation's way to top rankings in 15-year-old students' performance in science, mathematics and reading. Here we refer to the PISA program of the OECD organization. Prominent social innovations to be discussed here are (1) Compulsory Education (free to all citizens; legislation valid since year 1921); (2) Maternity Clinic System (free to all mothers from 1922); (3) Maternity Grant (free to needy mothers from 1937 and free to all mothers from 1949); (4) Free School Lunch (law regulated in 1943 and enforced in 1948); (5) Free Secondary and Tertiary Education (legislation in progress 1960s–70s); and (6) Student Financial Aid Act (first act enforced in 1972). From the above mentioned, the Maternity Clinic System was (in year 2012) voted the best Finnish innovation ever. According to the same survey, Free School Lunch was ranked the 4th best and the Maternity Grant the 8th best Finnish innovation. Our current concerns are related to the development of equality. In spite of the fact that Finnish women were granted full suffrage i.e. both the right to vote and to stand for nomination in national elections (this in year 1906), there is still inequality between the two gender. Actually, PISA results show that at the age of 15 years, girls perform better than boys at school. In the working life, however, women are in a weaker position than men, on the average. The least fortunate group of people in our society, nonetheless, seem to be the immigrants. Undoubtedly, we Finns are challenged to come up with new social innovations that will solve our inequality problems. Preferably, in the very beginning of the nation's second century of independence.

Keywords Finland 100 years · Social innovation · Gender equality · Equality · Inequality

I. Koponen (✉) · L. Isopoussu-Koponen
Oulu University of Applied Sciences, School of Business, Oulu, Finland
e-mail: ismo.koponen@oamk.fi; lea.isopoussu-koponen@oamk.fi

© Springer International Publishing AG, part of Springer Nature 2018
M. Peris-Ortiz et al. (eds.), *Strategies and Best Practices in Social Innovation*,
https://doi.org/10.1007/978-3-319-89857-5_11

11.1   Defining the Main Concepts of This Chapter and Introducing our Approach to Them

"**Finland** was a province and then a grand duchy under Sweden from the 12th to the 19th centuries, and an autonomous grand duchy of Russia after 1809. It gained complete independence in 1917. During World War II, Finland successfully defended its independence through cooperation with Germany and resisted subsequent invasions by the Soviet Union – albeit with some loss of territory. In the subsequent half century, Finland transformed from a farm/forest economy to a diversified modern industrial economy; per capita income is among the highest in Western Europe. A member of the EU since 1995, Finland was the only Nordic state to join the euro single currency at its initiation in January 1999. In the twenty-first century, the key features of Finland's modern welfare state are high quality education, promotion of equality, and a national social welfare system – currently challenged by an aging population and the fluctuations of an export-driven economy" (https://www.cia.gov/; with the authors' underlining). The underlined features of Finland are all social innovations.

"Finland has a highly industrialized, largely free-market economy with per capita GDP almost as high as that of Austria and the Netherlands and slightly above that of Germany and Belgium. Trade is important, with exports accounting for over one-third of GDP in recent years. The government is open to, and actively takes steps to attract, foreign direct investment (ibid.). "Finland is historically competitive in manufacturing – principally the wood, metals, engineering, telecommunications, and electronics industries. Finland excels in export of technology as well as promotion of startups in the information and communications technology, gaming, clean tech, and biotechnology sectors. Except for timber and several minerals, Finland depends on imports of raw materials, energy, and some components for manufactured goods. Because of the cold climate, agricultural development is limited to maintaining self-sufficiency in basic products. Forestry, an important export industry, provides a secondary occupation for the rural population" (ibid.; with the authors' underlining).

The above statements are factual ones, no doubt. As citizens we may, however, make the following two comments on them: (1) all the numerous small startup companies have not yet been able to replace the losses in production and national wealth caused by the recent close downs of a number of big industrial companies; (2) the relatively short annual growing seasons that both agriculture and forestry have to face in the country, can be seen as a quantitative problem; simultaneously, the short growing seasons and the cold winters in between result in very good quality production.

Social Innovation   Based on our own personal and social experiences and observations, we can say that social innovations are often non-tangible ideas rather than tangible things; they are there e.g. to ensure the wellbeing of either small minorities or the vast majority; social innovations contribute to democracy and equality in a society; their effect on individuals and groups of individuals can, simultaneously, be negative, neutral and/or positive.

External definitions on the concept are e.g. the following ones. "We can define social innovation as concepts, ideas and organizations that meet social needs of all kinds from working conditions and education to community development and health; and extend and strengthen the civil society. Social innovation can usually take place within governments, large organizations or within the non-profit sector. But usually social innovation happens in a space between these three sectors which is supported by open innovation. This can at times be related to social entrepreneurship but it need not always comprise innovation, but may lead to innovation" (Salim Saji and Ellingstad 2016).

As an outcome of the above suggestions, we would like to point out the following idea. Actually, all our nation – Finland – is one big social innovation that was made some time before the political independency was given to us. This innovation functions as an 'umbrella' for any social innovation emerging among people. "A social innovation is underpinned by an idea that is intended to change social practices which would contribute to overcoming social problems or to satisfy needs of specific societal actors" (Weerakkody et al. 2014).

Sometimes social innovations can, retrospectively, be seen as trials made. An example of such a trial was the prohibition law. It was regulated in year 1919 but was repealed April the 5th, 1932 at 10:00 a.m. (5-4-3-2-1-0), when the doors to the liquor stores were opened. This repealing may be seen as an example of just another social innovation, "an idea that is intended to change social practices which would contribute to overcoming social problems" (ibid.). The problem with the prohibition was that it triggered lots of criminality like smuggling. A final outcome of the prohibition was that Finns learned to consume strong spirits again. Something that e.g. the Åberg family had successfully fought against, starting just a few decades earlier (please, see the beginning of the following chapter).

Equality Versus Inequality One definition of 'equality' is: "The right of different groups of people to have a similar social position and receive the same treatment" (http://dictionary.cambridge.org/). Relevant examples here are: equality and inequality between the sexes and racial inequality.

Finland has, during the previous 3 or 4 decades, built a wide spread network of universities and other institutes of higher education. This contributes to geographical equality; it is not of primary importance to live close to one of the 4 or 5 biggest cities anymore. However, "Research and surveys suggest that cultures of higher education and science build inequality. Universities maintain ideals of manliness and masculinity. Female students experience inequality during their studies. Women also face hidden discrimination and harassment. Still, inequality appears at its clearest on the labor market" (Nieminen et al. 2014). A recent study suggests an explanation to the above: men in Finland work 15% longer hours than women. (Please, see: http://www.talouselama.fi/) According to Mr. Antti Kauhanen, the fact that women often are mothers, too, explains a great deal of gender inequality at workplaces. The rest of it is due to the fact that men are often more competitive and more willing to take risks than their female colleagues (2016).

According to Kolkka and Karjalainen, the principle of equality in our system of education mainly consists of gender equality and non-discrimination. They, thus, see it alarming that only 31% of our male citizens have graduated with a degree by the age of 30 years. From women, 48% have done the same (2013). We find it interesting to know that in year 2016, a vast majority (65%) of Finnish students who graduated with a master's degree in laws, were women (https://pro.almatalent.fi/juristikirje/2017/05/65-prosenttia-uusista-juristeista-naisia/). To our knowledge, the only schools and faculties in Finland with a significant majority of male students are the ones of technology.

11.2 Finnish Social Innovations That Have Affected Gender Equality in Our Country

Social innovations that date back to the times before our independence include OLVI, a brewery. "In 1878 Master Brewer William Gideon Åberg and his wife Onni founded a brewery in Iisalmi for the purpose of fighting drunkenness. They wanted to offer milder alternatives to citizens possessed by a lust for spirits" (http://www.olvi.fi/web/en/history). Was this – still active – commercial company a social innovation of its time? Indeed, it was. Women and children, too, were and still are the biggest sufferers because of their husbands' and fathers' alcoholism. This social progress was dramatically disturbed in year 1919 (please, see previous chapter).

"In a European comparison, Finland was unquestionably a pioneer of democracy. Norway, disengaged from Swedish rule, began to extend women's right to vote in 1907, and the reform reached the Finnish degree in 1913. Other Nordic countries soon followed; albeit Sweden not until 1919. Full political rights were granted to women in many European countries in the turmoil following the end of the First World War" (https://www.eduskunta.fi/).

11.2.1 From the Early Years of Independence Until the End of WW2

From the gender equality's point of view, are e.g. the following social innovations among the most important ones, for us Finns:

1. **Compulsory Education** (free to all citizens; legislation valid since 1921): the obligation to study and to learn, mainly, starts the calendar year when the adolescent reaches the age of 7 years. It ends the year when she or he turns 17. From all Finnish pupils, 99.7% graduate with a primary school diploma. Every municipality in our country has the obligation to arrange teaching for all children settled in their area. (http://www.oph.fi/koulutus_ja_tutkinnot/perusopetus/; see also: http://www.oph.fi/haku?searchtext=compulsory+education).

2. **Maternity Clinic System** (free to all mothers from 1922);
3. **Maternity Grant** (free to needy mothers from 1937 and later free to all mothers from 1949);
4. **Free School Lunch** (law regulated in 1943 and later enforced in 1948): "Finland was the first country in the world to serve free school meals. 1948 is seen as being the year when free school catering really started, though catering activities on a smaller scale had been around since the beginning of the 20th century. Until the beginning of the 1960's school food mainly consisted of soups, porridges and thin porridge-type dishes. Children brought bread and milk with them to supplement their school lunch, which was generally not very substantial. In the 1960's school meals slowly became more varied. Frozen and processed foods started to be used and more vegetables were served. In the 1970's the school menus often contained new food products, such as rice and spaghetti, that were yet to be popular at pupils' homes. Many children also learned to eat grated root vegetables, salad and fruit at school. The municipalities are responsible for monitoring and evaluating school meals in Finland. The statutory obligations are based on the following: The Basic Education Act (628/1998), The General Upper Secondary Schools Act (629/1998) and The Vocational Education and Training Act (630/1998). The common guideline is a free meal every school day" (http://www.oph.fi/download/47657_ school_meals_in_finland.pdf). At a university campus a student's lunch is not totally free but supported by the government. In our school canteen in Oulu, the student price for a set lunch was 0.88 € in the academic year 2016–17.

In general, we – the two authors of this paper – have experienced and all the above mentioned social innovations, and benefited from them, in the 1950s, 1960s and 1970s. Our children and grand-children continuously and onward. From the above listed social innovations, the Maternity Clinic System was (in year 2012) voted the best Finnish innovation ever (source: Yleisradio, Finnish Broad-casting Company; yle.fi). According to the same survey, Free School Lunch was ranked the 4th best and the Maternity Grant the 8th best innovation in the country (ibid.; n = 1027).

11.2.2   Rebuilding the Nation

The Second World War ended in the northern part of Finland no earlier than in year 1945. Social innovations like The Paris Peace Treaties in 1947 became very costly for our nation. By the end of 1952 Finland had covered so called war reparations to Soviet Union for a total value of 226.5 million American Dollars. Or as communicated on the web site of The Embassy of Finland in Washington D.C.: "Finland was quick to pay its dues, which took the form of war reparations to the Soviet Union … in the form of goods. Finland paid in full by … September 18th, 1952" (http://www.finland.org/). Despite being short of all possible resources at least all the 1950s and

1960s, to a certain extent even throughout the 1970s, Finland introduced and realized a few very remarkable social innovations for all the nation. These include:

1. **Free Secondary and 2. Tertiary Education:** Currently, there is no tuition fee for studying in Finland. From autumn 2017 on, non-EU/EEA students will have to pay tuition fees (for university courses offered in English). Each University will have its own fee and scholarship policies. All students, however, need to cover their living expenses. (Please, see e.g.: https://europe.graduateshotline.com/free-education.html).

3. **Student Financial Aid Act** (1994): In order to qualify for student financial aid, one must be a full-time student, make satisfactory study progress, and be in need of financial assistance. Financial aid is available in the form of study grant, government loan guarantee and some students can also be granted housing supplement. Study grant and housing supplement are government-financed monthly benefits. The study grant is taxable income. If a student has been awarded a government loan guarantee, one can apply for a student loan with a bank of one's own choice. (Please, see: http://www.kela.fi/documents/10180/681919/Optuinfo_engl.pdf/e1aba890-9bc0-4d77-a7ee-b1a7453a374e).

All citizens plus immigrant residents – subject to certain conditions and – with a student's status benefit of this legislation. The very idea has been to ensure that neither one of the two sexes and no particular social class be systematically without proper education.

O'Hara, still, reminds us about the following: "Since the late 1960s and early 1970s, most highly developed capitalist economies have suffered from a high level of instability and a sustained reduction in the rate of growth of real GDP" (1994). We, the authors of this paper, have experienced all the post war decades – since the 50s and 60s – in Finland. The global oil crisis in the 1970s became very real to all us Finns; so did the economical depressions in the early 1990s and in the early 2010s. O'Hara encourages us to study the "long waves of economic growth, each lasting between 40 and 60 years" and when doing so, "using interdisciplinary method, evolution, technology and institutions" (ibid.). If we did so, we would have to admit that e.g. being poor in our country is, today, very different from what it was 20 or 40 years ago. Social equality has developed, despite the repetitive recessions. Thanks to the many social innovations made.

11.2.3 Towards the Second Century of Independence

"Finland had been one of the best performing economies within the EU before 2009 and its banks and financial markets avoided the worst of global financial crisis. However, the world slowdown hit exports and domestic demand hard in that year, causing Finland's economy to contract from 2012–14. The recession affected general government finances and the debt ratio. The economy returned to growth in 2015, posting a 0.3% GDP increase before growing 1.4% in 2016" (https://www.cia.gov/). A short era of growth, even if it may continue, should not – necessarily – result in a raise in salaries and wages. Old debts should be paid back first. This is an idea that is not always understood throughout a democracy. Politicians provide Domestic Demand as a solution to economic problems. They, however, tend to forget that if demand focuses on foreign goods and services, we are – actually – not talking about a solution in the very meaning of the word.

"Finland's main challenges will be reducing high labor costs and boosting demand for its exports. In June 2016, the Government enacted a Competitiveness Pact aimed at reducing labor costs, increasing hours worked, and introducing more flexibility into the wage bargaining system. The Government was also seeking to reform the health care system and social services. In the long term, Finland must address a rapidly aging population and decreasing productivity in traditional industries that threaten competitiveness, fiscal sustainability, and economic growth" (https://www.cia.gov/). The aging of our native population, undoubtedly, is a big problem. Immigration may, however, partly solve this problem. Immigration may also contribute to solving the above mentioned problem of decreasing productivity. Simultaneously, it may – however – generate inequality.

Our nation's current social concerns are related to the development of equality in general and gender equality in particular. In spite of the fact that Finnish women were granted full suffrage i.e. both the right to vote and to stand for nomination in national elections (this in 1906), there is still inequality between the two gender. Actually, PISA results show that at the age of 15 years, girls perform better than boys at school. In the working life, however, women are in a weaker position than men, on the average. In year 2016, the median income of men in the Finnish private sector was 3620 € per month. The female equivalent was 2821 (please, see: http://www.stat.fi/til/yskp/2016/yskp_2016_2017-06-29_tie_001_fi.html?ad=notify). The least fortunate group of people in our society, nonetheless, seem to be the immigrants. While there is a general unemployment rate of 10.7% in the country (http://www.stat.fi/til/tyti/2017/05/tyti_2017_05_2017-06-20_tau_001_en.html),   the immigrants' unemployment rate may be double or triple of that, or even higher; depending on their nationality (http://www.eva.fi/).

However, "There is a growing consensus among practitioners, policy makers, the research community, and others that widespread social innovation is required to cope with the significant challenges that societies are facing now and into the future" (El-Haddadeh et al. 2014). Undoubtedly, we are challenged to come up with new social innovations that will solve our inequality problems. Preferably, in the very beginning of our nation's second century of independence.

"Development usually encompasses three dimensions – economic growth, social growth and human improvement. Thus scientific knowledge is divided into natural, social and humanistic dimensions. Hence innovation needs to happen not only in the natural dimension area – it needs to happen in the social and humanistic areas too. Innovation in the social dimension is usually connected to social innovation, and social entrepreneurship. Science and technology laboratories need to have a collaborative domain for interaction between these three dimensions to develop an innovation which is useful to mankind and the universe" (Salim Saji and Ellingstad 2016).

"The process in organizational innovation consists of three factors – individual, organizational, and environmental – all of which mutually complement and interact with one another, affecting the process of organizational innovation" (Li-Min 2014). From us two, Koponen investigated innovativeness in years 2002–2004. I came close to what Li-Min found a few years later. My measuring tool is a factor of four elements, namely: one's personal innovativeness, the innovativeness his or her work demands, one's organization's innovativeness and the innovativeness of his or her nation. Relatively innovative individuals contribute, firstly, to their relatively innovative organization and, finally, to their relatively innovative nation. Furthermore, innovativeness contributes to development, in general, and to welfare, in particular. Innovative nations, thus, have relatively good possibilities for developing their caring economies (Koponen 2004a, b). In other words: the factor's elements are interrelated, and an individual is influenced by his or her environment. An innovative environment encourages people to think and work innovatively (as in Koponen 2012).

11.3   Ambitious Aims and Decreasing Resources

The Government Programs in the 2010s emphasize education and expertise among Finland's most important elements of competitiveness. These elements were emphasized especially in Prime Minister Katainen's program in year 2011. According to the program, the best comprehensive school system in the world will be strengthen to guarantee equal opportunities for all. His government put their aim on making Finland the most competent nation in the world: "By 2020, Finland will be ranked among the leading group of OECD countries in key comparisons of competencies of young people and adults, in lack of early school-leaving, and in the proportion of young people and other people of working age with a higher education degree. The differences between the genders in learning outcomes, participation and completion of education will be reduced, and the intergenerational transmission of education will be reduced" (http://vnk.fi/documents/10616/622966/H0311).

As we have stated earlier, Finland's economy contracted between 2012 and 2014. Our current government, the one of Prime Minister Sipilä, reacted to this with their program in year 2015. According to this program, one of the five key projects is developing our population's skills and raising the level of its education. The economy, however, was dramatically poorer than in year 2011. Unemployment, in 2015, was high and the economic growth had waned. Finland's international competitiveness had dropped and was from 10 to 15 percent weaker than that of our key competitors. Despite all the effort put in education and in developing expertise of the people, expertise is not being converted into innovations and innovations are not automatically commercialized into products. We are in danger of losing our competitive edge. The ten-year objective of the current government, however, is: "Finland is a country that encourages people to continuously learn something new. Skills and education levels in Finland have risen, promoting the renewal of Finnish society and equal opportunities. Finland is in the vanguard of education, skills and modern learning techniques" (http://valtioneuvosto.fi/ documents/10184/1427398/).

In order to implement the above mentioned visions, Finland's Ministry of Education and Culture has launched a project with the aim of defining objectives for the Finnish higher education and research until the year 2030. A vision will be drawn up in broad cooperation with higher education institutions and other stakeholders. A parliamentary monitoring group will be established to support the work. The work is in progress and should be completed by September 2017 (http://minedu.fi/artikkeli/).

The two above mentioned government programs show quite different aims for developing education. This must, to a great deal, be due to the decreasing financial resources. This has been experienced in practice at our schools and universities, for quite some time now. For instance, academic staff has been reduced and student groups have been enlarged. Simultaneously, students' financial aid has been reduced.

References

El-Haddadeh, R., Irani, Z., Millard, J., & Schröder, A. (2014). Toward a coherent methodological framework for examining social innovation in the public sector. *Information Systems Management, 31*, 250–258.

http://dictionary.cambridge.org/dictionary/english/equality

http://minedu.fi/artikkeli/-/asset_publisher/suomen-korkea-koulutukselle-ja-tutkimukselle-visio-2030?_101_INSTANCE_0R8wCyp3oebu_languageId=en_US

http://valtioneuvosto.fi/documents/10184/1427398/Ratkaisujen+Suomi_EN_YHDISTETTY_netti.pdf/8d2e1a66-e24a-4073-8303-ee3127fbfcac

http://vnk.fi/documents/10616/622966/H0311_Programme+of+Prime+Minister+Jyrki+Katainen%E2%80%99s+Government+2011.pdf/41e14454-a2c2-4ed0-8179-e46801a37541?version=1.0

http://www.eva.fi/tyotjatekijat/maahanmuuttajien-tyottomyysasteet-kansalaisuuden-mukaan-2000-2013/

http://www.finland.org/Public/default.aspx?contentid=149650&nodeid=40956&contentlan=2&culture=en-US

http://www.kela.fi/documents/10180/681919/Optuinfo_engl.pdf/e1aba890-9bc0-4d77-a7ee-b1a7453a374e

http://www.oph.fi/download/47657_school_meals_in_finland.pdf

http://www.oph.fi/koulutus_ja_tutkinnot/perusopetus/oppivelvollisuus_ja_koulupaikka

http://www.stat.fi/til/tyti/2017/05/tyti_2017_05_2017-06-20_tau_001_en.html

http://www.stat.fi/til/yskp/2016/yskp_2016_2017-06-29_tie_001_fi.html?ad=notify

http://www.talouselama.fi/uutiset/naisen-ura-jamahtaa-jo-ensimmaisina-vuosina-miehet-tekevat-suomessa-15-prosenttia-pidempaa-paivaa-6644540

https://pro.almatalent.fi/juristikirje/2017/05/65-prosenttia-uusista-juristeista-naisia/

https://www.cia.gov/library/publications/the-world-factbook/geos/fi.html

https://www.eduskunta.fi/EN/tietoaeduskunnasta/kirjasto/aineistot/yhteiskunta/womens-suffrage-110-years/ Pages/historical-background.aspx

Kauhanen, A. (2016). The future of work: Challenges to men and women. ETLA Brief No 50. http://pub.etla.fi/

Kolkka, M., & Karjalainen, A. L. (2013). World's most competitive nation – Educational equality is a political and pedagogical question. In Mahlamäki-Kultanen, S., Hämäläinen, T., Pohjonen, P., & Nyyssölä, K. (Eds.). *World's most competitive nation 2020 – Resources, possibilities and solutions of the policy of education.* Koulutustutkimusfoorumi, 2013, 8, 50–67. In Finnish; the authors' translation.

Koponen, I. (2004a). Are organizational cultural distances affected by another human factor, innovativeness? *International Journal of Entrepreneurship and Innovation Management, 4*(4), 339–348.

Koponen, I. (2004b). *Evaluating e.g. Innovativeness in selecting an inter-national trading partner – Making use of the koponen manipulator.* Report presented to the ISPIM 2004 conference in Oslo, June 20–24.

Koponen, I. (2012). *Innovativeness measured within a triad of nations.* A paper presented to the 7th international symposium on business administrat-ion on May 11–12. Canakkale Onsekiz Mart Universitesi.

Li-Min, C. (2014). The social psychology of creativity and innovation: Process theory (PT) perspective. *Social Behavior and Personality, 35*(7), 875–888.

Nieminen, L., Tiilikka, P., & Tuononen, T. (2014). Higher education and equality – How does education support or prevent equality and righteous-ness in the society? *Oikeus, 43*(2), 215–221. In Finnish; the authors' translation.

O'Hara, P. A. (1994). An institutionalist review of long wave theories: Schumpeterian innovation modes of regulation and social structures of accumulation. *Journal of Economic Issues, 28*(2), 489–500.

Salim Saji, B., & Ellingstad, P. (2016). Social innovation model for business performance and innovation. *International Journal of Productivity and Performance Management, 65*(2), 256–274.

Weerakkody, V., Ghoneim, A., & Schröder, A. (2014). Social innovation in the public sector. *Information Systems Management, 31*, 184–186.

Chapter 12
Innovation and Knowledge in the Social Economy: ICT Accessibility

Amable Juárez Tarraga, Sofía Estelles-Miguel, Marta Elena Palmer Gato, and José Miguel Albarracín Guillem

Abstract Interest in social economy is growing rapidly for many reasons. There are many examples of this type of enterprise in Spain, and several are leaders at a European level. This paper examines the case of Technosite SA (a part of the Grupo Ilunion). Technosite specialises in e-business developments, business intelligence, usability, e-learning, integral management of web portals, and especially in web accessibility (aiming to ensure that a website can be used by everybody, regardless of whether they have a disability). Technosite SA also handles R&D projects: including the technical management of international projects and the creation of technological demonstrators. The company has achieved the above while remaining aware of its responsibilities as a member of the social economy. This chapter analyses innovation in social economy in Spain and presents the experience of Technosite SA.

Keywords Social economy · ICTs · Innovation · Usability · Disabled people

12.1 Introduction

According to data from the Spanish Social Economy Business Confederation (CEPES) the social economy sector is better at creating and maintaining jobs than the rest of the economy. There were more than 43,000 Spanish social economy enterprises operating in 2016 and they were responsible for more than 2,200,000 direct and indirect jobs. In the last 8 years, some 29,000 new enterprises have created more than 190,000 new jobs (CEPES 2017).

However, the Social Innovation Index published by The Economist Intelligence Unit (2016) ranks Spain in 28th position of a total of 45 economies analysed – placing Spain as one of the nations with the worst performances relative to income. Spain was consistently below average in the four dimensions analysed: institutional political framework; financing; entrepreneurship; and civil society (Anchuelo 2017).

A. Juárez Tarraga · S. Estelles-Miguel (✉) · M. E. Palmer Gato · J. M. Albarracín Guillem
Universitat Politècnica de València, Organización de Empresas, Valencia, Valencia, Spain
e-mail: soesmi@omp.upv.es

© Springer International Publishing AG, part of Springer Nature 2018   181
M. Peris-Ortiz et al. (eds.), *Strategies and Best Practices in Social Innovation*,
https://doi.org/10.1007/978-3-319-89857-5_12

Despite the low level of innovative activity in the field of social economy in Spain, there are successful Spanish social economy enterprises that are worldwide leaders in innovation in their sectors, as is the case of Technosite SA.

12.2 Conceptual Framework

The encouragement of the social economy through public policies is an objective of the European Union, as reflected in a resolution on social economy (European Commission 2009). Among the initiatives launched to expand the social economy is the Social Business Initiative that was created in 2011. This initiative was implemented in close partnership with sectorial stakeholders and EU member states (European Commission 2011) and aims to:

- Introduce a short-term action plan to support the development of social enterprises as key stakeholders in the social economy and social innovation
- Prompt debate on the avenues to be explored in the medium and long term.

Despite their diversity, social enterprises mainly operate in four fields:

- Work integration: training and integration of people with disabilities and the unemployed.
- Personal social services, health, well-being and medical care, professional training, education, health services, childcare services, services for the elderly, and aid for disadvantaged people.
- Local development of disadvantaged areas, social enterprises in remote rural areas, neighbourhood development/rehabilitation schemes in urban areas, development aid and development cooperation with third countries.
- Other: including recycling, environmental protection, sports, arts, culture or historical preservation, science, research and innovation, consumer protection and amateur sports.

In the case of Spain, the Social Economy Act (BOE 2011) is a pioneering example of legislation that defines the social economy as economic and business activities carried out in the private sphere by enterprises that pursue the collective interest of their members, or the general economic and social interest, or both. The social economy represents a distinct way of doing business with four main pillars (the primacy of the person and the community, the pursuit of general interest, positive economic performance balanced with social performance, and democratic procedures) that differentiate it from other business models.

The Spanish Social Economy Act encourages socially innovative initiatives – which according to Murray et al. (2010) can be defined as 'innovations that are social both in their ends and in their means. Specifically, social innovations are defined as new ideas (products, services, and models) that simultaneously meet social needs and create new social relationships or collaborations. In other words, they are innovations that are both good for society and enhance society's capacity to act'. Information and communication technologies (ICTs) are currently one of the main drivers of social innovation (DG Regional and Urban Policy and DG Employment 2013). The creation of social value consists in changing the lives of individuals for the better by achieving socially desirable goals (SEKN 2006; Rueda et al. 2017). Organisations are as efficient as their processes (Moreno et al. 2014) so these processes need to be made efficient.

Thus, for example, the internet offers numerous tools to combat isolation and unite people with various characteristics to achieve a common goal. Mobile telephony and smartphones are tools for change and improvement in the quality of life of the most disadvantaged and facilitate social integration. Applications for mobile devices can contribute to raising the standard of living and well-being of the inhabitants of developing countries, and communication networks enable the rapid and agile delivery of assistance after emergencies (earthquakes, floods, famines, etc.) (Murray et al. 2010). Moreover, ICTs break down barriers to knowledge, enable access to information, and facilitate the participation of traditionally isolated individuals and groups, thereby favouring collective action and the creation of new economic opportunities (Misuraca et al. 2015).

12.3   Social Economy and ICT Accessibility

Return on Social Investment (RSI) is a method based on the principles of understanding, measuring, and communicating non-financial value (i.e. the environmental and social value not currently reflected in conventional financial accounts) for resources invested. There are currently models such as corporate social responsibility that measure these types of action and reflect them in activity reports – but few companies use this approach.

RSI is a tool for both managers and investors in business initiatives to help make decisions based on optimising the social and environmental impact (Acosta and Egoávil 2014) and is therefore used routinely in social economy enterprises to assess projects.

Many studies in the specialist literature examine the incidence of ICT in the economic growth of nations, as well as its contribution to the generation of competitive advantages in enterprises that incorporate ICT in their processes. The development and use of new ICT is becoming one of the main drivers of the knowledge economy, and its contribution to the generation of intangible capital means it can become a source of competitive advantage (Barney 2010).

Environmental developments and an increase in social awareness have generated new business opportunities in sectors traditionally linked to the social economy: such as the care of the elderly or for people with disabilities. However, much more needs to be done to achieve a more inclusive society, and ensure that people with disabilities have equal opportunities. To this end, legislators from nations and international organisational are developing initiatives on disability and accessibility.

According to the standard 'Assistive products for persons with disabilities - classification and terminology' (ISO 9999: 2016), accessible ICT can be classified according to the:

- disability addressed
- process of making the product or service available to a disabled person.
- technology on which a disability product or service is based.

The above standard is divided into 11 classes and we focus on the class related to 'support for communication and information' (also known as accessible ICTs). It is divided into 13 subclasses:

- Support for vision
- Support for hearing
- Support for speaking
- Support for manual drawing and writing
- Support for calculating
- Support for managing audio-visual and video
- Support for face-to-face communication
- Support for telephoning (and messaging)
- Support for alarm, indication, and signalling
- Support for reading
- Computers and terminals
- Input devices for computers
- Output devices for computers

The possibilities offered by ICTs to eliminate or reduce communication barriers between people has made it possible for many social economy companies to base their activity on the dissemination and use of ICTs to contribute to their social goals. TECHNOSITE SA develops its activity on this basis.

12.4   Grupo Ilunion

Grupo Ilunion is founded on HOPE,[1] UNITY[2] and SOLIDARITY. These are the values sustained by ONCE for 82 years, and by its Foundation, for 32. This project for a socially responsible corporation, that is unique in the entire world, enriches and brings diversity to the business network and to society as a whole (ILUNION 2017).

Grupo Fundosa was founded in 1989 as a business division of the Spanish National Foundation for the Blind (ONCE in Spanish) to generate stable employment for people with disabilities. The group manages profitable business activities and negotiates strategic alliances (ILUNION 2016).

---

[1] Ilusión in Spanish.

[2] Unión in Spanish.

Thanks to a philosophy of innovation and continuous improvement, the group and its member companies have grown year after year. This growth is reflected in the social values of integrating people with disabilities into jobs (Rueda-Armengot et al. 2017).

Grupo Fundosa has established an inclusive and profitable business model. The ability and talent of its distinctive workforce is the engine that drives the organisation. The group in 2012 was composed of 36 subsidiaries and 21 affiliated companies with a nationwide network of 340 workplaces (including 274 special employment centres and 37 social economy centres). The group's growth and diversification are evidence of its sustainability and success in generating new resources and quality jobs for people with disabilities. It adds experience, capability, competitiveness, innovation, creativity, and diversity to corporate activities by offering more than 50 lines of business that are structured in five divisions: health and social care, comprehensive services, consultancy, marketing, hotels, tourism and leisure (ONCE Report 2012).

The ONCE Entrepreneurial Corporation (CEOSA) began operating in 1993 through participation and management in various companies. The company also generates employment for disabled professionals and operates in sectors such as hotels, physiotherapy, facility services, and insurance broking (ILUNION 2016).

On 31 December 2015 Grupo Ilunion and CEOSA approved a takeover of the latter by the former, and formed a single business group called Grupo Ilunion to strengthen its business and offer clients global proposals and solutions. Some 47.51% of the group belongs to ONCE and 52.49% to the ONCE Foundation. A capital increase of €296 million was made by the Grupo Ilunion to fund the merger (ONCE Report 2015).

The group resulting from this merger has 563 work centres throughout Spain, of which 264 are special employment centres. The group achieved a turnover of €753.4 million in 2015 (with an EBITDA of €32 million). Some 3% of turnover and 27% of profits come from the automotive industry. Approximately 35% of the Grupo Ilunion workforce are people with disabilities, a feature of the group that has received international recognition (ONCE Report 2015).

Grupo Ilunion is a pioneering and innovative reflection of the ONCE Foundation's social initiative and aims to maintain a balance between economic and social values.

12.4.1 Technosite SA

Technosite SA was founded 1998. It was an initiative of the ONCE Foundation and was started to develop projects for the generation of jobs for people with disabilities using information and communication technologies (ANEI 2011). Its original name was Fundosa Teleservicios. It is an ICT-service company specialised in facilitating accessibility for its clients. This business project is essentially creative and not based on imitation, nor on the external economies of other types of projects (EOI Foundation 2010). The company is firmly committed to the social economy.

The company started operations with just 20 employees but grew to employ 129 by 2009 (42% with disabilities). It made a profit every year – despite making large R & D investments (EOI Foundatio 2010).

The ONCE Foundation decided in 1999 to focus on the generation of the first Spanish-speaking internet portal for users with disabilities and the creation of a network of telecentres where people with disabilities could learn and become familiar with the use of new technologies. In this way, the Discapnet project started within the framework of the ONCE Foundation's Programme to Combat Discrimination and with EU support for the integration of people with disabilities. The company's activity in the early years included the design, creation, and evolution of the portal and its associated activities and tools. Discapnet continues to be the major Spanish site for content and services related to disabilities and other groups with special needs, such as the elderly or dependent people (ANEI 2011).

The enormous amount of experience acquired by the team at Technosite enabled a fast and solid growth in the various lines of activity that were gradually developed in the market. Its clients include public administrations, service and technology companies, banks, private companies, etc. In addition to the design and management of websites and technological services, ICT accessibility consultancy has become one of the strategic lines of Technosite since 2003 in response to the gradual development of legislation and corporate social responsibility practices that require the inclusion of people with disabilities in the new paradigm of the information society (ANEI 2011). The commitment to make a technical analysis of the user perspective and the definition of a very advanced methodology enables the company to present a unique offer in the marketplace.

A determined commitment from 2007 was made to research, develop, and innovate to improve the quality of life of groups with special needs by using ICT. The design of the INREDIS project and the responsibility for managing a consortium of 14 companies that manages an investment of €23.6 million to fund the joint participation of 18 research organisations has meant the definitive endorsement of this new line of work (ANEI 2011).

Social research and the internationalisation of the activity are also distinctive features of the company. An office was opened in Brussels in 2008 and this has led to European tenders and projects (EOI Foundation 2010).

Areas of activity:

- Research
- E-business development
- Business intelligence
- Usability and accessibility
- E-learning
- Portal integration

The competitive advantages that the company has identified are based on three interrelated factors: its ability to integrate technologies and devices for access to information and communication; its ability to integrate knowledge, technical standards, and Spanish and European standards (which because of their dispersed nature are difficult to manage in an isolated manner); and its ability to bridge the gap between ICT technological resources and the effective use of ICT resources by non-specialist users.

Technosite SA guarantees the accessibility and usability of websites through twice-yearly audits. It certifies the accessibility of technologies (web, mobile applications, etc.) and offers a recognition of quality to organisations that are committed to ICT accessibility. Certified client companies and organisations include: Alcampo, Mercadona, AXA insurance, Valencia City Council, Banco Popular, Caja de Ingenieros, Bankinter, Iberdrola, Regional Government of Castille and Leon, Endesa, Hoteles Sol Meliá, IMSERSO, AENA, CNMV, INJUVE, Ministry of Health and Consumer Affairs, Madrid Metro, Red Eléctrica Española, SANITAS, Fundación Vodafone, Fundación Universia, Fundación ONCE, and ONCE.

12.5 Conclusions

The recent increase in the contribution of social economy enterprises to European GDP shows the capacity of this sector to respond to increasing levels of social awareness. This social awareness can be defined as the knowledge that a person has about the condition of other members of the community (EOI Foundation 2010), and supposes that the individual understands the needs of neighbours and tries to cooperate through various social mechanisms so that everybody can play an active role in society.

Major legislative and normative advances that respond to the needs of citizens have been made in recent years to encourage the growth of the social economy.

The use of accessible ICT technologies helps various sectors of the population enjoy greater independence. This in turn creates a specialist market that has been exploited by numerous social economy enterprises that have efficiently detected and met the market opportunities.

Technosite SA is a limited liability company that is controlled by Grupo Ilunion and so belongs to the social economy sector. It is a profitable company competing in a technologically advanced sector with a growing volume of activity, and is a leader in consulting, research, and ICT accessibility services. The company offers quality services and has a deep understanding of its users (derived from people with disabilities who work as employees) and is committed to the social integration of people with disabilities (EOI Foundation 2010). Integrating people with technology is a motto that faithfully reflects the essence of the company's activity. This example demonstrates that social economy can be profitable from financial and social perspectives and can open paths that would otherwise have remained closed.

References

Acosta, C. S., & Egoávil, J. V. (2014). El retorno social de la inversión: ¿se puede medir el impacto de la difusión de un proyecto de responsabilidad social empresarial? *Universidad & Empresa, 26*, 29–62. https://doi.org/10.12804/rev.univ.empresa.26.2014.01.

Anchuelo, A. (2017). La situación actual de la I+D en España: el informe COTEC 2017. https://www.republica.com/sapere-aude/2017/06/28/la-situacion-actual-de-la-id-en-espana-el-informe-cotec-2017/ (28/06/2017) retrieved 29/08/2017.

ANEI. (2011). Technosite empresa del mes para la ANEI (06/04/2011) http://consultoria.ilunion.com/detalles_noticia.php?id=262&pag=31 Retrieved 02/08/2017.

Barney, J. (2010). Firm resources and sustained competitive advantage. Strategy Process, Content, Context. An International Perspective 290. doi:https://doi.org/10.1177/014920639101700108.

BOE. (2011). 5/2011, 29 March, Ley 5/2011, de 29 de marzo, de Economía Social. BOE n°76. http://noticias.juridicas.com/base_datos/Admin/l5-2011.html. Retrieved 29/07/2017.

CEPES. (2017). Listado de empresas más relevantes de la Economía Social. www.cepes.es/ranking. Retrieved 01/09/2017.

DG Regional and Urban Policy and DG Employment, S.A. and I. (2013). Guide to social innovation. *European Commission, 6*, 5–72. https://doi.org/10.1177/1473325007083354.

EOI Foundation. (2010). *Sectores de la nueva economía 20+20 Economía Social*. Madrid: Gobierno de España.

European Commission. (2009). Resolución del Parlamento Europeo, sobre economía social (19/02/2009) http://www.europarl.europa.eu/sides/getDoc.do?pubRef=-//EP//TEXT+TA+P6-TA-2009-0062+0+DOC+XML+V0//ES. Retrieved 26/07/2017.

European Commission. (2011). Social enterprises. http://ec.europa.eu/growth/sectors/social-economy/enterprises_es. Retrieved 26/07/2017.

ILUNION. (2016). http://consultoria.ilunion.com/area-corporativa/grupo_fundosa.php. Retrieved (02/05/2016). http://www.ilunion.com/es/conocenos/nuestros-origenes. Retrieved (03/06/2016).

ILUNION. (2017). http://www.ilunion.com/en/know-us/presentation. Retrieved (02/08/2017).

ISO 9999. (2016). Assistive products for persons with disability-Classification and terminology. https://www.aenor.es/aenor/normas/normas/fichanorma.asp?tipo=N&codigo=N0058322&PDF=Si#.Wcpzf8Zx1zk. Retrieved 29/07/2017.

Misuraca, G; Csaba, K; Lipparini, F; Christian, V, and Raluca R. (2015). *ICT-enabled social innovation in support of the implementation of the social investment package*. JRC Working Paper doi:https://doi.org/10.2791/9219.

Moreno, M., Estelles-Miguel, S., Merigo, J., & González Vázquez, E. (2014). In M. Peris-Ortiz & J. Álvarez-García (Eds.), *Management by processes-an effective tool for employee motivation in action-based quality management. Strategy and tools for continuous improvement*. Cham: Springer.

Murray, R., Caulier-Grice, J., & Mulgan, G. (2010). The open book of social innovation. *Young, 30*, 224. https://doi.org/10.1371/journal.pcbi.0030166.

ONCE Report. (2012). Informe de Valor Compartido 2012. Memoria de Responsabilidad Corporativa de Fundación ONCE y Grupo FUNDOSA. http://memoriarsc.fundaciononce.es/valor-compartido/reto-4-las-empresas-del-grupo-fundosa-valor-diferencial-y-competitividad. Retrieved (01/03/2016).

ONCE Report. (2015). Memoria Anual de la ONCE y su fundación, año 2015. http://www.once.es/new/sala-de-prensa/publicaciones-y-documentos/Documprensa/memoria-2015-de-la-once-y-su-fundacion/documentos/memoriaONCE2015.pdf/download. Retrieved (02/05/2016).

Rueda-Armengot, C; Estelles-Miguel, S; Palmer Gato, M.E; Albarracín Guillem, J.M. and Peris-Ortiz, M. (2017). Social entrepreneurship in the automotive industry: A Win-Win experience in social entrepreneurship in non-profit and profit sectors. Theoretical and empirical perspectives. Eds. Peris-Ortiz, M, Teulon, F. And Bonet-Fernandez, D. International studies in entrepreneurship, vol. 36. Springer. Cham.

SEKN. (2006). *Social enterprise knowledge network Gestión efectiva de emprendimientos sociales: Lecciones extraídas de empresas y organizaciones de la sociedad civil en Iberoamérica*. Washington, DC: Inter-American Development Bank.

Chapter 13
Management Systems for Sustainability Practices in the Wine Sector: The Case of Bodegas y Viñedos Fontana, S.L, a Spanish Winery

Félix Calle, Inmaculada Carrasco, and Ángela González-Moreno

Abstract Climate change is becoming a reality. As a consequence of human action, the increase in carbon emissions is altering the planet's climate patterns. The food industry generates and releases large amounts of greenhouse gases; in addition, the water consumed in these processes also has a large impact on ecosystems. More concretely, the wine sector has to manage its awareness of the close relationship between the sector's activity and climate change with the growing competition in the world markets. Companies are adopting different strategies. Some of them are defensive, with companies' stepping up production to increase sales and compensate for the lower profit margins, while at the same time, increasing their carbon footprint. Other companies, however, have opted to implement social innovations, seeking to reduce the impact of their production activities on the environment, while, at the same time, gaining in competitiveness.

This chapter reports a case study on Bodegas y Viñedos Fontana, S.L., a winery producing wines with the Uclés designation of origin, from the autonomous community of Castilla-La Mancha (Spain). This company has broken with the bulk production that is typical of the area, committing to a strategy dominated by a high level of environmental proactivity. In this way, not only has it increased turnover but has also managed to enhance its financial performance and position itself in

F. Calle
University of Castilla-La Mancha, Plaza de la Universidad, Albacete, Spain

I. Carrasco (✉)
Economic Policy Unit, University of Castilla-La Mancha, Plaza de la Universidad, Albacete, Spain
e-mail: Inmaculada.Carrasco@uclm.es

Á. González-Moreno
Department of Business Organisation, University of Castilla-La Mancha, Plaza de la Universidad, Albacete, Spain
e-mail: Angela.Gonzalez@uclm.es

© Springer International Publishing AG, part of Springer Nature 2018   189
M. Peris-Ortiz et al. (eds.), *Strategies and Best Practices in Social Innovation*,
https://doi.org/10.1007/978-3-319-89857-5_13

international markets. This case study makes a contribution to the literature on the economic profitability of environmental proactivity, within the framework of social innovations.

Keywords Social innovation · Sustainability · Case study · Wine sector · Environmental proactivity

13.1 Introduction

Due to human action, climate change is fast becoming a reality. The increase in carbon emissions is altering the planet's climate patterns. This has raised the alarm and the institutions have reacted by taking measures to prevent greater disasters and reverse, as far as possible, the damage already done. For example, among its Millennium Development Goals, the United Nations Social Agenda gives a specific place to the fight against climate change and the European Union has implemented its roadmap for a low carbon competitive economy by 2050.

The food industry contributes notably to climate change since all foods, before reaching the end consumer, must be produced, transformed, packaged and transported. All these stages generate and release large amounts of greenhouse gases. In addition, the water consumed in these processes also has a large impact on ecosystems. The agri-food industry is increasingly more aware of the close relationship between the sector's activity and climate change, resulting in the development of high-quality food products which respect the environment.

Thus, the wine sector is adapting its strategies which, in turn, directly affects the industry's economic performance, opening opportunities in the potential commercial exploitation of these strategies, enhancing environmental preservation and decreasing the sector's water, carbon and energy intensity footprint.

In the case of Spain, and particularly that of Castilla-La Mancha, the world's largest wine-producing region, the economic crisis and the suppression of the European Union distillation subsidies in the new wine CMO of 2008, have favored an exceptional opening to international markets, all of which has had an impact on the sector and on company accounts (Simón et al. 2015). This broadening of the business base towards foreign markets has undoubtedly had a direct effect on the environment, above all with regard to the carbon and energy intensity footprints (basically due to the increase in kilometers travelled per liter of wine), as well as the water footprint, as a result of the intensification of production to obtain higher yields and lower unit costs.

In Castilla-La Mancha, many companies have positioned themselves in the lowest price market, which has been made possible thanks to the competitiveness afforded by lower unit costs. In order to maintain their profitability ratios, companies have been obliged to increase production (with the subsequent environmental impact) as their profit margins are tight due to their focus on products with lower value added.

Some companies, however, have sought new sources of competitive advantage through environmental innovation and the incorporation of ecological issues in their strategies. This is the case of the winery Bodegas y Viñedos Fontana, S.L. The aim of this chapter is to analyze the reasons which have led the company to adopt this strategy and the consequences it has brought. Thus, we hope to contribute to the knowledge on how companies develop management systems which support social change and sustainability.

This chapter is organized into five main sections. After this introduction, the second section is devoted to present the information of the utmost interest and the maing figures of the world wine sector. A third section is dedicated to the revision of the academic literature in order to establish the theoretical framework of the research. The fourth section describes the methodological process used to obtain the information and presents the case of the winery Bodegas y Viñedos Fontana, S.L., and we discuss the collected information with relation to the literature insights, in order to conclude, in the fifth and last section, the main conclusions reached.

13.2   The World Wine Sector

The world wine market has traditionally been dominated by the three great wine-producing countries of the Old World: Spain, Italy and France. However, since the 1990s, The surface area of vineyards in other parts of the world has increased notably and new producers such as China, Australia, Argentina, Chile, New Zealand, South Africa and the United States have substantially expanded production (Figs. 13.1 and 13.2), gaining presence in international markets, especially in the premium segment. These changes have been made possible by technological advances permitting increased production and improved quality, while giving these new producers the opportunity to enter the world's wine markets (Barbara 2014).

The so-called New World (NW) wine suppliers pose a challenge to established European companies in both existing and emerging wine markets. The result is an expanding and increasingly competitive global market. China, specifically, has a substantial growth potential in terms of wine consumption, while also constituting a notable challenge to existing exporters as it has significantly increased its wine production (Thorpe 2009). In a few years, it has positioned itself as the world's fifth largest consumer (Fig. 13.3), the sixth largest producer and the second largest in terms of production area (Figs. 13.1, 13.2 and 13.3).

The transformations in the vineyards and wines of the Old World have been undertaken by a highly fragmented business sector, based on family wineries with large numbers of brands and wines made from grape varieties registered under a protected designation of origin or geographical indication. This is in marked contrast to the New World, which is characterized by strong brands associated with homogenous ranges of grape varieties under the control of big wine firms and the food industry, dominated by chains of production and distribution. The success of the production system in the new wine-producing countries has been facilitated by limited regulation and aggressive marketing strategies (Medina et al. 2014).

Fig. 13.1 Countries with
the largest vineyard surface
area. (*Source:* International
Organization of Vine and
Wine, 2017)

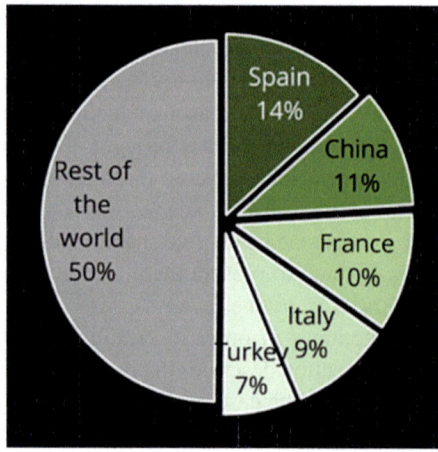

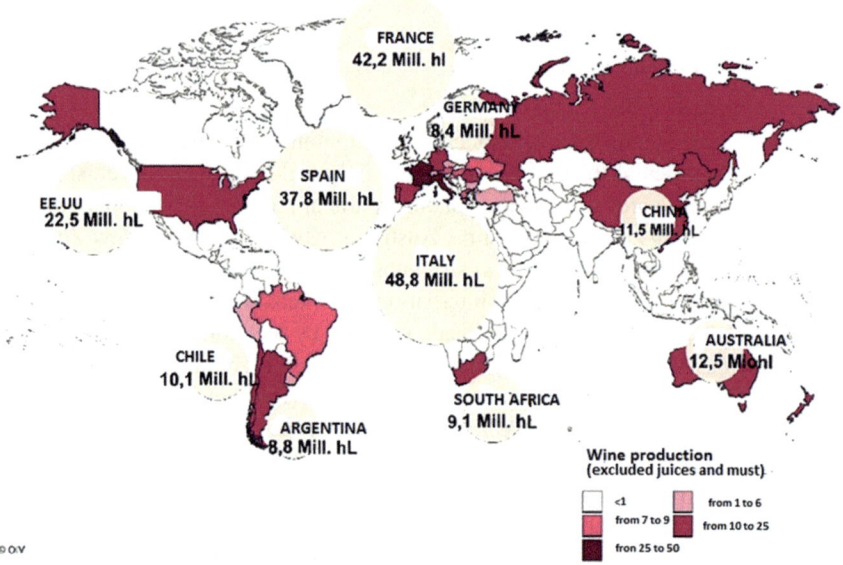

Fig. 13.2 World ranking of wine-producing countries (million of hectoliter). (*Source:* International Organization of Vine and Wine, 2017)

Global wine production is characterized by the existence of two partly contrasting models: European production, largely based on regulated designations of origin and quality indications, and the much more deregulated production in the new or emerging wine-producing countries. While the European Union regulates all aspects of production and manufacture and maintains strict control over wine-making practices, the emerging countries are much more tolerant. The European model focuses on differential quality, while the strategy in the emerging countries is based on high, homogenous quality.

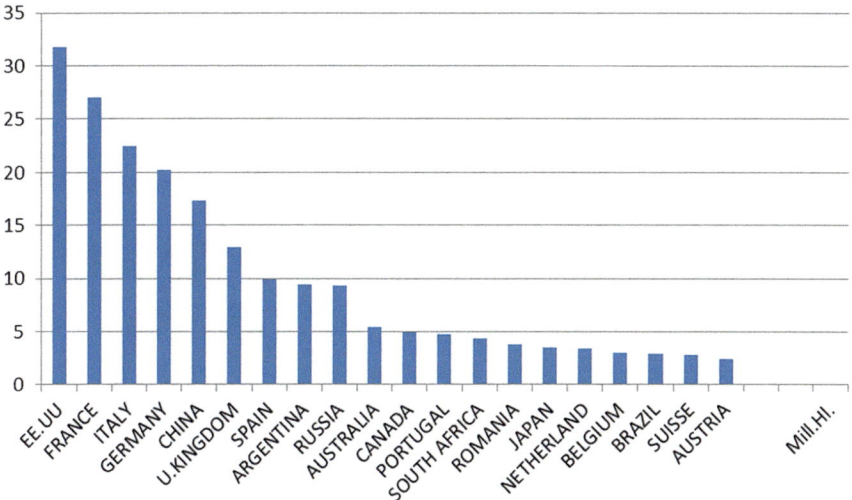

Fig. 13.3 Main wine-consumming countries. (Source: International Organization of Vine and Wine, 2017)

The general consumption and business trend is for fresh, light wines to spearhead growth, especially sparkling wines, followed closely by Cava, Champagne and others. Large amounts of relatively inexpensive wine will be marketed, increasingly in bulk, especially in more remote markets, where bottling and distribution are key factors influencing global producers. With regards to the general trends in production, if global consumptions remain relatively stable but there is a shift in location, production and structure will change. At economic level, the wine industry will continue to be a profitable and economically healthy sector. The evolution of profitability will largely depend on how producers, manufacturers and marketers adapt to the market's changing trends. The importance of the production and marketing strategies of the emerging countries has a double impact on the traditional wine-producing countries. The new wine producers have entered in the European market, especially in the Northern European non-producing countries and have affected the traditional sales of European producers in international markets (see Fig. 13.4) Fig. 13.4

Against this background of the expanding global wine market, wineries are under increasing pressure to enhance their environmental management for both individual and institutional reasons (Dodds 2013). Concern about climate change has put the spotlight on the food industry, since food, before reaching the end consumer, goes through different stages in which large amounts of greenhouse gases are produced and released into the atmosphere, as well as consuming water and impacting on ecosystems.

Wine consumers are increasingly aware of the environmental impact of the products they consume (Alonso 2010; Sinha and Akkorie 2010), and companies in the wine sector have begun to leverage environmental certification to seek a competitive advantage for their products (Doods et al. 2013).

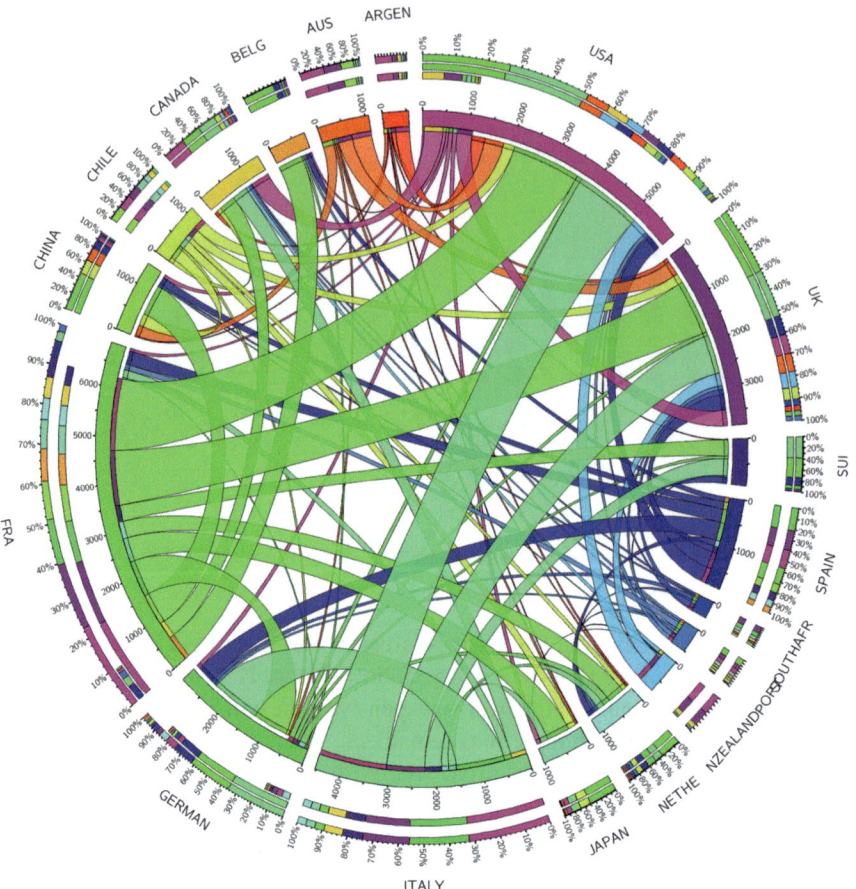

Fig. 13.4 Main wine international trade (Value in $). (*Source:* Own elaboration on OIV and GTA data, 2016)

13.3 Innovations and Environmental Innovations in the Wine Sector

Innovative activity has been the subject of extensive research in the field of business, and has been explained by internal factors (organizational characteristics) and external factors (contextual characteristics). Environmental innovation, also known in the literature as eco-innovation or green innovation, is defined as "the production, assimilation or exploitation of a product, production process, service or management or business method that is novel to the organization and which results, throughout its life cycle, in a reduction of environmental risk, pollution and other negative impacts of resources use compared to relevant alternatives." (Kemp and Pearson 2007:7).

Much of the literature on this topic focuses on the determinants of eco-innovation, comparing environmental innovations with other types (Frondel et al. 2007; Cai et al. 2014; Horbach 2008). Following Díaz et al. (2015), the determinants identified in the literature include factors of supply (technology-push), of demand (demand-pull) and of regulation (regulatory-push). Especially relevant are pressure from the supply side (Horbach et al. 2012), pressure from groups (Yalabik and Fairchild 2011), market trends and pressure exerted by consumers (Doran and Ryan 2012; Grunwald 2011; Horbach et al. 2012; Wagner and Llerena 2011; Tsai et al. 2012). The specific characteristics of the industry are also important (Peiró-Signes et al. 2011). In the concrete case of the agri-food industry, food processing companies (NACE10) and, especially, beverage processing companies (NACE11) drive most of the general innovative activity (Albisu 2014). However, there is little evidence of their behavior in the field of environmental innovation.

The internal factors of a company are also addressed, such as its resources or capacities, or its organizational culture. Most studies analyze the adoption of eco-innovation Eco-innovation across the entire industrial sector. There is very little literature on the development of eco-innovations in traditional sectors such as that of wine.

Broadly speaking, the endogenization of technological change (such as eco-innovation) may lead to win-win situations (Facheux and Nicolai 1998). However, there is a debate in the literature on the consequences for a company of applying environmental innovations. Despite having positive impacts in terms of business and the opening-up of new markets, for some authors, these benefits may possibly not compensate for the effect of the costs of environmental regulations on profits (Duchi et al. 1995; Marín 2014). In contrast, other authors posit that environmental technologies and innovations play a crucial role in the joint dynamic of environmental and economic performance (Mazzanti and Zoboli 2009; Ghisetti and Rennings 2014); that there is a positive relation between eco-innovations (in processes, products and organization) and business performance (Cheng et al. 2014); that they represent the key mediator between the severity of environmental regulations and financial performance (Lanoie et al. 2011); and they have a positive impact on job creation (Horbach 2010; Horbach and Renning 2013).

Major investment has been made in improving the installations and equipment in wineries. In many cases, they are no longer simply production centers but have become museums and spaces for lovers of wine tourism, and home to cultural initiatives. The entry of new wine-producing countries in the market has forced traditional producers to react and adapt to the challenges posed by these late production processes comers. It has led to their innovating and modernizing production processes on a new roadmap more in line with current demand Morrison and Rabelloti (2016).

Innovation in wineries has focused on identifying and eliminating pollution from the winemaking process, increasing analytical technologies to assess and optimize winemaking practices, understanding and controlling the chemical and biological processes related to sensory attributes and the development of objective measures of quality. The specialized literature recognizes that environmental innovations are not only technological but also organizational, social and even institutional (Horbach 2008). In the wine sector, environmental innovations have been associated with the introduction of improved, more environmentally-friendly production techniques, the use of disease resistant grape varieties, reducing the use of phytosanitary products, the use of waste for alcohol production or for the pharmaceutical industry and the reduction of bottle weight and packaging.

For new technologies to be adopted in the wine industry, certain conditions must be fulfilled: company owners must be willing to innovate; they must be convinced that innovation will benefit business, and they must have the material, technical and cognitive resources at hand and consider whether innovation is feasible (Calanit et al. 2012). Undoubtedly, however, including environmental issues in business strategies will depend on a company's environmentally proactivity (Aragón-Correa 1998; Buysse and Verbeke 2003). This complex concept may be understood as a dynamic capacity (Aragón-Correa and Sharma 2003) that materializes in the incorporation of environmental issues in all areas of business (Sellers-Rubio 2010) and is reflected the environmental practices implemented by the company (Barba-Sánchez and Atienza-Sahuquillo 2016). These practices in turn may also be associated with enhanced business performance (Leenders and Chandra 2013).

The vision of senior management teams, their strategic trends and the impression of the external environment foster or discourage innovation. Strategic intentions may be aimed at satisfying the needs of existing clients or seeking new clients and developing innovative products and services to satisfy their needs (Gilinsky et al. 2008).

In terms of innovation, wineries tend to introduce numerous internal and external innovative activities, based on a variety of information sources, with a clear distinction between competitive sources, governmental sources (laboratories, research centers) and higher education sources. They implement different types of innovation, including products and processes but also in organizational aspects (Doloreux et al. 2013).

In light of the above, we pose the following questions:

1. Does the company exhibit environmentally proactive characteristics?
2. What motivates the company to introduce environmental innovations?
3. How do the environmental innovations affect the company's performance?

13.4   Eco-innovations in the Wine Industry: The Case of a Spanish Winery, Bodegas y Viñedos Fontana, S.L.

The information presented below has been compiled from information provided by the company itself, the Commercial Registry, and that obtained during an in-depth interview at the company's headquarters with the Head of Winemaking Projects. This professional with extensive experience in the field also completed a semi-structured questionnaire, based on that designed by Aragón-Correa (1998) to measure environmental proactivity.

13.4.1 Presentation of the Case Study: Bodegas y Viñedos Fontana, S.L

Bodegas y Viñedos Fontana, S.L. was established on 6 June 1997, with its registered office at Calle de O'Donnel, 18–1° G, Madrid (Spain), with the corporate purpose of "producing, bottling, buying and selling, distributing, importing and exporting bulk or bottled wine", CNAE 1102 (National Classification of Economic Activities, with a subscribed and paid-up capital of 100,000 euros, and registered in the Commercial Registry of Madrid.

Production is located in Uclés, at an altitude of between 700 and 900 meters above sea level, in an area known as "The Álava and Rioja of Castille". The company's aim is to produce fresh, contemporary wines expressive of their origin, wines which are of great interest and attraction to a lover of modern wine, what is commonly referred to "authentic wines". The winery's operations are as environmentally, socially and economically sustainable as possible. Sustainability is an essential feature of an authentic wine, but also of accomplished wine professionals, good winemakers and solid entrepreneurs. The winery has modern, efficient cellars, focused on maximizing the quality of the wines and the competitiveness of the company. It also uses latest generation winemaking equipment to maintain the personality of the estate in the grapes.

It is currently listed among the Top 30.000 Spanish Companies, a distinction awarded to the leading Spanish enterprises based on annual turnover. It is also among the top 125 companies by turnover in its sector.

The annual accounts filed with the Commercial Registry of Madrid for the 2016 financial year present the following economic figures: (Table 13.1)

(a) Company culture and values:

For Bodegas y Viñedos Fontana, S.L., the consumer is the center of all its business, aiming to provide aesthetic and cultural pleasure, which it creates through authenticity, sustainability and competitiveness.

Authentic wines do not fit a specific mold. On the contrary, they embrace diversity in viticulture, winemaking and finished product. However, every authentic wine has at its heart a strong sense of place originating from respectful production. Authentic wines are not wines made to please journalists or win trophies. They are balanced and subtle wines designed for thoughtful appreciation rather than instant gratification on tasting. The practices to achieve it are practical and varied, depending as they must on the particularities of the individual vineyard and winery, as well as the style and market segment of each wine. In this way, the concept of authenticity

Table 13.1 Bodegas y Viñedos Fontana, S.L. Annual Accounts, 2016. (*Source:* Commercial Registry of Madrid for the 2016)

Income	5.668.240 €
EBITDA	698.747 €
Operating Income	424.597 €
Total Assets	13.889.597 €
Net Worth	5.179.936
Total Debt	6.612.266
Clients	2.623.434
Suppliers	2.097.394

in wine is inclusive and progressive. The criteria the company works in an effort to make more authentic wine are: vineyards with balanced yields; the fruit is picked early enough to retain freshness and definition; alcohol levels are in harmony with the rest of the wine; and free of faults and stable at bottling. The wines are produced with sympathetic winemaking, which is the path to a sense of place, enhancing an expression of origin in the wine itself. As such, it is the cornerstone of the making of authentic wine. At this intersection, nature is appreciated and respected, but the essential role of science is also acknowledged.

Sustainability is, for many, just another empty marketing buzzword. For Bodegas y Viñedos Fontana, S.L., it is much more. It is about taking responsibility – as viticulturists, winemakers and citizens – to ensure their actions now respect and protect the environment in the future. In our work, it means the vineyards are organically farmed and managed as integrated eco-systems that protect biodiversity, from the centenary oak trees and wild birds, to the micro-organisms in the soils. It means the wines are made with as little intervention as possible in a process that aims to minimize both carbon and water footprints, as well as waste generation. It also means creating viable market access for wines made from vineyards in risk of being abandoned, assuring a fair and sustainable income for growers and the communities that depend on them.

Finally, competitiveness. Bodegas y Viñedos Fontana, S.L. creates value for its customers by carefully aligning all assets and decisions from vineyard to market. It does not invest in anything that would make its wines more expensive without making them better, like empty marketing, expensive architecture or other unproductive costs or assets. It does, however, invest heavily and continuously in everything that contributes to the personality, sustainability and value of their wines, in particular human resources, viticulture, and lean, efficient winemaking facilities.

The introduction of ecological production was an ideological and not a business initiative, arising from the management's commitment to producing wines without impacting on the environment. That said, the ecological production subsequently led to entry into new markets, state aid for R&D, and creation of new customer loyalty especially in United Kingdom, Germany, Belgium, Netherlands and Luxembourg, where ecological wines are highly popular. This led to sales growth, higher profits and market share, which are all reflected in the company's marketing activities.

Consequently, environmental issues are regularly prioritized and defined through reviews and internal audits conducted by the company's environment experts, above and beyond the obligations of complying with current legislation. This has led to the company organizing environmental training programs for workers in direct contact with the design, development processes, maintenance and logistics involved in the end product.

The relationship with suppliers is of key importance to the company. They are required to comply with strict environmental criteria, their activities are monitored and they are offered personalized advice on crop cultivation processes. They promote and encourage ecological vine-growing among their suppliers (currently around 100 in number). They are paid higher than market prices to avoid old vines being uprooted (compensating them for the loss of income from subsidies for uprooting and planting new vines), and are regularly audited, protecting the land and maintaining its identity. The plant material in the old vineyards is of high quality and is reproduced by grafting.

(b) Products

The products are made and distributed under the following labels:

Mesta Wine. This is the winery's basic range, using Spanish grape varieties. The wine is ecological and the range includes white, red and rosé wines.
Gama Ovejas. The winery's dynamic, experimental range of red and white wines.
Gama Dominio de Fontana. This is the estate's own range. Its red and white wines have the distinctive personality of the location.
Gama Quinta de Quercus and Quercus. This range utilizes fruit from a particular vineyard, the company's favorite. Only red wine is produced.

The grape varieties used for white wine production are Airén, Chardonnay, Verdejo and Sauvignon Blanc. For red wines, the company uses Tempranillo, Cabernet Sauvignon, Syrah, Garnacha and Graciano.

(c) *Environmental innovations at Bodegas y Viñedos Fontana, S.L.*

The winery has invested in many research projects such as:

- R&D in biofuel generation from pruning waste. Although it provides no additional returns for the company, rather it costs them money, they implement the initiative as part of their commitment to the environment.
- R&D in clay barrels.
- R&D in oxygen management

- The estate has incorporated state-of-the-art technology. A weather station has been installed to provide constant information on humidity, rainfall and temperature. Humidity probes have been installed in the ground to predict and determine whether appropriate irrigation and minimum water use.
- The company has installed dendrometers, which measure the thickness of the plant trunks, provide information on plant activity (trunk size) and calculate the needs of the plants.
- They use satellite images delivered every 2 weeks to check the vitality of each parcel of land.
- A drip irrigation system to reduce use of irrigation water.
- The company is currently participating in the *"Wineries for Climate Protection"* program, organized by the Spanish Wine Federation, and has signed a commitment to reduce its water, carbon, waste and energy footprints, being subject to audits by external enterprises.
- The existing filters have been changed, as they contained highly polluting waste, and tangential flow filters have been installed.
- The wines are now bottled in lighter bottles.

13.4.2 Environmental Innovations at Bodegas y Viñedos Fontana, S.L.

The first of the questions we posed in the previous section referred to measuring the company's environmental proactivity. Based on the analysis of the 16 items from the questionnaire by Aragón-Correa (1998), which focus on internal factors in a company, it can be said that Bodegas y Viñedos Fontana, S.L. exhibit a medium-high level of proactivity, since:

- They place a high value on questions such as prioritizing environmental issues in the company's objectives; clearly and explicitly defining their environmental policies; considering environmental criteria in the design and development of products, processes, maintenance and logistics; considering environmental criteria when selecting suppliers; and taking into account the company's commitment to the environment in their marketing activities.
- They attach a high value to questions such as: the clear definition of long-term plans and objectives; periodic environmental inspections and internal audits; the existence of a head of environmental management, who actively participates in the development of company objectives and strategies; the participation of employees in environmental training programs; periodic assessment of the environmental impact of different products at differ stages of the product life cycle; the use of clean, environmentally-friendly technologies; and the consideration of environmental criteria in the selection of methods of transport and distribution channels.

– They give medium value to questions such as periodic measurement and assessment of environmental results by the senior management; the existence of a management position devoted exclusively to environmental issues; and demanding suppliers and subcontractors improve their environmental activities and compliance with the relevant environmental standards.

As regards the motivations which lead Bodegas y Viñedos Fontana, S.L to develop eco-innovations, the greatest influence is to be found in the business context, in question such as the need to adapt to current environmental legislation (although the company attaches little importance to the incentives available from the public administrations) and the need to respond to customer demands, as suggested by Horbach et al. (2012); Doran and Ryan (2012); Grunwald (2011); Wagner and Llerena (2011); Tsai et al. (2012). Commercial questions such as the wish to expand the range of products or maintain their competitiveness have a moderate influence. Finally, in the company's eco-innovation strategy little or no influence is related to the wish to increase returns or the pressure exerted by other stakeholders such as the workers or environmental activist groups, in contrast to the suggestions of Yalabik and Fairchild (2011).

Finally, according to Bodegas y Viñedos Fontana, S.L. the impact of environmental innovations on the company's performance is positive. The company recognizes a moderate impact on returns or profits (while also confirming that company performance is important in innovation), but considers the main gains are in commercial aspects, level and growth of sales and increase in market share (in line with Duchi et al. (1995). This perception is consistent with the findings of Junquera and Del Brío (2016) and Bansal & Roth (2000), who suggest that economic motivation is not necessarily the most important factor for a company when choosing to follow the path of environmental responsibility. In sum, this case study confirms the theory proposed by Mazzanti and Zoboli (2009), Ghisetti and Rennings (2014) and Cheng et al. (2014), for whom environmental innovations foster a joint dynamic which favors both business and environmental performance, while also permitting companies to mediate the limitations placed on financial performance by novel, and also innovative, institutional frameworks involving new environmental regulations, as suggested by Lanoie et al. (2011).

13.5 Conclusions

In a social context marked by growing concern about environmental problems and an increasingly more competitive global wine market, companies in the wine sector are adopting different strategies. Some strategies are defensive, with companies' stepping up production to increase sales and compensate for the lower profit margins, while at the same time increasing their carbon footprint. Other companies, however, have opted to implement social innovations, seeking to reduce the impact of their production activities on the environment, while, at the same time, gaining in competitiveness.

This case study reports on Bodegas y Viñedos Fontana, S.L., a winery producing wines with the Uclés designation of origin, from the autonomous community of Castilla-La Mancha (Spain). This company has broken with the bulk production that is typical of the area, committing to a strategy dominated by a high level of environmental proactivity. In this way, not only has it increased turnover but has also managed to enhance its financial performance and position itself in international markets. This case study makes a modest contribution to the literature on the economic profitability of environmental proactivity, within the framework of social innovations.

References

Albisu, L. M. (2014). Reflexiones en torno a la dinámica innovadora del sector del vino. *Cuadernos de Estudios Agroalimentarios, 6*, 141–152.

Alonso, A. D. (2010). How ´green´ are small wineries? Western Australia's case. *British Food Journal, 112*(2), 155–170.

Aragón-Correa, J. A. (1998). Strategic proactivity and firm approach to the natural environmental. *Academy of Management Journal, 41*(5), 556–567.

Aragón-Correa, J. A., & Sharma, S. (2003). A contingent resource-based view of proactive corporate environmental strategic. *Academy of Management Review, 28*(1), 71–88.

Bansal, P., & Roth, K. (2000). Why companies go green: A model of ecological responsiveness. *The Academy of Management Journal, 43*(4), 717–736.

Barbara, I. (2014). The evolving global wine market. *Business Economics, 49*, 46–58.

Barba-Sánchez, V., & Atienza-Sahuquillo, C. (2016). Environmental proactivity and environmental and economic performance: Evidence from the winery sector. *Sostenibilidad, 8*(10), 1014.

Buysse, K., & Verbeke, A. (2003). Environmental strategic choice and financial profitability: Differences between multinationals and domestic firms in Belgium. In M. Sarianna & Lundan (Eds.), *Multinationals, Environmental and Global Competition, (Research in Global Strategic management)* (Vol. 9, pp. 43–63). Amsterdam: Emerald Group Publishing Limited.

Cai, W., & Zhou, X. (2014). On the drivers of eco-innovation: Empirical evidence from China. *Journal of Cleaner Production, 79*, 239–248.

Calanit, B. A., Lapsley, J., Mueller, R., & Sumner, D. A. (2012). Grapevines of innovation: Ozone as a cleaning agent in the California wine industry. *Journal of Wine Economics, 7*(1), 108–125.

Cheng, C. C., Yang, C. L., & Sheu, C. (2014). The link between eco-innovation and business performance: A Taiwanese industry context. *Journal of Cleaner Production, 64*, 81–90.

Díaz-García, C., González Moreno, A., & Sáez Martínez, F. L. (2015). Eco-innovation: Insights from a literature review. *Innovation: Management, Policy and Practice, 17*(1), 6–23.

Dodds, R., Graci, S., & Walker, L. (2013). What drives environmental sustainaibility in the New Zealand wine industry?: An examination of driving factors and practices. *International Journal of Wine Business Research, 25*(3), 164–184.

Doloreux, D., Chamberlain, T., & Ben-Amor, S. (2013). Standing alone you can't win anything: The importance of collaborative relationships for wineries producing muscadine wines. *Journal of Wine Research, 22*(1), 43–55.

Doran, D., & Ryan, G. (2012). Regulation and firm perceptions, eco-innovation and firm performance. *European Journal of Innovation Management, 15*, 421–441.

Duchi, F., Lange, G. M., & Kell, G. (1995). Technological change, trade and the environmental. *Ecological Economics, 14*(3), 185–193.

Facheux, S., & Nicolai, I. (1998). Environmental technological change and governance in sustainable development policy. *Ecological Economics, 27*(3), 243–256.

Frondel, M., Horbach, J., & Renning, K. (2007). End-of-pipe or cleaner production? An empirical comparison on environmental innovation decisions across OECD countries. *Business Strategy and the Environmental, 16*, 571–584.

Ghisetti, C., & Renning, K. (2014). Environmental innovations and profitability: How does it pay to be green? An empirical analysis on the German innovation survey. *Journal of Cleaner Production, 75*, 106–117.

Gilinsky, A., Santini, C., Lazzeretti, L., & Eyler, R. (2008). Desperately seeking serendipity: Exploring the impact of country location on innovation in the wine industry. *International Journal of Wine Business Research, 20*(4), 302–320 https://doi.org/10.1108/17511060810919425.

Grunwald, A. (2011). On the roles of individuals as social drivers for eco-innovation. *Journal of Industrial Ecology, 15*, 675–677.

Horbach, J. (2008). Determinant of environmental innovation-new evidences from German panel data sources. *Research Policy, 37*(1), 163–173.

Horbach, J. (2010). The impacts of innovations activities on employment in the environmental sector-empirical results for Germany at the firm level. *Journal of Economics and Statistics, 230*(4), 403–419.

Horbach, J., & Renning, K. (2013). Environmental innovation and employment dynamics in different technology fields-an analysis based on the German Community Innovation Survey 2009. *Journal of Cleaner Production, 57*, 158–165.

Horbach, J., Rammer, C., & Renning, K. (2012). Determinants of eco-innovations by type of environmental impact-the role of regulatory push/pull, technology push and market pull. *Ecological Economics, 78*, 112–122.

International Organisation of Vine and Wine (2017). *2017 World vitiviniculture situation. Statistical Report on World Vitiviniculture*. OIV: Paris.

Junquera, B., & Del Brio, J. (2016). Clients' involvement in environmental issues and organizational performance in businesses: An empirical analysis. *Journal of Cleaner Production, 37*, 288–298.

Kemp & Pearson. (2007). Final Report MEI project about measuring eco-innovation. Maastricht.

Lanoie, P., Laurent-Luchetti, J., Johnstone, N., & Ambec, S. (2011). Environmental policy, innovation and performance: New insights on the porter hypothesis. *Journal of Economics and Management Strategy, 20*(3), 803–842.

Leender, M., & Chandra, Y. (2013). Antecedent and consequences of green innovation in the wine industry: The role of cannel structure. *Technology Analisis and Strategic Management, 25*(2), 203–218.

Marín, G. (2014). Do eco-innovations harm productivity growth through crowding out? Results of an extended CDM model for Italy. *Research Policy, 43*(2), 301–317.

Mazzanti, M., & Zoboli, R. (2009). Environmental efficiency and labour productivity: Trade-off or joint dynamics? A theoretical investigation and empirical evidence from Italy using NAME. *Ecological Economics, 68*(4), 1182–1194.

Medina Abadalejo, F. J., Martínez-Carrión, J. M., & Ramón Muñoz, J. M. (2014). The world wine market and the competitiveness of the Southern Hemisphere countries. *América Latina en la Historia Económica Revista de Investigación, 21*(2), 1961–2010.

Morrison, A., & Rabellotti, R. (2016). Gradual catch up and enduring leadership in the global wine industry. *Research Policy, 46*(2), 417–430.

Peiró-Signes, A., Segarra-Oña, M., Miret-Pastor, L., & Verma, R. (2011). Eco-innovation attitude and industry's technological level-an important key for promoting efficient vertical policies. *Environmental Engineering and Management Journal, 10*(12), 1893–1901.

Seller-Rubio, R. (2010). Introducción al Marketinge. Edit. Club Universitario.

Simón, K., Castillo, J. S., & García, M. C. (2015). Economic performance and the crisis: Strategies adopted by the wineries of Castilla-La Mancha. *Agribusiness. An International Journal, 31*(1), 107–131.

Sinha, P., & Akoorie, M. E. M. (2010). Sustainable environmental practices in the New Zealand wine industry: Analysis of perceived institutional pressures and the role of export. *Journal of Asia-Pacific Business, 11*(1), 50–74.

Thorpe, M. (2009). The globalization of the wine industry: New world, old word and China. *China Agricultural Economic Review, 1*(3), 301–313.

Tsai, M. T., Chuand, L. M., & Chao, S. T. (2012). The effects assessment of firm environmental strategic and customer environmental conscious on green product development. *Environmental Monitoring and Assessment, 184*, 4435–4447.

Wagner, M., & Llerena, P. (2011). Eco-innovation through integration, regulation and cooperation: Comparative insight from case studies in three manufacturing sector. *Industry and Innovation, 18*, 747–764.

Yalabik, B., & Fairchild, R. J. (2011). Customer regulatory and competitive pressure as drivers of environmental innovation. *International Journal of Production Economics, 131*, 519–527.

Index

© Springer International Publishing AG, part of Springer Nature 2018
M. Peris-Ortiz et al. (eds.), *Strategies and Best Practices in Social Innovation*,
https://doi.org/10.1007/978-3-319-89857-5

Printed by Printforce, the Netherlands